Also by Margo Howard

Eppie: The Story of Ann Landers (1982)

WARNER
BOOKS

LARGE
PRINT

A Life in Letters

ANN LANDERS' LETTERS TO HER ONLY CHILD

Margo Howard

WARNER
BOOKS

LARGE
PRINT

Warner Books, Inc., 1271 Avenue of the Americas,
New York, NY 10020

Visit our Web site at www.twbookmark.com

W An AOL Time Warner Company

Printed in the United States of America

First Printing: November 2003

10 9 8 7 6 5 4 3 2 1

ISBN: 0-446-53315-7
LCCN: 2003052592

The Large Print Edition published in accord
with the standards of the N.A.V.H.

Book interior designed by Mada Design, Inc.

Acknowledgments

One author's name appears on the cover, but no one writes a book alone. I offer my thanks

to Larry Kirshbaum, who wanted this book, edited it, and as fate would have it, knew my mother when we were all much younger. And to Molly Chehak, Larry's talented sidekick.

to Bob Barnett, for his expertise and guidance.

to Lynn Martin, for Bob Barnett.

to Kathleen Ryan, for listening to me.

to Daniel Smith, allegedly my assistant, but in reality, my twenty-five-year-old boss—and a gifted one, at that.

to Corby Kummer, for Daniel Smith. (As well as being an astute first reader.)

to everyone at Warner Books who made this all manageable.

to Mark Feeney and Alex Beam, who badgered me to do a book. Any book.

to Kathy Mitchell, for helping me remember, and for helping me, period.

to the writer girlfriends, Kitty Kelley, Jodie Allen, Judy Bachrach, and Carol Muske-Dukes, who gave me confidence, pep talks, and friendship.

And to the doctor, whose approach to me during the writing of this book was somewhere between gracious and saintly.

To the memory of my mother,
and
to the man who gave her such joy at the
end of her life, my beloved Ron . . .
her son-in-law, the doctor.

Contents

Introduction

My mother wrote this book. It took her forty-four years.

The letters in this book relate her side of an ongoing correspondence begun when I was eighteen and ended, upon her death, when I was sixty-two. Saving these letters since I was in college has been an unconscious act for which I have no explanation. It is the one area of my life where I've exhibited packrat-ism. The only reason I can think of is that the letters were just too good to part with. They were loving and tough and funny and gossipy . . . and of course filled with advice during any time of turmoil.

It dawned on me only in the mid-1980s that I was amassing an ongoing written record of my mother's thoughts. By then, I'd been living away from Chicago—and her—since 1977, when a new marriage took me to California. I never returned to

Chicago. In 1991, I moved to Cambridge, Massachusetts, where I lived for the balance of her life, and where I live still.

In addition to the letters occasioned by my living away from her, there was voluminous correspondence from her frequent travels. Mother loved pleasure trips and had friends everywhere. Her work-related travel was to build the Ann Landers name—to make speeches and meet editors. In this way she developed professional friendships across the country. When she died I was not surprised to hear from now-elderly editors and publishers, young themselves when Mother was just starting to write in 1955, at the age of thirty-seven.

For whatever reason, my mother had what amounted to a compulsion to stay in touch with me: to report on her life, remark on mine, discuss family matters, or just describe the passing scene. And being Eppie, it was some scene. Her influence, interests, and personality provided her with entrée to an eclectic group of accomplished and important people. And, of course, she corresponded with *them*.

Letter writing for Mother was never a chore; it was a joy, as well as a way to strengthen friendships. A note, a clipping, a "this reminded me of you," were the means by which she could reinforce a new relationship with people who interested her. Mother was known for being well connected, and letters were one way of maintaining the connection. Perhaps it is in the genes, because I, too, am a mad sender of notes and clippings. It is not work at all, but rather a way to express the feeling of friendship.

This collection of letters bespeaks different things, one of which is the bond between us. It was strong and we were extremely close. I had no siblings and my mother was heavily invested in me, emotionally. As I understand my early years, I was an appealing child in looks and intelligence—things that mattered to her. I was an attention getter as a little girl, with golden ringlets, creamy skin, and precocious verbal skills. Mother swore my first words were a sentence: "How are you feeling, Mr. A.B.?" (A.B. was her beloved father.) Perhaps more than some mothers, she felt that my persona reflected on her. And in a way, I was also a replacement for the heretofore primary relative in her life: her identical twin sister, Pauline, or "Popo" to the family. (It was she who was to follow my mother into the advice business as "Dear Abby.") First unconsciously, then deliberately, Mother refocused her attachment from her twin to her child. It was a choice she made not long after my birth and one from which she would never deviate.

Putting aside the fact that ours was a mother-daughter relationship that worked, perhaps the foremost factor distinguishing letters from this particular mother is that letters were her art form. Her life, literally, was about letters. Though an engaging and piquant conversationalist, the essence of Mother's personality was to be found in her correspondence. Stylistically conversational, her written communications used unvarnished, distinctive, vivid language—and a great deal of humor. Her feel for letters was no doubt refined by the sheer volume of mail she handled. Unlike other people who were faithful correspondents, Mother received huge amounts of mail, daily, from people she didn't know. And these she answered in newspapers around the world.

One thing my mother and I held in common, as writers, was the ability to write as we speak. This informality made her letters like a conversation that happened to be articulated through typewriter keys, a pencil, or a pen. And the look of her letters was, let us say, distinctive. When she wrote to me it was seldom on engraved stationery—unless it was a thank-you note for a gift. About these she was quite formal. Mostly, though, she typed on yellow copy paper, a newsroom staple. To dash off a short note, she would use the small, square notepads with her photo and the *Sun-Times* logo, later the *Chicago Tribune*'s—her two home papers during a forty-seven-year newspaper career. At the bottom of these notepads was printed "Ann Landers," which she always crossed out and substituted "Mother" or "Nonno." We were wild with nicknames in our family. Some of mine, given me by my father, were a spin on Margo: I was Mugs, Mugsy, J. Fred (inspired by J. Fred Muggs, Dave Garroway's chimp on the early *Today* show). And in many letters I am addressed as "Dear Thigs" because Mother found my handwriting mostly illegible, making my script signature "Margo" look to her like "Thigs." In later years, we called each other Shirley or Shirley Ann. Who even knows how these things start? I was also L.B., short for Lolly Baby, whom I believe to be the daughter of the radio heroine Stella Dallas.

Most often Mother's letters to me were typed, the rethought words or lines blacked out with the heavy editing pencils common at newspapers, precomputer. Although there may have been no "A" for neatness, there certainly would have been one for openness. The letters were always frank and straightforward—subtlety was no specialty of hers. I probably learned more of what she really thought from our decades-long correspondence than from in-person conversations.

A constant in her letters were the misspellings. We thought perhaps it might be a congenital defect that neither of us could spell. Our delinquencies were sometimes too far off the mark for even a dictionary to be helpful, and we considered ourselves lucky to have copy desks to clean us up. (I went into the newspaper business in the late '60s—accidentally, just as she had.) Alas, there was no copy desk when she would write to me, so there were innumerable misspellings that were not even consistent: the same word could show up over a period of time, or even in the same letter, with different spellings. For ease of reading I have chosen, in this book, to use correct spellings except when a [*sic*] spelling is particularly interesting or revealing.

In addition, I have redacted some names—those that would have no meaning for most readers or those that would be instantly recognizable. The names that appear as "[—]," or "Miss E." or "Mr. X.," for example, refer to people who are still living and whom I have no wish to embarrass with an unflattering reference or personal revelation. The stories do not suffer, however. Their meaning remains clear.

Some letters are not dated—they merely say things like, "Monday, doing the laundry," or "Friday— fish" . . . neither of which had anything to do with her. Often, though, I kept letters in their envelopes; hence I have postmarks to thank for dates. If she did not write dates I put them in brackets, having figured out the approximate time period. And at the top of some letters—on days during which she or I were away from home—I have written where she was or where I was. The frequent ellipses were her form of punctuation (as they are sometimes mine) and do not signify omissions. To denote a significant excision the ellipses will have their own line.

When I got deep into these letters, I realized that the organizing principle which made the most sense would be to follow events in *my* life. At first this struck me as too Margocentric for a book of Mother's letters, but then not. This way permits chronological clarity, as well as the chance to follow developing situations and changes of mind. The four sections include the Brandeis letters, written to me at college; letters from Mother's travels during my first and second marriages, when we both lived in Chicago; letters during my subsequent fourteen- year marriage, when I lived in California; and letters from the last eleven years of her life, when I was in Cambridge and remarried. These later letters were mostly faxed. Though Mother said "no thank you" to answering machines, computers, e-mail, or any innovation more technically advanced than an IBM Selectric, she did manage to get the hang of the fax machine—sort of—and then there was no stopping her. Mother often kept vampire hours, working until dawn. This allowed her to sleep late in addition to having a social life. It was not uncommon for her to come in from an evening event and work until three or four in the morning. And then the faxes would fly. Her office always had a stack waiting. And most mornings I, too, would have communiqués from the night. Letters—be they mailed or faxed—were all the same to Mother. She was simply hard-wired to stay in touch and be connected.

Arranging this correspondence as a continuum makes clear what could only be seen in retrospect—leitmotifs made apparent by their repetition. Money was one. The references are numerous: who had it, what things cost, my extravagance, hers, and the sometimes loopy penny-pinching we both engaged in. Mother's preoccupation with money came, as she well understood, from being a Depression-era kid. The wild card, however, was that my grandfather—a theater owner—received a good income even during the lean years, because, as someone put it,

"Everybody had a few nickels to go to the pictures."
Mother's explanation for this dissonance was that
even though her family experienced no real
hardship, the awareness of tough times was so
pervasive that she, like most of her generation, was
always afraid of a wolf at some future door. Then
too, when she and my father were young,
impecunious newlyweds, the belts were tightened
to a degree she had not known as a child.

Mother's Jewishness becomes another theme in
the letters. To have immigrant parents—from Russia,
no less, in Sioux City, Iowa, in the 1920s—was
certainly a way to feel set apart from the majority of
one's friends. The family's Americanization was so
gradual, in fact, that Mother and Popo, whose
birthday was July 4th, thought until they were about
seven years old that the fireworks and parades were
for *them.* Without paying too much attention to her
religious education, Mother felt her ethnic heritage
on a gut level. I probably have less knowledge about
the religion than she, but we both were given to
ethnocentricity—mine obviously coming from her.
Mother's attachment to Yiddish, I believe, came
from having immigrant parents speaking the
mother tongue even when they'd learned English.
The Yiddishisms Mother grew up with delighted
her, and she taught many of them to me. Because

her parents, Abe and Becky Friedman, died relatively young, I think continuing to use Yiddish phrases helped Mother feel tied to them and to her girlhood. Interestingly, the greatest compliment she could pay someone was to say that he or she was "a mensch." The following is from her first book, *Since You Ask Me,* published in 1961:

I grew up in an atmosphere electric with Yiddish adages. My father was a sort of Jewish Lin Yutang. My mother had a talent for fitting an appropriate expression to any set of circumstances.

One of her favorites (and perhaps the one which first stimulated me to think beyond the literal meaning of words) was "Zie a mensch." In English it means, "Be a person." Since everyone is a person I reasoned that "Zie a mensch" had to mean something more. So I asked. "A mensch," explained my mother, "is a real person."

A real person is one who manages to be himself. This sounds elementary, and perhaps even naïve, but don't be fooled. Being yourself is a challenging task because to be yourself you must know yourself. And few people do.

Another recurring pattern is her thanking me for my letters, loving them, asking for more, and apologizing that hers were not longer/better/neater. Her concern for my well-being, my children's, and whichever husband was in the picture shines like a beacon from one decade to the next. (My marriages and divorces never loosened our bond. In fact, even though she preferred my last two husbands to the first two, she was supportive of all of them when we were married, because that was her style.) Another feature of our letters, back and forth, was that we both sent clippings. They could be cartoons, political commentary, society dish, funny news photos . . . anything we thought the other might find amusing or useful. She teased me that I read *everything* because reading was my "job." This may also have been a remark on my having a lot more time on my hands than she did.

Mother's letters reveal, in broad strokes, the evolution and politics of the newspaper business from the mid-1950s on, as well as the beginning and early years of my father's company, Budget Rent-a-Car. Another ongoing thread is her desire, after her divorce from my father in 1975, for a stable relationship. (One might say that there were several, or none.) Mother was always open with me about her romantic life, owing both to the nature of our relationship and my being a "grown-up." I was thirty-five when my parents divorced. For a variety of reasons, I never cared for any of her suitors. Her choices simply baffled me, though I found some more appropriate than others. From conversations with her, my understanding was that she did not wish to remarry. The letters, however, make me think this was an incorrect assumption.

Also, of course, and all the way through, is Mother's ambivalence about Popo. She struggled with it her entire life and did not discuss it with many people. The tamped-down competitiveness between them had remained just under the surface *until* Popo followed Mother into the advice business, after which there were some very public, as well as private, eruptions. Popo's behavior placed Mother on a constant emotional roller coaster, which engendered very confused feelings. In the letters to me it was as if she were thinking out loud, or talking to herself, saying, "Well, on the one hand . . . but on the other hand . . ."

These letters, rich in impressions and real-time feelings, can be read as an unintentional diary sent to an only child with whom there had been a lifelong intimacy. The lack of intention to fashion a formal journal allowed for a spontaneity and emotional honesty that would have been hard to achieve in any form other than letters from home. This correspondence, which spans nearly half a century, is the most meaningful thing Mother left me; it is a record of our relationship, expressing thoughts we had about ourselves and each other at any given time. My letters to her are not included here because they would fill another volume. I was astounded to learn, however, after her death, that she had saved all of my letters . . . just as I had hers.

On June 22, 2002, my mother's voice was stilled. But editing these letters allowed me to go back and spend time with her again. They will let you spend time with her, too . . . only it will be a much more personal "her" than you knew from her column, her books, speeches, television appearances, or interviews. Even for people who knew her, I suspect these letters will offer a deeper, more nuanced understanding of who she was.

There is evidence, now and then, of a little "do as I say/not as I do," but I think that is common to all of us, famous and unknown alike. Mother never aspired to be seen as saintly or beyond human frailty. I have made no effort to make her, after the fact, politically correct, or to mythologize her. The woman in the letters is who she was. About mistakes she once wrote:

I have learned that each of us is capable of doing something completely irrational and totally out of character at some time during our lives. It simply means we are human.

Eppie Lederer never exempted herself. Though flawed like all of us, she was a dazzling original, an important influence on American culture, and certainly human. And it was a clear-eyed understanding of the human condition that allowed her to meet its successes, setbacks, and ironies with equanimity—and often laughter. That she was my mother surprises and delights me to this day.

Margo Howard, 2003
Cambridge, Massachusetts

"The party is within."

—Terrell Lamb Janney

Part One:
College

SEPTEMBER 1958–NOVEMBER 1961

INTRODUCTION

I was fifteen when Mother became Ann Landers. The excitement of a burgeoning career was still new, so her letters to me at college reveal the exhilaration of adding client papers, making speeches, and becoming a big-deal newspaperwoman. People have asked me—for decades—how I felt about my mother suddenly taking on a demanding, high-profile job. The truth is that it was like a gift from the gods. Finally, some of her focus was deflected from me. I was never one of those kids who could later complain I received short shrift in the attention department. On the contrary, my mother had always zeroed in on me like a laser. Probably because I was an only child, I was overprotected and the primary object of her concerns, hopes, and fears. I periodically rebelled . . . though in reasonably ladylike ways. I was considered "sophisticated" even as a high school girl. I smoked and I drank scotch on the rocks; I was well traveled and a magnet for men. It was all restrained and decorous enough, however, so that Mother never felt she had to lower the boom.

It is fair to say that my mother was ambitious for me, in the sense that she was, in spirit, a stage mother . . . without the stage. She wanted me to do well and to shine. She was similarly supportive of my father and his business endeavors. He loved to travel, and she never leaned on him to do less of it and spend more time with her. She was positive and optimistic. And when it came to me, she had an all-involved and unstinting love. Starting in college, and all throughout my life, those who knew us best and saw us together would remark that they'd never seen a mother-daughter relationship as close as ours. That closeness is the underpinning of the letters that follow.

I went to Brandeis University because it was the school my mother was pushing for. I do believe that on some subconscious level she thought it would serve as a belated Sunday school. (The reason I'd had no proper religious education was that during my grade school years we lived in Eau Claire, Wisconsin, a small town with only thirty-two Jewish families. The best that could be managed was a sporadic, makeshift Sunday school.) Not to put too fine a point on it, there weren't that many schools other than Brandeis to choose from. Vassar put me on a waiting list . . . too dicey a proposition to suit me. My "fallback school," the University of Pennsylvania, didn't even accept me. Sarah Lawrence was the only other school, besides Brandeis, to accept me on the straightaway. Mother pleaded with me not to go there; her argument being that given the kind of student I was, it would not be useful for me to park myself at a school that had no grades, no majors, and quite a bit of freedom. She was also concerned, given its location in Bronxville, that I would spend most of my time in Manhattan at Saks or Bergdorf Goodman. Having waltzed through high school with no discernible devotion to scholarship, it would be fair to say, quoting that sage, Diane Keaton, "I went to school as a social occasion."

In the late '50s Brandeis was a school for intellectual heavy-hitters. That would not have been me, but I suspect my lack of seriousness was counterbalanced by quite strong board scores, a really good interview with the dean of admissions, and recommendations from Supreme Court Justice William O. Douglas and then-Senator Hubert H. Humphrey.

This is the last paragraph of a letter from Senator Humphrey to Mother, dated January 24, 1958:

When are you coming to Washington? Tell Margo that I have written a recommendation for her to Brandeis University. She will not only be permitted to enter as a result of that recommendation, but most likely become the Dean of Women or Campus Queen on the day of registration. When Humphrey recommends they are recommended.

Best wishes,
Sincerely,
Hubert H. [hand-signed]
Hubert H. Humphrey

It worked! There was no offer of Deanship, or reign as Campus Queen, but I was accepted. My academic career can be tracked in the following four years' worth of letters. Well . . . not quite four years . . . and not always having to do with academics. What I now find most interesting is Mother's sliding scale of supportiveness, acceptance, or motivational browbeating about my various approaches to school. I was going to graduate; I wasn't going to graduate. Good grades didn't matter; they did matter.

Mother wanted me to date lots of different people—not choose a special one—but when such a person periodically appeared she was encouraging. She wanted me to take advantage of the social possibilities of the Ivy League, *but* she also endorsed putting schoolwork first. When it came to my college career, therefore, she was inconsistent and contradictory . . . but these approaches were indicative of her wish to be supportive. She was, I suspect, more involved with the social aspects of my college life than other girls' mothers. What I did not understand, at the time, was that my love life was being quarterbacked by a world-recognized expert in Chicago.

SEPTEMBER 20, 1958

Dear Margo:

Your letter from Boston was wonderful. Yes, I am saving this "gem" for Daddy. He will be home tomorrow morning. He couldn't get home on an afternoon flight so he must fly all night. (His arms will sure be tired. I told him next time to take a plane.)

I was struck by the neatness and accuracy of your typing. This made me very happy, as I am delighted you are a far better typist than your mother. Also, your phraseology was excellent. I guess it has been a long time since I have read a letter written by you. The last ones were from the camp days, and you have really grown up girl!

Nothing new. I am working like a little beaver . . . and the house is quiet . . . and clean. Too quiet—and too clean, if you know what I mean. I have already taken your old leopard flats . . . maybe for sentimental reasons. Anyway, they are comfy!

Bob the doorman asked if you had left . . . and when I said yes he expressed real sorrow at not having had the chance to say goodbye. Marshall [the other doorman] is still talking about your nice farewell. Miss Margo is a lovely lady he tells everyone.

Write when you can, doll, and so will I. Fill us in on what's going on. I am glad you find the roommates congenial. Bravo . . . and love,

Mother

In the following letter, "Martin" is Marty Peretz, a Brandeis senior when I arrived as a freshman. The proverbial "Big Man" on Campus, he was editor of the Justice, *the school newspaper, as well as a cause-oriented provocateur. We met during orientation week (of which he was chairman), dated briefly, and maintained a lifelong friendship. Himself the protégé of Max Lerner, a syndicated liberal columnist and an author, Marty essentially made me his Eliza Doolittle, involving me, for the first time, in things intellectual. When I mentioned in my first book that he'd played a big part in my education, he responded in the* New Republic *(which by then he owned and edited) that he could live without the honor and wanted no credit for my education! This referred to my social pose as a dumb blonde, a persona that later carried over into some of my writing. He was one of my friends who, while we were at school, met my mother and stayed in touch with her over the years.*

"Larry" is Larry Fanning, the gifted Sun-Times *editor-in-chief for whom Mother first went to work. He became her close friend and, in effect, her journalism school. "The Fan," or "Lare Bear" as we called him, polished her innate writing skills, helped her shape the column, and made her a star.*

Drew Pearson was a famous (and famously gruff) syndicated investigative reporter and muckraker.

Milt Caniff drew the comic strip "Terry and the Pirates."

OCTOBER 20, 1958

Dear Margo:

I am at the paper . . . and wanted to get this note off to you today. Your letter (the long one) was excellent, and showed real thought. I think you are reasoning things out well. I like particularly the notion that you are NOT pushed to make any decisions.

Marty's piece on the beat generation was excellent. I asked Larry to read it for an objective evaluation and he said the boy is brilliant without a doubt. He also said if he is interested in newspaper work to drop him a line. So, pass it on for all it's worth—which may be nothing.

I am leaving for Canton and Akron on Thursday . . . and will be at the Mayflower Hotel Thursday night . . . Akron . . . and Friday and Saturday in Canton, Ohio at the Soaper. . . . Last night Drew Pearson called me at home and Daddy answered. He said "This is Drew Pearson. Is Eppie home?" Daddy said "Of course it is. This is President Roosevelt!" Some joke. We didn't get to accept Drew's dinner invitation, as we had to go to a party for Milt Caniff. But it was good to talk with him on the phone. He wrote a new book called <u>USA</u>

Second Rate Power. Get it. I'LL PAY. . . . LOVE YOU . . . and am proud of your ability to think things through in a mature and patient way. Also, am very happy that you write to us so often. This demonstrates real consideration for us which is one of the great rewards of being a parent. There is no substitute . . . and you've got it.

Love,
Mother

I have no idea, now, of what the "jolt" was, but clearly it was of the college-girl-calamity variety. And I have no specific recollection of the professor being sacked, but I was always an enthusiastic acolyte to Marty's antiauthority actions. He involved me in campus politics, usually opposing the university president, Abe Sachar; the civil-rights movement; and Sane Nuclear Policy, which at first I thought was a group honoring Saint Nuclear. (I've had a lifelong proclivity for hearing things wrong.) Although my mother, pre-column, was involved in Democratic politics and anti–Joe McCarthy efforts, before Brandeis I had no real interest in or particular knowledge of public-policy issues.

Hubert Humphrey, from Minnesota, became a family friend when we lived in Wisconsin and Mother was a player in Democratic politics. They first met when she was in the Senate gallery listening to him deliver a speech and sent down a note asking to meet him.

[NOVEMBER OR DECEMBER 1959]
SUNDAY

Dear Margo:

I will try to phone you today and see how things are going. I know you will handle this last jolt well. It is all a part of the learning process . . . and I think you are getting a postgraduate there.

This letter that arrived today, about the anthropology guy being sacked. I am afraid you are letting Martin open your head and shovel things in . . . like a coal chute. There must be another side to this. That guy is a crusading type, which is fine. BUT . . . I think he likes to be a nonconformist better than anything else. So long as he has something to be against he seems to be happy. Don't let this attitude rub off on you. It is nice that he has "taught you to care." But please be sure you are caring about the right things.

All is well. Tomorrow Hubert comes to Chicago for a man of the year award dinner . . . (A Catholic group). He is going to spring himself after the dinner and the two of us are going to hide out up here for a nice long chat. He said on the phone yesterday he is not bringing any pals along. He just wants to talk to me . . . and I know about what. Last time he asked me if he should let them put his name up at the convention for V.P. I told him NO . . . but he didn't listen, and the results were disastrous. Now I think he is ready to listen. He is going to ask what I think about his chances for the top of the ticket. And I think they are pretty good. It's been a long time since the two of us have had a good political discussion without a bunch of hanger-oners around. The onlookers always fill him full of baloney and throw him into a state of megalomania. They tell him what a genius he is, and as a result, he lets them drag him into all sorts of losing situations. He can depend on me to give him the straight goods.

Gotta scram. Be well . . . Be good . . . love you, kitten,

Mother

Red Smith was one of the all-time great sports writers. My grandfather, "Mr. A.B.," knew him before my mother did.

Mike Di Salle was the Democratic governor of Ohio. Mother took me, as a pre-teen, to the wedding of one of his daughters, in Columbus, one week early. Just as I heard things wrong, Mother sometimes read things wrong. More than once she confused departure dates with flight numbers or times, until her secretaries started managing those kinds of details and simply told her where she was going, and when.

"Our Boy" is Hubert.

"Munnecke" is the late Wilbur C. Munnecke, a patrician gentleman of the old school whom I picked up on a train (the "400") when I was twelve. He became a family friend, and because he was Marshall Field IV's right-hand man when the Field family still owned the Sun-Times, *he was instrumental in getting Mother into the contest to replace the previous "Ann Landers," who had died suddenly.*

JANUARY 7, 1959

Dear Margo:

I will start on the unpleasant note and wind up in the key of C. Enclosed material speaks for itself. This is taking advantage and I won't go for it. I'll sail for one pair of "slippers" but not THREE. So send me a check for $9.90 . . . plus the $10 you owe me. Grand total $19.90. You are welcome.

I have a marvelous letter from Red Smith which I will also send on when Daddy has seen it. This is in response to my $100 in A.B.'s name . . . for the down-and-outers.

I'm enjoying the Steve Lawrence

record . . . which reminds me . . . where is Bobby Short? You got the record for ME and took it along, did you? Please, gonnif,* if it's around here tell me where to look for it.

See where Mike Di Salle came out for Kennedy . . . dammit. I had a nice letter from Our Boy. He said he wrote to you. So—what are you doing for him on campus? You can't just let it die on the vine now that you've committed. Got any bright ideas? Hubert is the only liberal in the race . . . so if Brandeis is a liberal school, he should be the front runner, the way I see it.

I'm enclosing something that looks like a thank you from Judy Levin [my best friend from camp]. Pretty soon she'll be a nice Jewish married lady. I can hardly believe that many years have rolled around. I can see her now . . . in the cubby . . . sitting on your bed!

Munnecke was sorry he missed you. He said you called "at the last minute"

---

*"Gonnif," which is spelled "ganev" in some Yiddish-English dictionaries, means thief.

whatever that means. I hope you can catch him next time. I think he feels put out a little. You can't keep friends and use 'em only when you need something.

Oh . . . the telephone credit card number has been changed to 97-M . . . 561-3200. Call when you want to, but leave us not abuse the privilege.

Write when you can, and remember the school work comes first.

Love,
Mother

―――――――――∞――――――――――

The Minneapolis–Charley Ward mention is interesting because it is relevant to Mother's relationship with her twin sister. Minneapolis was the home of Popo's in-laws, the Phillipses, a high-profile, prominent family. Having left Eau Claire (where my father was with National Presto Industries, a Phillips-owned business) for Chicago, basically to live apart from Popo, my mother certainly wasn't going to wind up in a town with her twin's in-laws. And Charley Ward fascinated me, even as a little girl. He was in jail, for gunrunning to Mexico, where he met a fellow "resident" who was one of the principals of Brown and Bigelow, a calendar company. Upon Ward's release, his jailhouse buddy brought him into the business, where he did exceedingly well, eventually becoming chairman.

The "Grandma" Mother refers to was Gramma Gustie, my father's mother who lived in Detroit.

[JANUARY 1959]

Dear Margo:

Your mother has been sort of a shlepper* about writing, but as I explained on the phone, I have had one helluva busy two weeks. The speeches really take the time. I never give the same one twice, and the preparation for the Ad guys was really a time thief. Will [Munnecke] wanted it to be JUST right. He spent one whole day with me, just going over it and suggesting alterations. Anyway, it was well worth the trouble, as the audience sat in the palm of my hand and stayed there.

---

*"Shlepper" translates, loosely, as a bum, a sad sack.

It was good talking to you on the phone last night. I think it is amazing that kids in college haven't got sense enough to move away from the phone when someone has a call. I KNOW you have better sense than that. Anyway, you are learning . . . PLENTY there. I am delighted with the academic strides. It would be nice if you could develop something of interest on the social side. Even if a guy has the personality of a fire hydrant, GO . . . he may have a friend or a roommate. Interesting that the N.Y. friend faded. You'll probably run into him somewhere. Don't forget to be pleasant. No questions such as "What the hell happened to you . . . did you drop dead?"

Drop Grandma a line if you have time. Also write to us. Daddy should be home Friday. Everything is going well. He ran into Charley and Yvette Ward in L.A. at the Beverly Hills Hotel. Charley wants your dad to go to Minneapolis and replace him as president of Brown and Bigelow. Don't worry. I won't let him do it. There ain't that much money in the world as far as I'm concerned. It is flattering, however, nonetheless.

Be well . . . Be good . . . write and I will try to do better.

Love,
Mother

--------------------------------- ◆◇◆ ---------------------------------

"The Puerto Rican venture" was a miniature precision ball-bearing factory my father built in a San Juan suburb. He did this when he was president of the Chicago-based Autopoint Corporation, an advertising specialty firm dealing in, among other things, ballpoint pens. He served as the company president after leaving Presto but before starting Budget Rent-a-Car. Advantageous tax laws at that time allowed U.S. businesses to manufacture in Puerto Rico. For whatever reason, the factory was not as successful as anticipated; it created a cash drain for him, and took quite a while to sell.

This letter carries just the first of many references to what my mother viewed as my father's indulgence. He was always extremely generous where I was concerned (*as he was with my mother*), but she felt he was doing me no favor. Mother, perforce, became "the tight one." They were playing good cop–bad cop with money. Even when I was at camp, bills would fall out of the envelopes from Father's letters to me. In addition, I received gifts such as a case of Bosco . . . I suppose his idea being, "Chocolate milk all around!" When I was in college, he arranged an account for me at Boston's Locke-Ober's, with the invitation to dine there with my friends whenever I wanted. And if I went to New York for a weekend, I was allowed to go to "their" hotel—the St. Regis—where the management almost acted in loco parentis. For example, when I went to visit prospective colleges as a high school junior, I went alone (*!*), and because weather changed my plans as to which school to visit and when, the head bell captain at the St. Regis took me to Grand Central Station and bought my ticket because I had no idea how to take a train by myself. (*That was the train trip during which I "picked up" Bobby Kennedy. He got on at Princeton Junction and took the seat next to me in the club car. We were both doing our "homework." Mine was Shakespeare; his was a thick file for a Senate committee. He said he liked mine better. This lovely* *man looked out for me, took me with him to the dining car, and was most kind to a kid traveling alone. In addition to which, the encounter became the main topic of conversation at my admissions interview at Brandeis.)*

Mother's speaking of my "resentment" toward my parents is now something I have to accept on faith. I have but a faint emotional memory of any rebellious feelings, but in hindsight it rings true because the selection of my starter husband could only have been an act of rebellion.

FEBRUARY 24, 1959

Dear Margo:

Just had a lonnnn-nng conversation with you. I think you do get some good out of our lengthy conversations, although there is a good bit of dead (though costly) air!

You mentioned Daddy . . . in detail. Your remarks were interesting, particularly in light of <u>his</u> enthusiastic remarks on the time you two spent together.

One of these days you'll appreciate

him for the great little guy that he really is. I've lived with him for almost 20 years and have seen him under every imaginable kind of circumstance. Take my word for it—he's a champion. He has real character, wonderful human qualities that you don't see very often in this day and age of frantic money-grabbing. He has a sense of morality in business that is very rarely seen in ambitious men. He has never stuck anyone for a dime in his life—and he never would. Every deal he's ever gone into has proven him to be a model of integrity. If this Puerto Rican venture didn't come through, he would be 10 years paying everybody back. This is the only way he knows how to operate.

But these good qualities are the least of it. He has a genuine goodness in his soul. The way he took care of his mother—when he was just a kid, living at the YMCA in Grand Rapids. He made $18 a week, and he sent his mother $12. He was only 18 then . . . and I defy you to show me many kids today who would do it. He never complained that life was rough, or that Fate had handed him a bum deal. There were days when he had to decide between breakfast and lunch—he could not afford both. He had two pairs of shorts and two pairs of socks. He washed one pair every night and put them on the radiator so he could have a fresh set every day. Yet these things never made him bitter or unhappy. He just dug in and worked harder and decided to make something of himself. I don't have to tell you that he's succeeded. But more important than the fact that he stands to be a millionaire pretty quick now . . . is the fact that everybody loves and respects him.

Of course he has his limitations and weaknesses . . . who hasn't? And one of his greatest weaknesses is YOU. He is so proud of you, and loves you so much that he has spoiled you badly. He is so eager for you to like him that he buys you off. He doesn't KNOW this isn't the way to do. He gets such pleasure from a smile or a kind word out of you that he keeps making the same old mistakes year after year. It's always been so, and it will never be any different.

I know you must feel guilty about some of your thoughts where he is concerned, and this is natural. You are pretty tied up with <u>both</u> your mother and father. After all, your parents are pretty young, and you, being an only child have had all the heavy artillery centered on you. This has been both good and bad . . . especially when you have a mother who is a plenty strong personality. True, I have influenced a lot of your thinking, but I have given you a great deal of freedom, too. There are times when I am sure you could cheerfully strangle me. I can understand this, and believe me, I don't mind. I understand.

I remember my own resentment against my parents. It wasn't as deep as yours, but it was there. I recall well . . . when I didn't do well in school one day, I came home and said to my father "You failed your children. You didn't give us <u>CULTURE</u>. There is never anything to read in this damn house but Elks magazines." I can remember the hurt look in his eyes. After all, what did A.B. [her father] know about "culture"? Nothing, I can assure you. But he knew an awful lot about how to love people and make people love him. He was a master at this. And he taught me a great deal that has made me able to do the work that I am doing today. When a future candidate for the highest office in the land can write to me and say, "Eppie, please steer me and guide me. I value your opinions very much. I need your thinking," . . . this means something. And where did I get it? A lot of it came from A.B. . . . who didn't have any culture.

If I had been honest with myself, I would have admitted that there were thousands of books in the public library. All I had to do was go get them. It was easier to blame A.B. It took me 10 years to wake up to this.

So don't be so critical of your dad because he doesn't measure up in every department. The important things he has. He has heart. He cares about people. And he has character and principle. He's kind, and sweet, and good. And the world is a better place because he's in it.

Love,
Mother

"The Bandler deal," as I look back on it, was just remarkable, and today seems like something that might have happened in the early 1900s. Bernard Bandler was chief of psychiatry at the Massachusetts General Hospital. I wound up seeing him because I was concerned about having become romantically interested in a handsome, homosexual upperclassman. Both my mother and I thought this was rather strange behavior . . . hence the psychiatrist! My only rationalization for this, some forty-plus years later, is that the thinking was very *different then. In any case, I veered away from my unavailable love object and bamboozled this eminent shrink into thinking that the standard five-course load was too taxing for me. His recommendation, which the school accepted, was that I*

be allowed to become a "special student," taking only three courses a semester. It was at this point I made the decision that I was at school for a custom-tailored education, as opposed to a degree. (My custom tailoring included failing a freshman requirement, Physical Science, three years in a row by simply never showing up. I didn't understand science then, and I don't understand it now.)

FEBRUARY 25, 1959

Dear Margo:

Hurray . . . your letter made the <u>Justice</u> [the student newspaper]. I enjoyed seeing it, and I think it is quite a tribute to you, in such competitive surroundings to have made print. Apparently they put the personnel guy's picture in upside down, I take it. A very shoddy trick, to say the least. Your letter was very good. The only thing I would have edited out would have been the sentence about "breeding." Breeding is strictly for animals. I never did fancy the idea that breeding was a factor in judgment or behavior . . . <u>training</u>, yes . . . but breeding no.

About the Bandler deal: If he decides you should go on a 3-a-week routine you had better learn where the bus stop is, and acquaint yourself with a schedule. A car you ain't gonna have, and taxis are insane.

Glad you see the sense in contributing something of your allowance in the way of a stipend. This will insure you getting more out of it. I would like to make something clear about money that apparently I have failed to get across to you all these years. What we can afford <u>has nothing to do with</u> how much you can have at your disposal to spend. These things are totally unrelated. The Rockefeller kids were brought up to save one fourth of their allowance and they were also taught to tip everybody a DIME. The Ford boys had less money to spend than any kids in their fraternity. As a result they are now amounting to something. It's the nouveau riche and the fools who throw dough around, don't know the value of a dollar. Naturally, there is <u>never</u> enough . . . and they succeed only in becoming bored and jaded, and to others look like jackasses. So, if Father should strike uranium you would still not get one more dollar. Your allowance is more than adequate. Make it do. And incidentally, if Martin has not crashed through with what he owes you, it is time now to remind him.

Speaking of him . . . his editorial (his last one upon leaving) fairly drips with negativism and pessimism. If ever he writes anything big it will be the Great American Tragedy. Oi what a merchant of gloom and doom!

Well, petrenella, this is it . . . be well . . . and write when you can and I will do the same.

Love,
Mother

———————————— ⌒∞⌒ ————————————

[FEBRUARY 26 OR 27, 1959]
FRIDAY

Dear Margo:
I knew you would be excited to know

that the <u>St. Louis Post Dispatch</u> . . . second only in excellence to the <u>New York Times</u>, bought my garbage.

And guess what letter will be the first to appear in that paper? My definition of love! You liked it very much, I recall. It was a good omen.

Love,
Mother

[Here is Mother's definition of love]

Love is friendship that has caught fire. It is quiet understanding, mutual confidence, sharing and forgiving. It is loyalty through good and bad times. It settles for less than perfection and makes allowances for human weaknesses.

Love is content with the present, it hopes for the future and it doesn't brood over the past. It's the day-in and day-out chronicle of irritations, problems, compromises, small disappointments, big victories, and working toward common goals.

If you have love in your life it can make up for a great many things you lack. If you don't have it, no matter what else there is, it's not enough.

-------------------- ✎ --------------------

"The Pest house" was Mother's term for either the infirmary at school or a hospital.

Ralph Starr was a business friend of Father's who Mother always held up as an example of understatement. He was a mainline Philadelphian whose father or grandfather (I forget which) was a backer of Andrew Carnegie. He not only eschewed finance and mortgage banking to run a spice company, he often appeared looking a little down at the heels. I remember one visit when he arrived with part of the hem of his coat hanging down. Mother retrieved the coat from the front closet, sewed the hem, then hung it back in the closet.

FEBRUARY 28, 1959
SATURDAY

Dear Margo:

Your last phone call came from the Pest house. I hope you are feeling better now. Me—I am back to normal . . .

laughin' and scratchin' (more scratchin' than laughin', however . . .) and I hope soon you will be back on the intellectual line . . . making with the pearls and the gems.

I hope this letter reaches you altogether. I have no stamps to speak of . . . so had to salvage a few "seconds" from the drawers. You know . . . no glue. I pasted them on . . . with a hope and a prayer. Father mails his overseas stuff like crazy with MY stamps, and when I want to write a letter to my only child I have to look in the garbage can.

Monday night the caterers move in and put on the party. I hope it will be nice. They have a good menu and it is costing a left lung . . . but the Cory Corp is paying so I am not too concerned. They charge $7.50 a head . . . and we have to supply the booze. Of course the menu IS tenderloin steaks, and they will have five in help buzzing around, so I should not complain. A butler, two maids, a cook and a supervisor. Too bad you wont be here to "direct things." This would be your cup of tea!

Ralph Starr is in town . . . have to take him to dinner tomorrow. Rat soup. I hope the weather is nice or I may wind up cooking. I am pretty well over my cold but I don't want to take any chances.

Wednesday Pops and I are taking the syndicate to the Pump room for dinner . . . first cocktails here . . . this is long over-due . . . so I thought in celebration of the St. Louis Post Dispatch and the 300th paper, I would crash through. It should be fun.

Enough drivel for now. Just wanted to get a line off to you as you are probably still in the bed. And after all, this IS better than a poke in the eye with a sharp stick.

Love,
Mother

"E and P" is Editor & Publisher, *the trade magazine for newspaper and magazine people.*

[APRIL 1, 1959]

Dear Margo:

Your letter today was wonderful. You DO write well. Now . . . How about writing often? (I'm a fine one to talk.)

I am enclosing something which may interest you. It is a promotion from <u>E and P</u> on <u>Charlotte's Web</u>. Remember? Where is that book anyway? I recall it was one of your very most favorites.

. . .

Hubert just called. He's in town for a dinner. Will Daddy and I be free tonight? Of course. Daddy will be home from Puerto Rico in about an hour. He missed the g.d. plane by THREE minutes. He called madder'n a hornet's nest.

NOW . . . a BEEF. Did you or did you NOT write to Bertha Olehausen. Immediate action requested! I went to see her for a few minutes last night (poor thing had ANOTHER operation) . . . . and she didn't say you had written. If you didn't . . . do it right now, or your name is mud with Mother. She always says such nice things about you.

. . .

Well, doll . . . this letter isn't short . . .
the type is just small. Write to me . . .
and I will do the same. The important
thing is the WORK . . . school I mean . . .
keep at it. It's that day at a time
plugging that makes the difference . . .
a drop of water at a time can wear away
a rock . . . so GET BUSY ROCK-HEAD.

Love you,
Mother

———————————— ⌘ ————————————

*Mother's use of the word "goyem," while not
politically correct then—or now—was the way many
Jews of that generation referred to Christians. It was
the most widely used Yiddish word for "other," in
terms of religion.*

Dear Margo:

Here are some stamps . . . not stolen . . . paid for . . . or should I say "charged to" . . . after all . . . what's a mother for?

Also, a check for $70 rocks . . . Since I am paying for the straightening of the INSIDE of your head, I think I should pay for the straightening of the outside. Also, have a heart to heart with ol Doc Pandhandler . . . [the psychiatrist, Bandler] or whatever his name is and learn if this thing is going to continue . . . because if it is, you will have to start figuring ways and means to cut down on expenses so you can help lift that barge and tote that bale . . . (get a little drunk and you land in jail).

We had a long winded conversation today . . . in which you accused me of not liking ANYBODY you liked. Name me TWO. The only one I ever knocked in the head was Mr. P. and I have a sneaking hunch you unloaded him emotionally long before I ever got into the act. And besides . . . like I said earlier . . . "What's a mother for?" I just don't want to see you get tangled up with <u>ONE</u> guy for a while . . . and this goes for anybody. You just <u>MUST</u> learn how to handle fellows casually for a while. I think you are in love with love. Just keep your feet on the ground and all doors open. You don't have to make any commitments or give anybody the idea he has the inside track. At this stage of your life . . . the more the merrier.

Wednesday I am going to the <u>Life</u> Mag party at the Gaslight. [Singer, actor] Maurice Chevalier is going to be there and other celebs who are in town. It should be fun. I shall report.

All is well. . . . I will have Feuers send the fur piece along and they will clean it before they send it, natch. You will need it in Florida. Otherwise, how would they know you were Jewish? Goyem come with yarn stoles . . . Jews have fur.

Well . . . doll, this is it. Love you like

ca—razy . . . even though at times I am sure you don't think so.

Mother

———————— ⌘ ————————

Mother never drank or smoked, having decided when she was young that alcohol and tobacco could do nothing good for her body. On the other hand, I did both. This letter is an example of how she was able to be tougher in a letter than in a face-to-face conversation. This "stay out of the hay" lecture, for example, would not have been as easy for her at the breakfast table.

[APRIL 9, 1959]

Dear Margo:
Well last night was the <u>Life</u> party, and your old beat-up mother had a ball . . . a matzo ball, that is, as Passover is just around the corner. Several pictures were taken and I will try to snag you one or two.
One of the more interesting guests was a guy you used to love . . . in your

high school days, that is. Hank Bloomgarten. Remember? He is doing Public Relations work for Life and came in especially for this party. When I was introduced to him I told him my daughter used to love to watch him on the $64 thousand question—and I was pleased that she became enamored of "a brain" rather than Howdy Doody or Gunsmoke's hero. We got to talking about politics and he is an ardent (and active) Democrat . . . and a really very bright and interesting boy. He asked me if it would be all right to call you as he is in Boston very often . . . and I said yes, and gave him your number. Now he may or may not call . . . but I wanted you to know that I said it was all right. He even suggested taking you out to dinner . . . and I said I wasn't exactly sure about THAT as he is married, has a son, and is 30 years old. He assured me that as far as HE was concerned it would be a very pleasant way to spend a couple of hours . . . and nothing else.

As he spoke I churned over a few things in my mind and decided to O.K.

it. So . . . if he calls and invites you to dinner I think it would be nice to go. This is, in my opinion, a real sign of progress, so far as <u>YOU</u> are concerned. It means that I have enough confidence in you to know that you can handle yourself well under any and all conditions. I think you have the maturity now to begin to establish some good platonic relationships, and that you need no longer think of all males as potentials for the romance department. In other words, you can now operate on a good level—three steps higher than the most feminine plateau, which is of course clobbering 'em with the sex appeal.

You know how, over a period of the last several years, I have been able to maintain very good relationships with men in many fields, and I would like to see you begin to do the same. Hank could be one of those people. He is extremely bright, wonderful company and well worth knowing. I learned very early that if you have the stuff—and <u>I HAD IT</u> . . . and <u>you have it, too</u> . . . the same stuff, kiddo . . . that you can establish relationships with men at any level you want to. Most men will take what they can get. The really worthwhile ones like Hubert and Will [Munnecke] and Soapy [Williams] and Pearson, to name just a few, operate at a high level and they are not interested in making everything they see. Being human they could probably be knocked over the head and dragged into the boudoir, but once that happens, the relationship gasps a few dying groans and then dies. Nothing is as fatal to a relationship as getting intimate with people of high reputation, good conscience, or someone who is well known to the public. They can't afford to be involved . . . so the minute they get back to their senses, they start to get panicky . . . then the guilt and the fear move in, and the friendship is kaput. I learned this lesson early. My instinctive good sense always kept me out of trouble and it really paid off. Wherever I go I have very good friends at the top, both in politics and the newspaper field.

My friendships have lasted through the years . . . and I am constantly making more friends. Also, the word gets around. One tells another. This is why the no drinking and no smoking has fit into the picture so well. It adds an aura of wholesomeness that is somehow incongruous to a good-looking sexy woman. That is what I would like for YOU. A girl who can look like you . . . and speak well and intelligently . . . and not drink or smoke . . . and not lean on her sex appeal as her major weapon . . . well, this could be a gasser.

This is a long letter, but it could be an important one. I just want you to get the fun out of life that I am getting . . . and I think this is one of the big secrets. Just keep this one tattooed on your cerebrum. . . . If you want a relationship to fold up fast—just hop in the sack with a guy and I can guarantee you something will happen to sour it. It may look like something that is completely unrelated, but it will definitely fall apart. If on the other hand, you want a relationship to flower and grow . . . remember that you are a real lady and that you have enough on the ball so that YOU can call the shots . . . and be in command of the situation, and you don't have to give away a damned thing.

Love,
Mother

————————— ∽∾ —————————

Felix (McKnight) was a Dallas newspaper editor whom I knew and liked. He would later, to Mother's way of thinking, double-cross her professionally, at which point she moved Ann Landers to the Dallas Morning-News.

The summer school session was Harvard Summer School, between my freshman and sophomore years. This turned out to be one of my more elaborate scams— though I had not planned it that way. Mother was in Russia that summer writing a "straight" series about the problems of Olga and Igor, the generic Russian citizens. This meant she couldn't *check on me, and my father, being his usual preoccupied, peripatetic self, wouldn't check on me. So it became possible to withdraw—after only three weeks—just in time to get significant money back and spend the balance of the summer at the Cape with a charming Oklahoman. Miraculously, my mother did not find out until YEARS later that my summer at Harvard had been severely truncated.*

Popsy Topsin is my father. The YPO (Young Presidents Organization) is a prestigious business group that continues to this day. To join, one had to be president—before the age of forty—of a company that did a certain volume of business and employed a specified (minimum) number of employees. During my father's tenure, I was the oldest "YPO brat," and perhaps because I was an only child my folks often invited me to the annual conventions. Father joined while I was in high school and I have memories of business stars like Warren Avis and Al Rockwell, and men who ran companies with household names like Pine Sol and Holiday Inn. I occasionally would ask one of them for a little assistance with my homework.

[MAY 7, 1959]

Dear Margo:

Decided to use my best stationery on you. After all . . . why not? Who is closer?

The phone conversation was fun. You sound as if you are buckling down and working. Good. . . . I know your next set of grades are going to be better than the last. If they aren't, you will need police-protection. Seriously, I know Brandeis is a very tough school, but I know, TOO, that you can do a first rate job if you want to. Those characters who are pulling down the honor grades are no smarter than you are. They just work harder.

I had a gushy letter from Bob Brodkey [a cousin]. I guess Ron [his brother] wrote him what fun he had at our house, so Bob had to get into the act, too . . . sibling rivalry you know. He couldn't let his brother get TOO far ahead of him. This is interesting when you consider how they can deny any competitiveness whatever. Like I said . . . bull. The minute I hear brothers and sisters rave about how "close" they are . . . I get suspicious.

Dallas was great fun. Felix and his wife Lib were marvelous to me. They had a dinner party at their home . . . shipped me to their country club and made it very special. I gave five speeches in two days, so you know I worked my can off. Southern Methodist is a beautiful school. The campus is lovely and the kids look a lot different from Brandeis students. These kids REALLY look presentable . . . no Bo-Ho . . . leotards or far out stuff. Of course S.M.U. is a Methodist school . . . and most of the kids are blonde Swedes and at the worst red-headed Norwegians. A darling Jewish guy came up to me tho . . . he lives in Philly . . . he told me he played basketball for Wharton last year and hurt his back so he was down at S.M.U. "resting up." He also asked for your address . . . and I told him no soap.

The summer school session sounds like it's going to be fine. Let me know where to send the money. It maybe wouldn't hurt to take a couple of courses that you can use for credits. No point in putting money down a rat hole. As long as you are going you may as well make it pay off. And one day, you may NEED a few credits. Hoo nose?

Popsy Topsin will be home next Tuesday I HOPE. The poor boy has really been beating the bushes. He tells me that things are good, however, and the Autopoint Company may be a real outfit yet. I hope you took care of ordering the pictures from the YPO convention, as I didn't even SEE 'em. Much less take action. Also . . . is your dress for your friend's wedding being sent home? And who is to pay for the alterations? Did you put it on the bill, or what?

This is a far-shtunkina* letter to say the least . . . but Mother is on her bicycle as usual. Today I must go to the wallpaper house and make a few selections. Need I say, my head is twirling?

---

*"Far-shtunkina," often spelled "farshtinkener," means lousy in Yiddish.

Love you . . . like ca—razzzzzy, ...
. . . . . .

Mother

P.S. Please write to me, baby.

———————————— ❧ ————————————

Mother's mention of a new car is funny because, in approximately three years, my father and I would be standing in the "1000" garage saying good-bye to her. For whatever reason, we stood there and watched her pull out into Oak Street traffic, and my father had the realization that she was a menace to others—as well as herself—and soon thereafter engaged a chauffeur for her. Mother promptly forgot how to drive, and she never took the wheel again.

"1000" is 1000 Lake Shore Drive, the building we moved into when we came from Eau Claire. My parents would live there until after I was married, when they moved about a block away, to East Lake Shore Drive.

[MAY 8, 1959]

Dear Margo:

I know you will just hate this . . . but I am sending it anyway. The time to think about these things is NOW . . . not 15 years from now when you may go to a doctor and he starts to call in consultants to look at the exrays [*sic*]. This damned cancer thing is no joke anymore. I hope you will give it some consideration. I really became alarmed when I noticed in Florida that you honestly <u>wanted</u> to lay off the weeds for a few hours because I had asked you to—and then you actually had a helluva time because of the addiction to the stuff. This is bad. The only thing you can do now, if you want to emerge victorious over this lousy habit is to substitute mints (or a pipe . . . and I recommend mints . . .) . . . plus a lot of will power . . . rooted in common sense that the cigarette habit is no damned good for you. Particularly since you have a bronchial history . . . with asthma in your early days.

The new car is in today . . . and I will be driving it to the office. Hooray. I must be a big hick, but I get a big bang out of a nice car. Father had been trying to talk me into a smaller one . . . like a foreign job, but I like a Cadillac. Must be my Iowa background. I told him if HE wants a small car to get one for himself and leave the Caddy for Mugsie and me. I promise to drive carefully so when you come home it will be in good shape. And by the way, doll, when ARE you coming home? Your room is lovely. I picked out some stunning new papers for your bath, the guest bath, our room and bath . . . and I know you will just love it. Your bedspreads are gorgeous . . . and Mr. Gersh is delivering your benches today. I can hardly believe we are going into our fifth year at 1000. . . . And a good five years it has been, too. We have no complaints believe thee me.

Gotta run. Write when you can . . . and don't hit Mother for enclosing this clipping. I just want you to be around to enjoy your grandchildren.

Love,
Mother

Willie (Washington) was our housekeeper who stayed with us until she retired. "Ellya" is a nickname for me that I only faintly remember.

As for Mother's entreaties to stop smoking, I finally succeeded. When I was forty-four.

The Trezevants were Dick and Dorothy. During this time, Dick edited her, informally, before the copy went to Larry Fanning. Dick would later become her editor. He had a dry sense of humor, and Mother was extremely fond of him.

[MAY 14, 1959]
THURSDAY

Dear Margo:
Yesterday was a red letter day. Two delightful letters from the baby. Father will be home tonight and I'll put 'em right on top of all the bills . . . gevald!*

Your dress came from Miami. It is a beaut. And now. . . where are the shoes? Did you take them or are they to be mailed? Oops, I just asked Willie and she tells me they came in the Florida

*"Gevald" was Mother's alternative to "oy." She had individualized

suitcase. I looked them over and they are lovely.

So—you are going to be living at 19 Everett Street [my Cambridge address for summer school]! Mazel tov. I just hope the place is nice enough to be an inducement to study . . . and not SO nice that you will want to be entertaining all the time. Like I said . . . I expect you to perform well in summer school and make it count.

. . .

Now about the weed habit. I am praying you will hack it because I KNOW if you can't lick it now, you'll never be able to do it later. I will always worry. Every time I heard you cough in Miami (and you cough a lot and don't realize it) it was like a little knife going through me. You just MUST stop completely, Ellya. If I sound like it's a matter of life and death—it's because it is, in a good many cases. It just isn't worth it, Baby. The first couple days you'll be climbing the walls, I know, but after that it will be completely over. You must alter your thinking and approach it from a positive point of view and not say "I'm going to try . . . and see how it goes. . . ." Just make up your mind that you're <u>going to win</u> and you will. It takes a lot of guts and tremendous self-discipline, but I know you've got it. Please report on the progress and don't let anyone sell you on the "gradually stopping or cutting down method." It doesn't work. In two weeks you'll be back at a pack a day. You just must say to yourself "I am through with cigarettes for keeps. They are my mortal enemies. I will have nothing more to do with them. Period." Whenever you feel like a cigarette— take a mint. I promise your entire physical condition will improve.

So—this is it for now. The Trezevants are in New York on their way to Europe. Daddy fixed them up at the St. Regis and I had Andy Lyons [St. Regis general manager] send him a single rose from me with a card: "This is a rose—for your ear. . . ." In your absence I read the copy to him . . . and I call this "giving me his ear." I know he'll get a bang out of it.

That mink suggestion from you is

gorgeous . . . and I am taking the picture down to Suzy's today. I want her opinion and if it doesn't cost a million dollars we may do it. I am having a new silver blue coat made this FALL you know, and I don't want to be too much of a pig. I must say, Kiddy, you have a very good eye on you . . . and your taste is sensational. (That model looked a little like you, by the way. Did you notice?)

Gotta run . . . (and in the new car is a pleasure). Be well . . . BE STRONG . . . and write,

Mother

———————— ⌒∞⌒ ————————

[JULY 4, 1959]
THURSDAY

Dear Margo:

Thanks for the wonderful letter . . . and the delightful cards. You are a dear child . . . and we are so happy that God didn't drop you on the Groruds [our next-door neighbors in Eau Claire]!

So . . . you had a reception committee

of vermin and mold [in the Cambridge apartment]? Remember, dear . . . it's better to be in bed with bedbugs than all alone . . . when you are lonesome. As for mold . . . a guy named Fleming made it pay off. He called it penicillin.

All is well here. Twenty years today I have been married to your Pa.* I just can't believe it. I couldn't have done any better if I had known what I was doing.

You seemed to be having a ball in O. City . . . I won't preach, but just remember . . . NOW you have a completely clean slate . . . the canvass is white . . . without a single line on it. Make sure you don't put any marks on that canvass that you wouldn't be happy to look at in 20 years from now. I don't have to get any more specific than this. At this very moment YOU are in control . . . so play it right. Don't close any doors, spit in any wells or burn any bridges. Build all new relationships slowly . . . and with your eyes wide open and your head squarely on your

---

*Mother was actually married on July 2nd, but the birthday and anniversary, being two days apart, were always celebrated together.

pretty shoulders. You can have anything you want . . . any way you want it. Take my word for this. Time is your greatest ally. Use it wisely and well. If you want something worth having . . . and something that will LAST . . . build it slowly . . . and carefully. . . . In fact, the slower, the better. Again I repeat . . . the OPEN DOOR policy is the best one to follow. When the door is open you can come and go as you please . . . and close it when <u>you</u> want to. Once you close the door . . . it can become a prison if you make a mistake.

Be well . . . study . . . work hard and have fun. Write often. We miss you already. . . . When you coming home?

Love,
Mother

P.S. Your cards made my heart leap for joy! I can't think of a lovelier gift. Thank you, ketzel.*

---

*"Ketzel," or more commonly, "kets'l," means kitten.

[JULY 6, 1959]
MONDAY

Dear Margo:

I have one million things to do—the desk is heaped like crazy.... Queen Elizabeth is coming for lunch ... (I told her all I had was salami, and she insisted on coming anyway ...) Well ... what can you do? At any rate, I am throwing everything aside and writing to my darling daughter.

Your letter is the reason. It was short and sweet ... and heartwarming. You said your mailbox was haileh,* and I just couldn't stand THAT. So, here I am.

I got a slew of darling studio cards for the birthday and anniversary. I may pile them into an envelope and send them on to you for laughs. Yes, I think I'll do that!

I thought about you a lot yesterday ... the 5th ... wondering if you made it up to Newport and back O.K. I hate the thought of highways on these lousy weekends. The Festival must have been a gasser. Daddy told me your friend's

---

*"Haileh" means naked, bare.

mother was trying to get you sleeping quarters up there. I hope you succeeded. You could always go and sleep in the basement of the country's oldest shul. Did you know that Newport has the oldest synagogue in the USA? It's true. . . . They built it in 1640! (I happen to know because I was there!)

Now, about the roommate sitch. I hope to hell you have one by now because time is getting short and I can't see a girl moving in when the semester is half shot. We won't go into detail, but it will be an expensive goof for you if you don't locate a buddy. Like I said, Vic . . . $150. You are welcome.

Daddy left for New York this ayem. He is now in fine shape and I wouldn't be surprised if he sold the factory this trip. He has had a tough time of it and the fact that he has kept that damned turkey afloat to the point where someone wants to buy it . . . is a goddamn miracle. He's a genius!

Beauty Parlour Scuttlebutt:

I went to the Basil Shop last week to get de-flead and de-loused. Ingrid they told me is no longer there . . . also . . . ditto Neil . . . and Ruby. They quit with NO NOTICE . . . just walked out. They had vacations coming up, and this is the scoop. Neil is opening a shop over Bregy's . . . and in August. He took Ruby and Ingrid with him. I just can't understand why a gal as nice and ladylike as Ingrid would walk out on Basil with no notice. After all, when he brought her to this country she could not speak a word of English and she didn't know doodle-dee-boo about hairdressing. This is gratitude? I am eagerly awaiting the chance to get the real dope on this. There must be more to it than meets the eye.

Well, doll-face. This is it for now. Call when you can and pay attention to your work. Keep me posted and I will do the same.

Love,
Mother

[1959]
WEDNESDAY

Dear Margo:

This is a GREAT day. Father sold the plant. I am sure you know it by this time as he said he was going to call you.

He is a goddamn genius ... to have been able to keep that turkey afloat until the one guy in this whole world who would want it ... came along. I couldn't be happier. He didn't come out too bad financially, either. So—do a jig in honor of your old man's victory. I am THRILLED!

Now, about the roommate situation. SO, you got a girl to move in with you ... but she does not pay any rent. Right? But she does have a car ... and she will pay the household expenses, food etc. Right? This means that she will be paying the expenses that you ordinarily would have to pay. Right? You then exchange her the rent money for the other expenditures which you will be relieved of? Right. So—send me the $150, please. Thank you very much.

Bill Blair (of the McCormick Blairs) is setting me up travel connections through his agency. When we were in the Pump Room on our anniversary . . . (with Lou and Maryjane Kohn) he joined us and he is very hip to Russian travel. He was there with Adlai [Stevenson] last year. This is quite a break. Daddy keeps saying he can't go, but I'll bet he does! [He didn't.]

Guess who joined us in the Pump that night . . . but briefly, thank God . . . [longtime acquaintance] Baily Ozer. He is still the same infantile bag of wind . . . reminded us once more about how you and Mike [Baily's son] spent $36 for dinner . . . and we laughed about it all over again. His memory is pretty good . . . he recalled the menu . . . artichokes and so on. It was kinda funny at that. Mike goes to school in Tucson, but didn't like it . . . so he'll go somewhere else next term.

Write when you can . . . keep Maymo posted . . . and remember what you are there for, kiddo.

Love,
Mother

My mother briefly mentions "that Irisher Driscoll," but he was important in my Brandeis life. Phil Driscoll was the dean of admissions who accepted me, and who also, I suspect, ran interference for me. He was a dear and shy man whom I am certain I embarrassed with an original song I wrote and had a few girlfriends sing under his office window. The song began, "How'd you like me in your life, Mr. Driscoll, doll? How'd you like to leave your wife, Mr. Driscoll, doll?" Coincidentally, I hadn't known that Mother and Popo, when they were in college, had serenaded a math teacher with "Don't blame me . . . for failing geom-et-ry. . . ."

Mother most likely mentioned "the quiz stink" because Charles Van Doren's brother, John, was my English professor, and one of my all-time favorite teachers. A reticent man to begin with, the scandal involving his brother and The $64,000 Question *was very hard on him and made him even more introverted.*

George Abrams (S. George) was a close friend from high school.

Dear Margo:

Just had a lonnnng conversation with you and it was good to talk to you, although this wasn't one of our peppiest conversations, to say the least. But like I have always said . . . life is one godam thing after another.

It will be good to have you home for a few days. Let us know what flight you will be on. If it's possible Daddy and I will meet you . . . altho' this meeting is for the birds. I think you are smart to get away a day earlier and beat the mobs. I hope you thanked the dean of women adequately. It was VERY nice of her to write you that note which you sent on to me. She really extended herself to give a pat on the back to a student for doing something which is damned well EXPECTED in most places. I was greatly impressed with her thoughtfulness. I hope you are aware of it.

Don't be discouraged about the damned grades. Just keep plugging. If you get two years of Brandeis under your hat this is an achievement. After this school year is over you can go to school anyplace this side of the moon. But like I said, Vic, you gotta finish this year and make passing grades. Try to get some info. on the various European schools so you won't be operating in a vacuum. Geneva sounds good to me although I don't know much about it. I just don't want you to waste the year dizzying around.

The important thing is to hack the assignment at hand, which is Brandeis. Keep at it and I guarantee you the results will be there. Also, keep your oars well exercised in the social waters. When you do well in the social wars, your school work does better, too.

Keep writing and I will do the same. I will put the $125 for travel in the bank today so your balance won't suffer.

I was surprised to hear that Lynn Guthman is going to the U. of C. She must be living on campus. Do you hear from Freya or Ina? Has S. George written to you? It's good to keep the contacts up so when you come home you have not lost the thread of friendships.

Did you know I was speaking in Washington for the Brandeis chapter? This will be in April, toward the end of the month. If you want me to come to see you on campus this winter I will. It's up to you. I'd like you to introduce me to some of your faculty members. I'd love to meet that Irisher Driscoll.

What do the kids think of the quiz stink? Please let me know what the opinions on campus are on this subject. I am interested.

Enough for now . . . be a good Ellyasita and writer to your father and mother.

Love,
Mother

[NOVEMBER 1959]
[THE DAVENPORT WESTERN HOTEL
THE HOTEL WITH THE ROOF-TOP POOL
SPOKANE, WASHINGTON]

Dear Neglected Daughter:

Your poem arrived, also the other letter in which you weep buckets because you ain't had no letters from your roaming ma.

Well . . . I have been no rose, but we have done so much yakking on the phone of late I rather thought it covered everything. But this IS a lame excuse . . . and I should not have even mentioned it. Just try to understand that I have been on a real merry-go-round all October and I am not thru yet. Things have been so close time-wise that I actually had to mail Larry two days' copy from Des Moines. I didn't finish the week by the time I left on this trip, so I left Sunday through Thursday on his desk Saturday as I ran for the airport . . . and I had to mail him the remainder.

Des Moines is a gasser. I had a ball. We had over 900 people there . . . more than came to hear Mrs. Roosevelt last year, which was amazing. The Des Moines paper did a wonderful job of promoting it, however. They gave me every break. After all, I am their property, why not? So, it worked out very well and the dinner party was great, too. Art [Sanford] invited the Governor and his wife. He is a living monument to the theory that ANYBODY can get elected if he has a weak enough opponent. What a jerk. When the newspaper editor asked him questions about politics he looked to ME for support! The guy must be living in a closet. His wife is lovely, however, no brain hemorrhage, but a sweet person who helps him a lot. His name is Herschel Loveless, the gov. that is.

The suite I am now living it up in is really gorgeous. It is one of the plushest I've seen anywhere. They met me at the airport and I am getting the really red rug. tra la la. This is part of the reward for working like a damned dog. You know, it's like that old song "Love and Marriage . . ." . . . It goes "You can't have one without the o . . . . . thuuuuur!" If you want the benefits . . . you gotta put out the work. And that goes for everything in life.

Chew on THAT one for a while.

I love you and your letters have been wonderful. Keep it up and keep me posted.

Your ever-lovin',
Mother

──────── c❧꙳ ────────

Kup (Irv Kupcinet) was Mother's longtime friend and colleague at the Sun-Times. *For years he wrote the premier gossip column in Chicago. His daughter, Cookie (Karyn), was in our best-friends-group in high school. A starlet, she was murdered in Hollywood when we were all twenty-three.*

[NOVEMBER 1959]
[HOTEL STATLER
DETROIT, MICHIGAN]

Dear Margo:

This is Mother . . . reporting from Detroit. You aren't the only one who has a smith-corona portable. I have one in my room, compliments of the Michigan Medical Society.

I had a ball in Toronto . . . it was great fun, and tonight I speak to the croakers and their wives. Tomorrow I am off to Battle Creek . . . and then home.

I had a very interesting time with Margaret Truman Daniel . . . She spent the day with me and we talked politics for three solid hours. Then I took her to the <u>Sun-Times</u> and they fell on her in large numbers . . . including Kup. The word got out that we were in Fanning's office and the avalanche descended. She is such a pleasant person and it was an enjoyable day.

Then on Saturday night Father was in Puerto Rico so Margaret knew this and phoned to ask me if I would like to come out to the theatre and see her in the play . . . and also, HER husband was in town for the night, and since she had to go to the theatre very early . . . how would I like to have dinner with him and come out later? So . . . this we did . . . and it was really most enjoyable. I knew Cliff before I knew Margaret you know. He took me to the Cape Cod room (my suggestion) . . . as I didn't want to go into the Pump room with a strange man, especially Harry Truman's son-in-law. So . . . then I hired a car from the Ambassador to pick us up at 8 and drive us to Drury Lane. It was too long a hall [*sic*] for me to drive . . . and I decided to let the moths out of the change purse and spend the dough. It was well worth it.

Well, the play was simply terrible and Margaret may be a wonderful girl but she's no actress. It was rather embarrassing in fact. SHE SANG, too, yet. Murder. After the play the three of us and Margaret's leading man, George Vesico, went to the Bonepart room for something to eat.

All in all, a most pleasant evening, but I sure wish she would get off the stage. I am going to be interviewed and photographed in a few minutes . . . and

I have to call up my relatives and look over my speech . . . so . . . be a good girl and write when you have time, and so will I. Your letters are a real joy to us, and we appreciate hearing from you.

Love you,
Mother

[DECEMBER 1959]
FRIDAY . . . BENSHT LICHT AND MAKE A BROCHEH!*

Dear Out-Patient:

Well . . . the five-page gasser from the Fountainbleau arrived today. In fact . . . I yanked my column out of this typewriter so that I could make with the very prompt reply. I am plenty happy you are coming home next week. YOU NEED HELP! My stars (and garters) . . . after the phone conversation reporting on Mr. S's behavior [a problematic beau] . . . you are finding him delightful!!! All I

---

*"Bensht licht," from "bentshen," to bless, and "licht," candles—the Friday night tradition of lighting candles and saying a prayer. A "brocheh" is a blessing.

can say is c'mon home before they put you in restraining irons and call the cops. Your feeble explanation is that there's nothing better around. I want to ask you just one question. IS THERE ANYTHING WORSE? Please collect your money from the guy and make a resolution not to float any more loans.

You were right . . . I said he was BRIGHT . . . and he is . . . in fact, he is one of the brightest yet. But I didn't say he was sane. He is attractive, too . . . one of the most, but what difference does that make, really? All right, now . . . enough on this subject until you get home. If you want to continue here on the pink bedspreads I am willing. After all, what's a mother for?

Daddy reported on the Florida trip via phone (he'll be home tonight . . . in fact this afternoon) . . . and he said you were a joy and a pleasure. He filled me in on the details and I think it was good that you made the trip . . . if only for this one reason. You made him feel awfully good. He was thrilled with the way you conducted yourself . . . your kindness and friendliness to people and your attitude toward him. This is good good good.

Daddy's business ventures are flowering and blooming. He is feeling very good about miny miny things.

Willie [her houskeeper] is fine . . . got new uniforms in anticipation of your arrival home. She thought it was TODAY. I told her it is NEXT FRIDAY. She said "Oh, a whole week yet? Remember to get the flowers for her room."

Enough for now . . . more later. Write and bring home clothes that need shortening or altering as we have Rose Kaplan coming.

Love,
Mother

The "Stolars" are Frances and Bob Stolar. Bob Stolar was the Washington physician who was known as my mother's "Svengali"; it was he who guided and encouraged her to forge an identity separate from her twinship. He acted informally as family shrink to Father and me, as well. Though not a board-certified psychiatrist—he was a dermatologist—he had become well versed in psychiatric issues because so many skin problems were of psychosomatic origin. (Not that we had rashes . . . just plain old everyday problems.)

"The Wall Street romeo" is still the Oklahoma chap. Mother saying, "You learn by doing as they say in Parker" refers to the motto of Francis W. Parker, my small, somewhat eccentric, private high school. Over the front door of the original building was the dictum "We learn by doing."

"Trez" (or "Trezl") was Dick Trezevant.

[DECEMBER 8, 1959]

Dear Margo:

This is the first minute I have had to sit down and write anything that may vaguely resemble a letter. The Stolars were house-guests . . . Frances left but Bob is still here. The YPO [Young Presidents Organization] formal Saturday . . . trying to keep up with the office and writing work . . . making plans to go to Omaha and Lincoln (where I speak at the U of Nebraska) . . . fittings (new suit . . .) . . . and multiple things banging me on the head at one time. On top of all this, Hubert is coming . . . he asked me to set up a news conference with him at the paper Friday at 3:00 . . . I have done it. I hope Marshall [Marshall Field IV, owner of the Sun-Times] appears as is hoped. Then a dinner for Hubert at Elmhurst school . . . a rally. I know it will be fun if for no other reason than Hubert is on hand to whoop it up. Maybe we can steal him after the dinner and take off our shoes at the apartment. The only trouble is, that guy doesn't know what it is to go to bed, and with him morning comes very fast. Then . . . Blatnik [congressman from Minnesota] will be in Friday for lunch. This is a ritual. He always drives back to Washington from Duluth . . . and stops to spend a couple hours with us. Soo-oooo. . . .

The YPO formal was scrumptious. . . . Eighty thousand dollars worth of gowns. Many people asked about you. It was a Las Vegas night set-up . . . phony money and gambling tables. Every one got a thousand bucks in Confederate money and the 15 people who had the most $$ at the strike of midnight got prizes. I

went broke on the fourth roll of the dice
(my money and pa's, too) . . . (he was
busy refereeing a new war between Lu
and Arnie Meyer) . . . so I had a few
dollars left which I gave to John Patton
who went tap even before I did . . . and
then I visited around with a few people
and had a nice time.

I am eager to know: Are you rounding
up anything in the way of support of
Hubert.

The last phone conversation with you
was excellent. . . . It is very GOOD that
you are able to be honest about your
feelings regarding the Wall Street
romeo . . . and that you do not feel
compelled to cover up your doubts and
disappointments is indeed a sign of
maturity. HOORAY FOR YOU! You know
I am not enthusiastic about this guy but
yet you know, too, that I want YOU to
make these decisions based on your
feelings and your findings. This is the
only way you will feel right about it.
So—you learn by doing as they say in
Parker. I just don't want you to get too
many lumps in the same place.

Your white kid gloves came back from

Bregy as good as new. So please stay out of Lederers of Paris and leave my credit alone. Thank you, Sylvia Porter [a well-known financial columnist].

The weather is gorgeous. Bob [Stolar] and I have been doing a very generous amount of talking. In other words I am getting my psychological valves ground and my mental crank case drained. It is WONDERFUL to have someone to evaluate and guide and help. He is, indeed, a very old angel.

So, doll, this is it for now.

Do you want to have some fun when you are in N.Y.? Call University 42700. This is the Crown King hotel in N.Y. Trez is there for a two week course in advanced journalism. . . . It is a national editor's school put on by Columbia U. Call for Mr. J. Trezevant and say "TREZEVOONTI. . . . have you got an ear?" He will die dead as a doornail as this is MY greeting! Just say hello and ask him how he's doing in jail there. These editors cannot get out of the joint. They are under campus regulations and can't leave unless they go awol!

O.K. Doll, more later . . . when I can,
for now this is it,

Love,
Mother

Mother's high dudgeon at "Mr. Capp" referred to a plane I was on (Boston to New York), where Al Capp—the creator of the comic strip "Li'l Abner"—not only tried to pick me up, but he invited the man in the seat next to me to sit somewhere else so he could try. I knew him by sight, and when I saw the way the conversation was going, I told him he knew my parents. He didn't care!

Her mentioning the "smokey tones" was part of an ongoing discussion we had for decades. *Well, actually a discussion she had. Mother was heavily invested in my hair from the time I was a little girl with ringlets. I remember her once saying to me, "Your looks are in your hair." And blond was the color she preferred for me . . . the color I was, in fact, for quite a bit of my life. The last couple of years she was alive, however, I was a redhead, and this is no joke: during the next to last visit we had together she asked me, "When are you going back to being a blonde?"*

[JANUARY 19, 1960]
TUESDAY

Dear Margo:

The typewriter man just left . . . new ribbon . . . I'm cuttin' like a diamond . . . as Trez would say.

You woke me up this morning. But after all . . . what's a mother for?

The child is sounding better better better . . . all the time. I know the real reason you called was because you were worried about the plane wreck in Virginia. Those damned accidents do unstring a person, but it's always been that way and it won't ever be any different. You just can't go around living in fear. When you consider how many thousands of planes take off every day from hundreds of airports, it's a wonder there aren't a lot more accidents. In 10 years there will be virtually no train travel . . . it will all be by air. So . . . we live every day at a time, the law of averages is on our side, and remember that more people get killed at home, falling off ladders, chairs, slipping in bathtubs, catching fire from Christmas trees and falling asleep with cigarettes than in plane wrecks. The moral of that story is—quit smoking.

About Mr. Capp: All I can say is . . . the nerve of him. Just take his phone number and feed it to the nearest goat. You know what I think of the lecherous old bastard . . . I see he believes in working every generation. There will be others just like him—so don't be surprised. Life is just filled with little surprises—and big jerks.

Norma [an assistant] is making reservations for me. I plan to be in Boston on Sunday, February 7th. . . . You and I will stay at Somerset and Monday I'll attend classes with you. I want to meet [Stanley] Kaufmann if possible and that lady dean of girls . . . and of course see Goldie and Judy and Emily [my roommates]. Don't put the B on anyone to meet me at the airport. You can be there in a taxi . . . or I can meet you at the hotel. Please . . . get a reservation for a nice double room for the two of us . . . twin beds. We don't need a suite, unless you plan on having someone over . . . or if someone is with you at the airport we would need a sitting room. You noodle it out. Are you interested in seeing Hal Berman [Harvard Law School professor]? If so, let me know. I almost forgot about him. I do think he would be a good one for you to know.

About the shreck department: This is the occupational disease of a student. All kids everywhere (except maybe Miss Finch's or Pine Manor) are shrecked at exam time. The key of course is to work moderately hard all through the year instead of trying to do a semester's work in one week. So-oo-oo . . . you do the best you can and forget it.

I am not heartbroken that you are not a top student. I believe you are getting more out of school even on a half-assed basis, you should excuse the crudity, than you suspect. The Brandeis experience has been wonderful. I am thrilled you went there and in the years to come you will appreciate what it has really done for you. I do feel you could have gotten more out of it if you had been able to harness yourself a bit better. But there's no sense in beating on a dead horse. I do hope that something, somewhere, will kindle a spark in you and that you will take your next semester more seriously and prove to yourself (not me . . . I KNOW what you can do) that you have got something on the ball. This would be a great achievement as well as a real victory.

But it's the total product that I am interested in and in this regard I am very happy with Margo. I have seen too many educated damned fools, maladjusted odd balls, book-smart egocentric pains in the neck . . . and so have you. The important thing is the total package . . . and this I like. It's HOW you fit into life with the people around you that counts. You have proven that you can and are developing meaningful, honest relationships with people . . . particularly you have done well with the girls. This is more of a victory than you know. For years this was an impossibility. You were so self-centered that you simply couldn't manage a decent relationship with girls. Now you have many friends forever. Your relationships with boys are getting better all the time. You are making better selections by far ... controlling the situations much better, and dealing with the male animal on YOUR TERMS. I have no fears or doubts in this department. You are over the hill. You know what to look for and you no longer have a fear that you have to make any definite decisions. You have finally realized that this world is full of people who are worthwhile and that you haven't met EVERYBODY yet.

I hope you will keep all doors open, not waste time on foolishness, explore, learn, investigate, and give yourself every opportunity to make new friends and keep the ones that are worth keeping.

It will be wonderful to see you again. I hope you've given up on the smokey tones and are a golden-headed doll once more. Write to me when you can and if you can't can ... buy frozen foods.

Love,
Mother

The "skip the gym/wart on the foot" business, like my blond hair, was also an ongoing story with us. Mother was totally nonathletic, and so am I. It appears that in those days one could opt out of physical activity, which was part of the curriculum—even in college—with an excuse from home. I know we did this, to some degree, in high school, but it surprises me now that such was possible in college.

[JANUARY 29, 1960]

Dear Margo:

You are getting so goddamn wonderful I can hardly stand it. The letters have been deeeevine. And now this one which says if you have to come through with the $50 for Hubert, out of the allowance, you will do it. I am so proud of you I am busting my buttons. There is this business of talking big . . . and doing nothing, which many people do. But it looks like you are a kid who comes through, and is willing to put her money where her mouth is. I want to be kept posted on this . . . and also tell me if you meet any interesting kids through the politics. The current <u>Time</u> piece shouldn't hurt our boy at all.

I am sending stamps. The astringent you will have when I get there if I don't send it with Daddy in advance. And . . . if you make Dean's list (full course load, of course) you can have a Jaguar.

. . .

Now about HISTORY . . . I IMPLORE you to please stick to it. Don't tell me it's too late. The money is already paid for a full course. In fact, you can skip the gym if you'll take the history. I'll go that far . . . even support the wart on the foot . . . if you will please stick to the history and get the full year's credit.

It is shocking the difference in the tone of your letters as well as your voice, when you are working hard at your school work. You are a different person. The feeling of achievement, which can come only from putting out the energy, is marvelous for you. I urge you to stick to this ship, kiddo. You will be glad you did, and I will consider it a personal victory.

All is well . . . Daddy leaves Sunday. . . . I will let you know from N.Y. when to expect me. I don't know what the flights are but I'll grab something that will get me into Boston about 5 on Sunday. O.K.?

Gotta run. . . . Be a good pussy-cat and write to me and keep plugging away.

Love,
Mother

———————— ⌀ ————————

My mother regretted not seeing the musical I was in at Brandeis and she talked about it for years. It was more of a problem for her than for me. She felt she had let me down . . . and also perhaps wondered why Eliot Norton, the legendary drama critic at The Boston Globe, *had called me a "mercurial talent."*

[1960]
SUNDAY

Dear Margo:

It was so good to talk to you today . . . both Daddy and I agreed that you are sounding better than ever. We are happy that your musical comedy is coming along so well that you want us to be there. I just wish we could make it . . . but at the minute, it looks pretty doubtful. We have both been away from home for almost two weeks. Daddy has to go out again in a week for another TWO weeks. As you know, he is trying to put the distribution system in shape before he leaves the company [Autopoint]. This is no small job. So . . . a hop to Boston is not in the cards.

The last conversation from the road wasn't a very good one . . . and I'm glad you recognized it. Now—about the weeds. It means a whole series of things besides just puffing away. When you are able to REALLY quit, it will mean a lot more than just cutting down your chances for lung cancer 900 to 1 . . . (this is the average). It will mean that you are the master of your ship and the captain of your soul—to borrow a phrase. And more than that . . . it will mean that your attitude toward me is a much more mature one. The weeds have been a symbol of your hostility. You have smoked through the years knowing that I didn't want you to do it. It has been in effect, an act of defiance and rebellion. Now . . . this is all right— if you <u>need</u> it, and as you know I can tolerate a helluva lot. I always felt that there would come a day when you would not need to hit me with this brick . . . and apparently the day is here! So—hallelujah . . . praise be the Lord! This is a major victory for you and for me, too, in a way, because when _you_ do better, then it means that _I_ have done better. It's a bloody battle . . . becoming a whole person . . . and I see wonderful evidences that you are making the grade. And NOTHING in this world gives me the satisfaction and pleasure of seeing you win over your weaker self. I want you to have GUTS . . . to be in command . . . to be in control. You can never win the major battles if you can't handle the minor skirmishes—and winning you are! I see it in many areas. You are thinking better. Your selection of friends is better. Your school work is doing better. Your attitude toward Daddy and me is better. You are able, now, to think in terms of the big picture . . . the long haul. The notion of staying in school for four years does not terrify you . . . as once it did. You may _not_ do it . . . true . . . but at least the thought of facing the challenge doesn't turn your knees to water.

I am really pleased with you and what you are becoming . . . and more important . . . I am thrilled with what you CAN be.

Love,
Mother

———————————— ❧ ————————————

[APRIL 4, 1960]
MONDAY . . .

Dear Margo:

When I heard your little whimpering voice on the phone I had to laugh. . . . You are so much like me in the shteeklock* department that it is frightening.

The <u>Justice</u> arrived [student newspaper] and I saw your letter. IT WAS GREAT. YOU CAN WRITE. I WILL BE HAPPY TO POINT OUT A COUPLE LITTLE AREAS IN WHICH IT COULD HAVE BEEN A SHADE BETTER—(a word or two deleted) . . . but let me tell

————————————

*"Shteeklock," probably "shtick loch," means, loosely, little things, or mannerisms; the commonly used term "shtick" derives from it.

you, Girl . . . I think you've got it. By
Jove, she's got it!

Today is Monday . . . only a few more
days and tra la la . . . la. . . . Call me
from the airport!

Love,
Mother

[APRIL 29, 1960]

Dear Margo

What the hell did you do in the beauty
shop for $31.59? You are too young to
have had your face lifted but I just can't
figure out what you charged dorton.*
Now, please do not send me a check for
this because it is paid and it is not your
fault if your mother is crazy. All I can
say is, I hope you instill in your
daughter a more solid appreciation for
a buck than I did in mine.

Lots of luck,
Mother

---

*"Dorton" means there.

The trip and the small towns Mother mentions refer to her speaking engagements. She did a great deal of platform speaking as the Ann Landers column became widely syndicated. I remember being on airplanes with her, when I was in my thirties and forties, and hearing many of the flight attendants say to her, "You spoke at my high school."

[MAY 14, 1960]
SATURDAY

Dear Margo:

It was wonderful talking with you last night. You are doing BETTER BETTER BETTER. Back to Brandeis with you, child. The total product is beginning to shine through!

The enclosed letter is from M. [an old friend] . . . well . . . judge for yourself. This is a bit of a lesson. I misjudged them both, which I realize now. This was a bit of a shock because I always felt I was pretty shrewd about people . . . but even the old master can get taken in, which I assure you, I was. I should have had the ticket when I heard they were here for a weekend and didn't call. Notice in this letter, she starts Popo dear, and then she goes on to say Eppie dear. Well . . . if she can't even keep the names straight I feel sorry for her. As if this letter wasn't enough, Daddy called them about a week after the big party took place. He talked to [the husband] on the phone. . . . (Daddy, big shmo <u>always</u> called them . . . on every trip, but he won't again. . . .) Well . . . anyway, [he] never even mentioned the telegram. Here I slaved on the damned thing, phoned him long distance to get the facts and figures so that it could be accurate . . . and now I wonder if they bothered to read it at the party at all. I'll bet my life they did not! You know, the most valuable thing <u>I</u> have is time, and when I took that much time to compose the wire, and it WAS good . . . it just burns me up that I was such a big yokel. I feel like a hick at a county fair—with egg on my face.

Enough of that. All is well. It is good to be home. Father took me to Jacques for dinner last night. We just sort of celebrated. My trip was a lulu . . . but then they always are good—it is just a matter of degree. The small towns are great. Everybody turns out, rain or shine, and we had RAIN all over, and plenty of it. But they came in herds anyway, which is always a good feeling. . . .

Love . . . and write, you beast!
Mother

———————— c❧ɔ ————————

MAY 31, 1960

Dear Margo:
You called last night, and I decided to write a few lines about your letter rather than wait until you got home. We can still talk about it in person, natch, but I just read it for the second time and think that while the thoughts are fresh in my mind I will try to translate them to paper.
First—the letter was extremely well written, from a literary point of view. You expressed yourself well, and the composition was surprisingly good. You

are really learning how to write—and this is wonderful.

Some of your letter made good sense . . . particularly the part which started "I didn't raise myself." Yes . . . I accept the blame (or the congratulations) and whatever criticism you may have to offer. However, this reasoning can be extended to any area of failure, by any person who doesn't want to accept responsibility for his own actions. So, I don't think your argument is completely valid, but I liked the way you put it.

As for David . . . well, let's skip him for the time being. I think your description is an interesting one because you talk about things that matter. You didn't say whether or not he was short or tall . . . whether he had more than one suit, or if the girls think he is darling. He certainly sounds solid—and this means you are making better selections. Mazel tov. I remember meeting his brother in Mr. Emanual's [Frank Manuel's] class. I think he sat near me and opened and closed the window a couple dozen times.

It's too bad that I can't show Daddy your letter because it is a good one, but that bit about [S.] rules out the possibility.

And speaking of Daddy brings me to an important point. We both know how you've got him shnoggered, so no need to go into detail. It's a damned shame but there is nothing I can do about it. Because of his insecurities, he feels that he must cave in every time you want something. I have failed completely to make him understand what sort of a position this puts him in. All I can say is, you should be thankful that you can't maneuver me as you do him. Your girl friend who is now at Menningers would surely have a roommate.

And now about the earning. We are having a problem with semantics. Earning does not mean the same thing to both of us. I shall define my terms. When I say I want you to EARN the freedom that you want . . . (you can call it a trip to Europe if you want to but a poor example since you've been there—) I don't mean I expect you to behave yourself or make all A's. I mean by earning . . . I want you to show me that you are capable of mature judgments and that you have harnessed your unbelievable potentialities so that you can achieve something. THIS is what I call earning.

In this you ARE doing better. Much better. I think this is your best school year yet, from a standpoint of being able to discipline yourself and get something real out of your studies. Also, I think your male selections are getting progressively better—much better.

You will reach a notable level of maturity when you can accept total responsibility for your school work, and not put the blame on a teacher. One day this will come.

You are correct when you say Daddy can afford to buy you anything you want. I'm glad you don't want a Rolls-Royce, because I think Daddy would probably see that you got it. And I agree with you when you say "the determining factor should be the ability to pay for it and the need." It's the last word that is the clue. NEED. I do not feel that you need a car. It would only serve to distract you . . . and maybe make life easier for a fellow who didn't have one.

As for your declaration of independence, I don't think you had to declare it, since you have been more independent than you know, for a lot longer than you think. What irks you is the feeling that you are not <u>completely</u> independent— you want complete freedom to do as you please. This I can't give you. Freedom to a point . . . yes, but carte blanche to come, go, do, have, . . . no. I am still your mother and it is <u>MY</u> responsibility to see that nothing spoils my masterpiece. Not even you.

Love,
Mother

P.S. The roses will be waiting.

The late Tom Ross was a Sun-Times Washington *correspondent. Mother was obviously on a husband-hunt on my behalf. She also cared very much that any future husband be Jewish. Her personal and professional opinion was that marriage was tough enough without introducing religious differences. But she was to change her mind about this some years down the line. It is interesting that two developments in my life caused her to rethink the issues of divorce and intermarriage. Knowing the situation intimately, Mother concurred that my first marriage should end, and being so fond of my third husband—who was Christian—she reversed her view on that subject.*

In the summer of 1960 I was an intern in Hubert Humphrey's Senate office when he ran against John F. Kennedy for the presidential nomination. In those days, interns were unlikely to rendezvous with their bosses; what we did mostly was fetch doughnuts for midmorning coffee. In fact, I remember riding in the senators' elevator on two occasions with John Kennedy. He never looked at me twice, let alone tried to strike up a conversation. When his amorous habits became well known years later, I was deeply embarrassed that my twenty-

year-old blond, svelte self had not interested him at all. All I could think was, "What's wrong with me?"

Dear Margo:

Your letter was a gasser . . . and I loved every minute of it. Write to me at home from now on. I leave here on Friday. Daddy gets out today.

I met a friend of yours from Harvard. His name is Howard Miller. A doll. He said he had asked you for a date . . . and you were booked up for six months. What's the matter . . . are you a nut or something? I told him to <u>TRY</u> again. He said he would.

I met Tom Ross. He is a honey . . . but he is <u>CATHOLIC</u>. However, I gave him permission to call you, and he said he would . . . just for coffee . . . but he knows lots of swell fellows who are bright and Jewish and he told me he would FIND YOU A HUSBAND FOR SURE. A <u>Herald Trib</u> guy from N.Y. is his dearest friend and he said this guy would be the one for you. So . . . it's a connection.

I have seen Hubert and Muriel . . . and have spent quite a lot of time with him in fact . . . and he is in great spirits. Also, he is delighted that you are in his office. I hope you are doing something useful.

I must run now, doll . . . I will write more when I can.

For now . . . love and kisses . . . and enjoy . . .

Mother

Newton Froelich was a young Washington lawyer to whom I became unofficially engaged during the summer I worked for Hubert. Newton was a serious and scholarly young man, the kind of beau to please one's parents . . . certainly the kind of beau to please **my** *parents. We found ourselves in interesting situations that summer, including one when he represented a nightclub owner at whose club Sammy Davis Jr. was* *going to perform. On opening night, white supremacist picketers were outside making a terrible racket and a scene. In response, Sammy Davis performed for one hour and forty-five minutes in which he sang, danced, played instruments, and worked his heart out. It was a superb, amazing, and moving performance. The second odd footnote to history with Froelich was that he was a friend of John Chambers, Whittaker Chambers's son. At a party one night, where we all were, someone introduced me to Tony Hiss—the son of Alger Hiss. I asked if he'd ever met John Chambers. He said no. I introduced them.*

"Bob" is Bob Stolar, the aforementioned family adviser.

JULY 27, 1960

Dear Margo:

First . . . your letter in which you have told me that Newt is "the one."

I couldn't be happier.

Daddy gave me a full report when he got home from Washington. When he said, "That kid has a smart eye on him" I knew that was <u>it</u>. Those were the words A.B. used when I introduced him to Daddy.

Bob's reports have been excellent. He used all the meaningful words—potential, bright, mature, well balanced. The only thing that troubled me in the beginning was the pace. It seemed too fast. Too much . . . and, I still feel the tempo could and <u>should</u> be cut down for the sake of the relationship. It would be much better for you and for Newt if you could give each other one or two breathers a week. . . . Night and Day is a beautiful song. But, I don't think it's the best way to court.

About the Man: I am eager to meet him, but that must wait. I have a fairly good idea of what he's like. In fact, I think I could pick him out of a room of 100! The thing I like best about him is that he brings out the best in you. I have always known your potential, although I'm sure you still are unaware of "the tiger in your tank" to get a bit commercial.

I feel, too, that you can do many important things for him. Just loving him would be enough, but being my daughter, you know how to give beyond the call of duty. Strangely enough, however, in your romantic relationships you have never actually done it! You've never gone with a fellow that brought out your true potential for giving . . . or loving. You were always the one who was loved. You were the adored . . . the one who did the taking. Now at last, I think you can be both adored and the adoring one. And THIS is a <u>marvelous</u> combination. If I could have just one . . . I would rather love than be loved. For loving is giving, and the one who loves becomes whole, fulfilled, and complete. <u>Being</u> loved is someone else's history. I think you have found the one who cast you in the dual role of the loved one and the loving one. How wonderful!

And how do I know? Because, you told me on the phone, "He doesn't have any dough, but he has lots of potential and I am willing to work. I know there is nothing we can't do together."

What a glorious time you'll have. There is no fun that can match working together, facing a challenge, doing without a few things, counting nickels. You'll have an appreciation for things you used to take for granted. It will be exciting and it will add a new dimension to your character and it will give you a better understanding of what life is all about.

What makes me happiest is that you, in your final selection, have looked for the right things—the real values. You made the decision knowing that he didn't have any money. You haven't met the family . . . and you said right off he wouldn't win any beauty contests. So . . . what is left? Just the most meaningful things.

My most important job is almost finished. And I can say with a feeling of real satisfaction and pride, I have done it well.

Love,
Mother

"Ka-Noot" was Mother's nickname for Newt Froelich.

Referring to John F. Kennedy as "the punk" was a function of her friendship with, and loyalty to, Hubert. She would later become a supporter of JFK, as well as Ted and some of the other Kennedys.

Steve Reiner was a pal at Brandeis.

[SEPTEMBER 14, 1960]

Dear Margo:

You are a chiseling beast . . . but here are the stamps. More later—IF YOU WRITE HOME . . . and not use them all on Ka-Noot.

And speaking of Ka-Noot . . . he wrote Larry [her editor] a loverly letter which shows he has some couth and knows how to do things. SO—<u>this</u> you will not have to teach him. In fact, maybe he will have to teach YOU. Have you written to the Stolars to thank them for the last hospitality?

I hope you got that big fat envelope that I referred to on the phone. By the by, we saw (the morning after your call) that Boston was hit by the hurricane. I am surprised the Kennedys would allow it. Incidentally, it looks like Nixon might beat the punk.

Last night was my Guild Hall speech and I done good. Marsh [Marshall Field V, the son of her publisher] was my dinner partner and it was very pleasant. He is a lot brighter than most people give him credit for. We did have a relaxed and interesting evening, although the broad on his right tried to get his ear on many occasions . . . but failed.

Who is Steve Reiner? Besides transportation, that is. And . . . did the dress come?

I'm enclosing a letter which may swell up your head, but I think it will serve a useful purpose in illustrating something that I have been trying to get across to you. You have a basic insecurity on how you are going over with people . . . and you must GET OVER IT. Just because they don't fall dead at your feet does not mean that you are a flop. You must conduct yourself well . . . and then be satisfied that the results will be good. I hope this teaches you something. It took me 40 years to learn it.

Topsin bought three gorgeous suits

and wore one of them this morning. He looked like a fashion plate. I told him that if he loses five pounds he can forget about acquisitions and mergers . . . and just be a fashion model for menswear.

He went to Eau Claire yesterday to see Hale Publishing company (the hale he did!) . . . and it is progressing NICELY. Then he went over to Presto [his earlier company] to say hello, and said he got a great big hello from one and all. He said he was awfully glad he went. So am I. I always like to leave a "good feeling" behind. The Autopoint Co. is having two lunches for him . . . today and tomorrow. The gift for his farewell . . . LUGGAGE!! Hooray.

Love . . . write when you can and so will I.

Mother

Mother's carrying on about math reminds me that she and I had many of the same strengths and deficiencies. Neither one of us could deal with numbers, or spell. (We couldn't read a map, either. We both thought north was up.)

SEPTEMBER 17, 1960

Dear Margo:

. . .

Now, Doll . . . about the school . . . math, etc. As they used to say in Sioux City . . . "Feed it to Sweeny." Just get to work and hack that math course and don't tell me the math teacher told you it was too tough for you and you'll never make it. You probably took one look at the book and decided . . . "What the hell . . . why should I knock myself out . . . ? I'm not going to graduate anyway."

I am telling you that you are being unfair not only to Topsin and me . . . but to yourself, when you goof off. It may well be that you will decide after you get to Washington permanently that you want to get your degree. It will be one hellova lot easier to get the math credit at Brandeis . . . so please don't be so short-sighted as to think it doesn't matter. . . . With a LITTLE bit of effort you can make at least a D . . . and maybe a C. So, get with it, Kid, and see what you can do.

. . .

Bick [Irwin Bickson, business friend of Father's] congratulated me on your engagement today. I told him if you got engaged he'd be among the first to know. He said Arnold Root [friend of mine] told him. I told him, so far <u>as I knew</u> you were not engaged. Now, look, until you get your ring you are not engaged so please, kid, let's keep this thing in hand. I don't want this leaking all over the country in advance of the announcement. So, please keep your trap shut until we have something for your left hand . . . and I don't mean a wart.

Daddy bought three gorgeous suits and a magnificent cream-colored camel's hair coat. (yeah . . . from a real camel . . .) He looks sharrrrp.

I got myself a few choice rags, too . . . you shouldn't be ashamed of us when we get to Washington to meet the mahoots.*

Love,
Mother

———————— c◇◇◇ ————————

[OCTOBER 1960]
SUNDAY . . . (MASS)

Dear Margo:

Just got home this morning from Akron and Canton, where, I, of course killed all the people.

I read your letter complaining of the "three liners" [short letters] . . . and I suppose I should take five lashes with a wet noodle for neglecting my dotter.†
But honestly, I think I have been very good through this whole ugly mess.

I have been traveling. In fact I have more miles than the average United

---

*"Mahoots" was Mother's version of in-laws. The real word is "me'chutaneem." But "mechutan," the word for father-in-law, is probably what she was shortening. There are many versions of the same Yiddish words, depending on where people came from in Europe. And families sometimes "personalized" words and phrases.
†One of Mother's generic phrases.

pilot this month. So have mercy. I don't go anywhere until Nov 5th, and then it is only Milwaukee for a day. Then Michigan for two days ... then St. Louis ... and Florida on November 16th ... for two days. I will be in Eden Roc and living it up to the hilt. But it is the Southern Publisher's Convention and will be great fun for me.

Father is in Puerto Rico at the moment, and expected home today. He is fine and bizznizz is good.

NOW ... are you deaf er something? Why don't you answer my questions! Did you go to the Smiths' for dinner? Who called for you? How was it? Please, kid, pay attention when mother speaks.
. . .

You mentioned the dean's list. If you should crack this I would probably be forced to give you a Jaguar out of sheer pride. It is almost too much to hope for that you would do so well academically at such a stiff school. Do your best of course. We will settle for that.

I have a column to write and two more speeches to go over in the next couple of days ... so this is a long letter. In fact . . . <u>34</u> lines . . . so there. Can't wait til Thanksgiving . . . I am LONE-SOME. . . . LOVE,

Mother

———————— ⌒∞⌒ ————————

However embarrassing, "tamps" (for stamps) and the "toidy paper voice" have to do with the baby talk we sometimes used. The latter began when one or the other of us would run out of toilet paper (for which she was famous in another context: should it be hung over or under?); the one in need would call out, "Toidy paper!" This silliness actually went on for as long as I lived at home.

OCTOBER 3, 1960

Dear Margo:
I loved talking to you last night . . . and I did promise a long letter today. Well . . . I am waiting for a call to come in from Will's [Munnecke] office . . . so I don't know how long this will be. I'll type until the jingle . . . however. Can't guarantee anything. It could come at any moment.

Will is now on the fourth floor again . . . hooray . . . with HIS people. He is general manager of both papers, which means he's in up to his hocks. I LIKE this as he is also automatically head of the syndicate. Russ Stewart had this job for the past five years, and all the good he did ME, you could put in your left eye and still see pretty good. I asked him for three things, and he laid three large goose eggs. Now that Uncle Willie is at the helm, things will go easier. Altho' I used to go right over Russ' head and run to Will anyway.

I am enclosing the "tamps" which were requested in your "toidy paper voice." Now—let's see you use 'em . . . on US, I mean. This is sort of a token of love . . . half and half. Part of them came from Daddy's office, and part from mine. What are you doing with your allowance . . . buying a building?

My Omaha trip was fine. I told you most everything on the phone and it's a good thing, because I just got a call from Will . . . so I am runnnnnning. Be good, and write and keep up the good work. I think you are doing beautifully in all areas.

Love,
Mother

———————— ❦ ————————

The story that Mother liked so much about Erich Fromm—the then-elderly humanist, psychoanalyst, peacenik, and book writer—was my report of something that happened after a rally for "Saint Nuclear" and his policy. (I was taken there, of course, by the rabble-rousing Mr. Peretz.) Fromm was the speaker, and afterward there was a party. We were talking in a corner, he and I, and he asked where I went to school. When I told him Brandeis, he said he had been a visiting professor there in 1935. "But the school wasn't founded until 1948," I told him. With a twinkle and a smile he said, in his wonderful accent, "Vell, den, I am lyink to you!"

OCTOBER 7, 1960

Dear Margo:

Well . . . you've really got the whip-hand over me now. You have been just wonderful about writing, and I have been terrible. Two letters from you yesterday . . . and one the day before. Me—well . . . I have sent you a magazine, a crummy clipping and a few lame excuses for mother love. One thing you must admit . . . I am very secure to think that I could ignore you so completely for two weeks and not fear for violent outbursts of hostility. Nu—so I am a secure mother—and I hope you are the same. (Not for a while, tho', please.)

Things are humming right along. I have been a real loafer for the past two days . . . I mean like no work, just entertaining myself like ca-razy. This was the program: I got a phone call from Father Paul . . . you remember that living doll of a priest from Eau Claire. . . . Well, he is a Monsignor now in La Crosse. He wanted to know if I could spare a minute . . . so I said . . . "Come right over." I have not seen this

Catholic Rock Hudson in three years and I must say time has done him no dirt. He is still plenty beautiful. So . . . he hopped in a taxi and arrived in time for lunch. I had Willie run to Stop and Shop and get corned beef . . . etc. At 1:30 I get a call from Trez . . . Pierre Salinger (Kennedy's campaign manager) is in town with Kennedy. . . . They are across the street at the Drake . . . can they come over? "Sure" I said. "I may even give you a nip of booze." So . . . over they came. Ten minutes later Lare Bear [Fanning] calls. . . . He heard I am having open house . . . can he come over? He had lunch with Sid Yates [a congressman] and is two minutes away. . . . Natch, I shrieked. . . . (that Irishman can smell an open bottle of Scotch a mile away . . .) So—we had the most terrific hour and a half of visiting ever. The conversation was great and Willie stayed with me to keep the glasses filled and the ash trays clean. (It was getting on to four o'clock!)

Then after they left I got a call from a gal I used to know in Sioux City. She is about Sister Helen's age . . . lives in California and I liked her very much. She is here for a convention of Doctor's wives. . . . She is Calif. state president and this is a national convention. I asked her over as she was across the street at the Drake. We had a lovely visit . . . (hadn't seen her in 20 years) . . . and she said "I saw Popo last year in San Francisco. You are the same Eppie I knew in Sioux City. She has changed." I did not wish to go into detail, but it saddens me to hear old friends say these things because the word gets around and it gets worse in the telling, and she is just NOT that bad. I never thought I would see the day when I would defend the situation, but believe me . . . she isn't.

. . .

Your report on Erich (Ear-ache) Fromm was great. I ROARED . . . and I am so happy that you are attending extracurricular things. This year at Brandeis is going to be far your best yet. Atta girl . . . keep it up.

. . .

Daddy is going great guns. His ad in

the <u>Wall Street Journal</u> pulled like magic. He is in a state of Euphoria. (By the way, this may be the 51st state, yet.)

Now . . . you can't say this is not a long letter. Well, you can SAY it, it won't be true. Of course I am over-compensating, as you well know. You probably fell asleep ten minutes ago. Please write to your old grey-haired parents. We love you. And . . . I ordered a few extra pictures of you from Maurice Seymour [a theatrical photographer from Chicago] . . . but I would like you to try for an engagement picture one more time . . . either in Boston or Cambridge. . . . I hate to use your high school picture. We will if we can't improve on it, but please get your hair fixed and try it again.

Love,
Mother

⁓⊰⊱⁓

OCTOBER 9, 1960

Dear Margo:
This letter is being written the day

following the phone conversation. You told me you aren't ready to announce your engagement.

I can't say I was surprised. The silence these past few weeks on the subject of Knoot and the plans made me wonder. I figured you may be having some problems dorton, and since I have become an expert at keeping my nose out of your business I didn't want to ask what was wrong. In my conversations with Bob these past few weeks (mostly about my book) he didn't give me any hint that all was not well. (Yeah, I think you are right about him. He's on YOUR side, kid.)

I wouldn't, for the world, attempt to give you any advice. I want you to feel perfectly free to make your own decisions. You have the right to do what you want with your life—even wreck it. But I hope for only one thing, that you make your decisions based on mature thinking.

Life is no pipe-dream. It's no hayride, and it's no joke. Life is real, and it can be plenty rough for the best of us. There are no shortcuts to the road to glory.

You must cut your very own feet on the rocks. And rocks there will be a-plenty, because this is part of the price of the trip. But you'll cherish the scars because they will be the reminders that you did grow up—experience by experience. I wouldn't remove the rocks from your path if I could, because I believe everyone should learn his own lessons. And you ARE learning. Your progress this past year has been magnificent. You are twice the girl today that you were a year ago. And I hope you continue to develop and most of all, to accept in your guts, solid values.

Maybe Knoot isn't the one. Nobody knows this but you. But if you <u>do</u> reject him, do it with mature reasoning. If you think things through honestly, you won't be kicking yourself in five years. You're still pretty young and I'm not worried that you'll be an old maid. But please, use that smart head on your shoulders. If you hold a precious jewel in your hands, a jewel that has been appraised by experts to be worth millions, but to you—it looks like a hunk of pop-bottle, then that's all it's worth. It's the value that <u>YOU</u> put on something that makes it worthwhile.

I love you,
Mother

———————————— ✦ ————————————

My mother was fond of the young man I had been planning to marry. Newton Froelich was a person of quality, and perhaps I was just too young to appreciate his solidity. Her relaxed position on broken engagements, however, was no doubt influenced by her own, more than twenty years earlier. At truly the last minute, when the twins' double wedding was deep into the planning stages, she "switched" grooms . . . with her father's blessings. Mother was engaged to a lovely guy from California when she met my father. My dad was the one who sold her and Popo their wedding veils! He was then the very young millinery buyer for the TS Martin department store in Sioux City.

OCTOBER 11, 1960
TUESDAY

Dear Margo:

Your little "angel mother" note came today and it meant a lot to me.

No . . . you have not shaken my confidence . . . in fact, if anything, it has increased. I would be a failure, indeed, if you had gone thru the motions . . . not meaning it . . . just because you were afraid of letting me down.

Just keep your feet on the ground and think things through. If it doesn't work, well, it is not the end of the world. You must not let what others think be the deciding factor. It matters only what YOU think, and how you feel. Give it a fair chance this weekend, and don't be ashamed and feel that all is far-shmodret* because you did or said a foolish thing. Believe me, whatever it was, time will take care of it.

Keep me posted, and if you tell me you are coming to conclusions based on

---

*"Far-shmodret" means soiled (her version). Probably a variation on "farshmutsen," to make dirty.

logic, then I will be very happy . . .
regardless of how it goes.

Love,
Mother

———————— ⁓⊗⁓ ————————

Mother enclosed in this letter a clipping about James T. Farrell, a novelist and critic whose most famous book was Studs Lonigan. *The clipping said Farrell worked "in pajamas, barefoot." This, she underlined.*

OCTOBER 12, 1960

Dear Margo:

I'm sure you'll get a kick out of this.

I haven't heard from this kook in ages. The last time I gave him a kind word, I couldn't get rid of him for two years.

The thing I do like about him, though, is that he contributed to your growing up. Remember when he came to St. Regis Hotel looking like a bum and we took him out for coffee? You were about twelve years old and you decided that he was very smart even though he looked like a tramp.

Oh well, enough of this trivia. Back to work.

Love,
Mother

———————————— ⌘ ————————————

OCTOBER 19, 1960

Dear Margo:

Mother has been no great shakes at letter-writing this week, but then we have been on the horn incessantly . . . so that should keep you from feeling too much like an abandoned waif. I would say we have chatted in the past week, a total sum of 1,000 man-hours.

. . .

The weather is gloomy and sunless. It's a good day to stay at home and work, which is precisely what I am planning to do. I have spent several days on columns . . . and now I must go back to the book. My next chapter is NOW TO CHOOSE A MATE. Got any red-hot suggestions? I am serious . . . no joke. If you would like to outline a few thoughts or give me an idea of what YOU think belongs in the chapter I shall be happy to have your suggestions. After all, who knows better than one in the process of making such a selection? It's been quite some time since I chose a mate, and maybe my memory is a little dim.

. . .

Nothing new . . . since my surprise party [for her fifth anniversary as Ann Landers]. It was a real thrill. Will was the Master of Ceremonies. He read the wires and took charge in general. There was quite a sweat about who to invite and who to leave out . . . because the Tap Room holds only 17 people.

Phone just rang. . . . It was Coop [Bob Cooper, head of the syndicate] . . . we got Whittier, Calif. . . . (Nixon's home-town . . .) but I took it anyway . . . count now 402 . . . onward and upward . . .

Love,
Mother . . .

P.S. Pa just came home . . . wheeeeeee!

Max Lerner, devotee of De Tocqueville, taught at Brandeis two days a week, in addition to writing his syndicated newspaper column from New York. His department was American Civilization, which was my major. Marty Peretz was a grader and section man for him, and he also had a significant part in writing Max's book America as a Civilization. *Max, Marty, and I went a lot of places together. I think Max just liked to troop around with young people . . . and perhaps thought one of them should be a blonde. This gave people the idea, erroneously, that Max and I were an item . . . when actually I was just along for the ride.*

This second mention of the WSJ ad—meant to rustle up Budget franchise holders—is interesting, all these decades later, because many of the original franchise holders went on to make millions.

"Toilet mouse" meant, in our family, "really clever person." I have no idea about the derivation of this inelegant compliment.

OCTOBER 21, 1960

Dear Margo:

Tell Max Lerner to look again. BARKIS is a man . . . not a woman. He is a character from David Copperfield all right but he was the guy who wanted to marry the nurse . . . and his message to <u>her</u> was . . . "Barkis is willin'. . . ." My source is Will Munnecke and I'll put my money on him any old day.

From the looks of all the polls it's Kennedy. The only really good thing about this election is ONE of those jerks has to lose. They BOTH can't win. Of course I'll vote for Kennedy. You, doll . . . will have to wait till next time.

Father returned from the financial wars with a few dazzling scalps on his belt. He has had terrific response from the <u>Wall Street Journal</u> ad, and people are fighting over the franchises. The toilet mouse really picked a winner with this car deal.

The Jaguar in the meantime is ready for the fox-farm. Damned thing is the worst car mechanically we have ever owned. It is in the garage again . . . stopped dead on me. If it isn't the spark plugs it's the carburetor, or the clutch. Daddy said "There's nothing seriously wrong with that car. It's just a small problem.   Probably   something mechanical." To which I replied . . . "Of course it's mechanical. It's not emotional." If this isn't breaking you up, it is losing something in the translation.

Snow due here tomorrow. Hooray, that means I'll wear my Russian hat! Write when you can spare the time, and I'll do the same.

Your Very Own,
With Love yet,
Mother

———————⚬✖⚬———————

OCTOBER 25, 1960

Dear Margo:
The "BEAST" card arrived today and father and I screamed! It is a lulu. . . . We would have it framed, but we don't want anyone else to see it. So—we'll hide it in our room, and take it out from time to time to enjoy.

Several bits and pieces of news. First

a comment on [an ex-beau's] letter. The kid is semi-literate. No comment beyond that. Maybe one. In YOUR words . . . he has all the qualities of a dog except loyalty. The guy wants you to ditch [his friend] . . . but the jerk leans on a very slender reed when he makes the proposal that you cannot go with <u>BOTH</u> of them. Over-confident. Oh well.

Good news: Our car finally runs. The complaint was . . . water in the gas tank. It was to be sponged with a powder puff instead of washed with a hose. Also we have been using the wrong kind of gas. Anyway . . . it runs like a top, the guy said. <u>NOW</u> . . . if it would just run like a car.

Prediction: Kennedy is going to win. Who said so? I did.

Love,
Mother

OCTOBER 30, 1960
SUNDAY

Dear Margo:

Well . . . that was some conversation we had last night. I hope you can call again tonight so we can have another good laugh. HONESTLY . . . you had to go to New York for hor deaurves [*sic*]! Well . . . as they say in Francis Parker . . . we learn by doing.

It will be wonderful to have you home for a few days. I'm really looking forward to it. Please make your reservations as soon as possible as there will be lots of people trying to get places right before Thanksgiving and after.

This won't be much of a letter but I just wanted to drop you a line and remind you that this New York trip should be a landmark. . . . The New Margo. Deal from strength from now on . . . not from weakness. YOU decide who you're going to associate with and how you're going to spend your time.

HOLY KIMONO . . . YOU JUST THIS MINUTE CALLED!

. . .

If you can't spend an hour or two with somebody who is at least in his right mind . . . then be alone . . . so you can maintain a semblance of stability yourself. Kooks do only one thing for you . . . they make you doubt your ability, your potential and your own sanity. Also, add to the list Max Lerner. See him in the classroom only. He is using you for window dressing and you're a damned fool if you let him get away with it.

Love,
Mother

[OCTOBER 31, 1960]

Dear Margo:

Hooray . . . you are coming home for Thanksgiving! Get your reservations confirmed because there will be a mad rush at that time of the season . . . and you want to make sure you are ON.

Your last letter was great. You are actually attending classes. For a while there I thought classes were holding forth in the beer joint . . . or in Pittsfield . . . or that guy's apartment where you eat lamb chops.

. . .

It's actually hot here today . . . and I have a million things to do. I just got back from a week's trip . . . and the work is staring me in the face. (I am staring back.)

Write when you can, and love to you, doll. It will be so good to see you again. I am counting the days.

Love,
Mother

———— ⚭ ————

NOVEMBER 1, 1960

Dear Margo:

Some parents' kids get mixed up in the hospital. Not us. We got our own. Your bill from the Hotel St. Regis arrived yesterday. I would say that $74.81 for two days is over doing it a bit. You have one item there, $12.56 which looks like drug store purchases.

Also, you have a breakfast for $4.80 and a meal for $9.70—now really, Kid, the total of these expenditures means you owe me $15.00 the way I figure.

This amount will be deducted from your next allowance check. But, I don't think you will have to start selling apples . . . or anything . . . on the street.

Love,
Mother

NOVEMBER 11, 1960

Dear Margo:

I <u>HATE</u> people who say "I told you so. . . ." . . . but I told you so! Kennedy is in like a burgalar [*sic*]. You knew of course that Orville [Freeman] got swept out with the garbage. I can't say I'm heartbroken. Maurine Neuberger made it . . . also Gaylord Nelson . . . back as Wisconsin's governor. There was a real upset in Iowa. That jerk Governor Loveless thought he was a cinch for the senate . . . but he got broomed out by a young guy who used to hang around me at Morningside College. A nice Republican shnook named Jack Miller. I'm sure he never thought he'd ever make <u>THIS</u>!

Enough of politics. Guess who's in Larry's office at the moment? Max Lerner. The other night Rhoda [Pritzker] told me that Max was in town and called her but she was busy that day and couldn't invite him over. He was supposed to call her again. I don't known if he did or not.

Your letters have been wonderful and I feel like a crawlin' furley not doing any better by you this past week . . . (and the week before I was not exactly The Mother Of The Year either). However, you will just have to know I love you madly even if I don't write you long magillas . . . and bake brownies like all the other mothers.

I just glanced at the paper and see where Marilyn Monroe and Arthur Miller are pff—fft. So, now I wonder who will marry this nice Jewish girl. I'll bet the Frenchman [Yves Montand] is in there pitching. It is all denied, but weezel see. When I have to start in with movie star gossip, it is a new low.

Tonight I leave for Minneapolis. Daddy is going to Cincinnati tomorrow so this makes it nice. We'll both be home Monday . . . and Tuesday night we go to a party for Rod Serling. It is going to be at Frankie Atlas' [a neighbor in the building] and I know damned well HE didn't think of us as guests. It must have come from Rod. So, it should be a lot of fun. It's a dinner party.

I have so many little shteekloch to relate when you come home . . . so please be well rested as we will stay up all night talking. I told Willie to rest up as I will be working her plenty hard. So far the car is running. . . . It makes tea at four o'clock and popcorn in the morning. But it does run, and you can't expect anything more from a $5600 automobile.

. . .

Love,
Mother

NOVEMBER 14, 1960

Dear Margo:

Your letters are a delight. The one today, in which you had to do some "mental gardening" was a treasure. We roared.

I am sending this air special delivery because TUESDAY is Topsin's birthday and I know you have not forgotten but if no gift is on the way . . . a telegram (prepaid) will be very welcome.

We will be going over to Frank Atlas' place for the Rod Serling dinner that night . . . (I decided to let Frank give Daddy his birthday party) . . . so please . . . something . . . a kind word . . . like.

I had a lovely time in Minneapolis . . . got back this morning . . . but before I go into that. I <u>did</u> see Max Lerner. . . . I had to drop copy in Larry's office Friday and when I walked in, there Max was . . . needing a shave and a haircut. He was very friendly . . . in fact, warm, I would say. He told me that you sit right in the front row, and provide excitement in the class room . . . by "entering the lively discussions . . . etc." He also said . . . "She looks very beautiful . . ." and I replied . . . "Yes I know that she can do THIS all right . . . what I would like is for her to develop the mind." He assured me that you were doing well.

. . .

The perennial nightmare of every public speaker became a reality last night. I was to be in the ballroom of the Curtis Hotel at 7 bells . . . and I had a suite upstairs. At 7 flat I kicked the TV guy out of my room and ran a comb thru my hair in preparation for meeting the dinner audience. I went to get my speech . . . and I COULD NOT FIND IT. Well . . . I knew I had left it somewhere . . . but WHERE? Beauty shop, Drugstore, coffee shop? I didn't have time to look . . . so . . . I went <u>without</u> a speech. Believe it or not . . . I spoke for 35 minutes from a few last second notes . . . and it went off without a hitch.

[In pencil, she wrote, in very squiggly letters: "WHO'S NERVOUS?"]

The [—] saga is interesting. We will talk when you get home. I see you have Goldie's [one of my roommates] support and that means something. I have learned one thing in my 42 years of living. I don't expect perfection from people . . . and I am never disappointed. She is colorless, un-bright . . . lazy in the mind, but above all . . . she is a real neurotic. So, why expect much out of the kid? If she can shlep her beautiful face and frail bag of bones from one class to the next, this is a great deal. Be content to accept her limitations . . . and see her when you can stand it. I'm quite sure she never had any REAL deep affection for you because she is not capable of a really stirring emotion. This is her whole trouble with boys. She can't give anything . . . it isn't there. So be nice . . . don't look for her company, but keep in mind she has plenty of trouble and you should not add to it.

The panel at Sholem was indeed political. It was an afternoon version of <u>At Random</u> . . . with Kup moderating. It was fun . . . and I opened up a mouth on Nixon the likes of which nobody heard before <u>anyplace</u>.

The YPO formal was fun. Pa looked great in his boiled shirt. He is a doll.

Tonight he left for Cincinnati. He'll be home tomorrow.

Enough for now. Even the mothers who bake brownies don't write letters THIS long. So . . . nu . . . go, and do likewise . . .

Love,
Mother

⸺ ❧ ⸺

[NOVEMBER 1960]

Dear Margo:

A note in haste to say

1) it was nice talking to you today. Too bad a date with an Assistant Professor at Harvard doesn't count for a half-credit at Brandeis for Bio-Chemistry. Now HERE is a way to get thru school, kiddo.

2) I got the nicest phone call this evening. Smokey [Mann, an old friend]. He called to see how I was and just visit a little because he "misses Margo."

. . .

Daddy is in El Paso. The sheep is in the meadow and the cow is in the corn and upstairs, downstairs, in my lady's chamber, which makes no sense at all. But then it is midnight and I am beat.

Oh . . . one more thing. The lobby is finished and the tenants are taking up sides and the WINES ARE MOVING OUT OVER IT. Mrs. Wine says she will not live in an apartment where the lobby looks like a whore house. Now, I'd like to know how <u>she</u> knows what a whore house looks like.

Love,
Mother

NOVEMBER 15, 1960

Dear Margo:

Here's the guest list for my N.Y. speech. We invited four people from <u>Reader's Digest</u>. Three refused and the fourth didn't even answer. I must really rate over there.

Love,
Mother

"Essee" was Kup's wife, and in a true sense, his partner. She was involved with both his column and TV show, as well as many cultural events in Chicago. In addition, Essee was the mother of Cookie, my close friend from high school. Following Cookie's death three years later, Essee had a wistful connection to me and the other "best friends."

"Metrecal," for those readers too young to remember, was a diet aid. The violin Mother speaks of is the one she played as a child. She and Popo took lessons . . . but because Popo was the better musician— and because they were identical twins—Popo would walk out of her lesson, walk right back in as Mother, then take a second lesson.

NOVEMBER 17, 1960

Dear Margo:

Don't let the envelope fool you. It's your cheap mother . . . using up one of her reader's envelopes. Some dope sent an envelope with a stamp . . . but no address.

The Rod Serling party was a gas and a half. Kup was the host and it was at Club Alabam. This is a dive from the word go, but the food is delicious. It has one distinction . . . it is the oldest nightclub in the United States. I am sure they have the original entertainment. Some old has-been . . . dyed red hair singing. . . . "My red-headed Mama Anette" and a few numbers that even I don't remember.

The saving grace was that Rod sat next to me . . . so we got to talk a little. The TV guys were bashed out of their drunken skulls, totally incoherent, and I didn't say anything beyond hello to them because they would not have understood.

. . .

Essee sat next to Daddy and they had a long conversation. She asked him if we ever looked at At Random. He told her frankly, we don't stay up that late. She answered: "You're smart . . . and that accounts for the way you both look. You and Eppie look like a couple of kids." I really felt sad when he told me that because I know that she must realize she's aging fast, and when you don't have much else to fall back on it can be a devastating thing for a woman, especially. I still cannot figure out why she is so unpopular in this town.

The weather is deevine. Too warm for a fur coat. Daddy and I went hat shopping yesterday and we bought two lulus. Wait till you see! Sweet of the old tycoon to knock off in the middle of the day to take his old broad millinery shopping. He's a dear child and I don't want you to be mean to him when he comes east. He does the best he knows how with you. It's not his fault if he is an easy touch. He thinks he's being nice. I am talking about the $19 for Metrecal, which was foolish ... followed up by candy yet!

Willie is shining up your room as if Queen Elizabeth was moving in! She has been polishing the floor since noon! By the way, we have been invited to the Pritzkers for Thanksgiving. This means we won't have to cook a toikey!

Daddy had my violin overhauled. He took the violin into Lyon and Healy and the man said to him "Do you know your wife has been playing with a cello bow all these years?" Well ... I KNEW something was wrong, but I didn't realize it was THAT! If the U.S. Committee of String Instrument Geniuses hears of this they will take away my membership!

The car is feeling fine, thank you. We have tea at four and popcorn at 6, but it does get us where we are going, and we've had no complaints since the last one.

I'll send this special delivery mail just to prove to you that I DO know how much it is, and that I am willing to pay the price.

Love,
Mother

NOVEMBER 28, 1960

Dear Margo:

I think your plane was the last one out. The fog settled in down to the ground about 10 minutes later and the birds were walking.

. . .

Daddy is busy with his Washington people and I am hard at work solving the world's problems. If you need any help, please send a self-addressed, stamped envelope.

Love,
Mother

———————————— c⦚ꝋꝋ⦚ ————————————

[DECEMBER 4, 1960]
SUNDAY

Dear Margo:

I know you think I just SAY I'm going to these various cities to make speeches . . . and that I really sit in the bar and drink beers with the editors. Here is proof that I really did make a speech.

We had a lonnn-nng conversation today and she was hostile to Mother. I suppose you do get tired of hearing me harp on the same old things. It must be boring as hell. I think it's fine that you call but maybe we had better cut the conversations down to a 20 minute limit. Maybe the sheer repetition gets on your nerves. Let's try it.

In spite of the way the conversation

wound up, I think it was a good one. You are sounding a lot more sensible these past few weeks.

I think we'll plan on leaving Chicago Dec. 20th . . . and grabbing a few extra days of sun. I have a lot of work to do and so do you. Maybe we can both work better in sunny Arizona. Please go on a diet NOW because food there is the most devine ever and I am planning on gaining five pounds.

Love,
Mother

JANUARY 30, 1961

Dear Margo:

After that lovely conversation I intended to sit down and write you a nice long letter, patting your fur and stroking your Benzedrine-fevered brow. Still I have not been able to get off that longie to you so accept these two hilarious clippings and call me step-mother.

. . .

Keep in touch with me—which is a helluva lot more than I've done for you lately but then, I just know that you love me for my sweet adorable self and not for the lovely letters I write.

Jeff Stern got back from the army and is now employed at the <u>Sun-Times</u>. He asked after you yesterday like this, "Where's your beautiful daughter?" "Is she engaged or married or anything?" I told him that so far as I knew "no" but then I had not talked with you since yesterday at noon.

I will phone you soon and we will settle the affairs of the world.

Your father joins me in saying "dearest love and multiple kisses to our darling daughter who is growing old gracefully with us."

Mother

―――――――――――――― ⌒∞⌒ ――――――――――――――

FEBRUARY 13, 1961

Dear Margo:

. . .

Daddy and I are planning on coming

to Parents' weekend on Friday. We got a brochure and the first event is Friday dinner. . . . Also . . . they have a large hole in the schedule Saturday afternoon. We'll think of something. Father will probably open up a business of some kind. It should be fun . . . and we are looking forward to it.

. . .

This is no letter . . . but it IS better than a poke in the eye with a sharp stick.

Love,
Mother

FEBRUARY 22, 1961

Dear Margo:

Well, report me to the Juvenile Protective Association if you want to. I have been a lousy mother. If the state wants to take you away from me, they have a good cause. I have used every subterfuge known to man . . . I have sent clippings . . . cartoons . . . even seven cent stamps. . . . Everything but a letter. Now, I hope this will make up for it. At least I am going to continue to type to you until Will Munnecke comes up behind me and says "Come on. . . ." Nobody can say "COME ON" quite like Will Munnecke. He has an air of authority about him that is unmatched. Class I call it.

Sue Feuer [neighbor and Mother's furrier] has been a basket case. . . . We have tried to keep her afloat. There have been lots of people around which helps, but very soon she will be alone and on her own, facing reality. Daddy and I have been in and out of there a lot . . . we don't spend hours, but we pop in and out . . . liven up the joint and that serves the purpose.

Well. . . . Will just appeared. I must leave, but I will write again tomorrow. So, sue me. I am a failure.

Love,
Mother

Mother's "Mark" reference has to do with the Jewish tradition of naming children for the dead, either by using the actual name or first initial. My paternal grandfather, Morris, died when Father was thirteen, and it was for him I was to be named. For whatever reason, my folks were sure I would be a boy—and the name they had picked was "Mark."

The key to the city referred to Mother's collection, which just sort of happened, as she visited more places and was considered a visiting dignitary. Her favorite keys were ultimately mounted in a huge frame, which hung on a wall in her office at home . . . opposite an entire wall of honorary degrees. In fact, many of the keys were very impressive looking (and obviously some were not!). The exclamation "Nu, mach-a-nini" came from a television show (I don't remember which). Mother adopted it for a couple years, in her conversation and in her letters alike.

"Chapter Three" describes her visit to the Florence Crittendon Home—the national shelter for unwed mothers—a group for which Mother did much over the years. This kind of facility had also been a pet charity of her father's. In fact, in Sioux City, Mr. A.B. would send over movies, with a projectionist, to the Catholic *home for unwed mothers so the girls would have some entertainment. Mother's report about which girls were clients reveals another example of her ingrained ethnocentricity.*

[FEBRUARY 27, 1961]
[THE COMMODORE PERRY HOTEL
TOLEDO, OHIO]

Dear Margo:

Daddy adored your latest "Dear Topsin" letter. . . . You signed it Mark. I am in Toledo. . . . I spoke last night to the Episcopalians and this afternoon I am going out to the Florence Crittendon Home. Tonight I speak to the Sigma Delta Chi group . . . this is the journalist's national fraternity. The phone just rang. I gotta run . . . going over to the mayor's office to collect the key to the city. I hope it's a nice one. I'll leave ya' know later. Bye now. . . .

Chapter Two: Mother Returns

Well . . . the key may go in the drawer . . . alongside the piece of chaserie* from Oklahoma City. It was

---

*"Chaserie," also written by Mother as "mozzerie," means junk.

the crummiest piece of junk . . . plain wood . . . painted gold . . . (O. City, that is). You'd think with all the bragging they do about their wealth they could come up with something decent for visiting firemen. The mayor was very nice, however, and he gave me a gold-plated jeep which isn't bad. (Table model, natch.) . . . The Willys jeep is made in Toledo. The mayor told me it has been given only to Nixon, Kennedy and now me. Nu, mach-a-nini! Off to the home for unwed mothers . . .

Chapter Three: Mother Returns

Well . . . that experience is not a chapter—it's a volume. More in person. I couldn't do justice in a letter. They have 48 girls in there . . . and some are just dolls. One 16-year-old who could win any beauty contest. She is from a very fine family . . . and is supposed to be in Europe going to school. They have three Negro girls . . . one Japanese. They have no Jewish girls. This is interesting. Mrs. Walters who is the head of the home told me that in her 30 years of experience with the home . . . she hasn't seen 10 Jewish girls.

The girls were all wearing tags . . . "Ann Landers Day" and they baked me a lovely cake, all decorated beautifully. I spoke to them in an informal get-together in the dining room and they had a prepared list of questions. I am saving the questions. They are very revealing. Many of the girls are wearing wedding rings. Mrs. Walters says Woolworth is very nice. They send over as many as the girls want.

So . . . this is it for now.

More later. . . .

Love,
Mother

MARCH 16, 1961

Dear Margo:

So you have discovered morning! It really is a lovely part of the day—and I heartily recommend that you see more of it. Honestly, girl, a kid with your brains sleeping away the years is really criminal! For God's sake get out of that sack and accomplish something.

Daddy called me from Houston last

night. From there he goes to Dallas. I am home until I leave for Tyler, Texas, a week from Sunday. The sheep's in the meadow and the cow's in the corn and that accounts for the whole damn family; where are you?

Why are you using the St. Regis Hotel stationery when I remember a $42 bill from Saks for special Margo Lederer stationery. And speaking of Saks—those thieves, I went through the last 18 pair of hose in 14 days. I swear they must have been left over from the black market days of World War II. I would put on a pair, they would tear before I got to the door; I'd have to go back for a second pair and they would be torn before I got home.

. . .

All right. This is it for now. Be a good kitten, write often and lots, newsy letters, and make your summer plans and your winter plans—knit for Britain and Vote Democrat!

Love, your
Mother

Mother's asking for the green light to have coffee with Newt Froelich was indicative of two traits—one we shared, the other we usually did not. The shared impulse was to follow through and make good on our word . . . even if the particulars of a situation might have changed. Where we differed is that she often, either from pity or affection, stayed in touch with men who were past tense for me.

APRIL 15, 1961

Dear Margo:

I leave Monday for Norfolk, Va . . . Washington and N.Y. QUESTION: shall I call Newt when I am in Washington . . . for a cup of coffee at the Statler? When I talked to him on the phone . . . (you put him on, recall) I said I would. If you say no I won't . . . after all . . . it was MY interpretation that he was the mouse that died. Let me know. Write to me at the Statler. I'll be there Tuesday thru Sat. I will be on the run plenty from now until Mar 3rd. I will call you from the variety of places that I hang my hat. No point in your trying to call me. It is going to be one great big rat race.

Your recent notion (expressed on the phone) that you ought to scrap all the men you know and start from scratch is an interesting one. Tell me, do you think that somewhere, someone is raising a brand new kind of human male just for YOU? People have been basically the same for a few million years. I'm all for meeting NEW people . . . the more the merrier, but don't expect perfection. If you make good basic selections, the next step after that is arrange your own set of values so that you can appreciate the good in people . . . and be happy with what you <u>know</u> is first rate.

Your new school attitude sounds terrific. This year you have really done well. If you had your present ideas the first year you would have been Dean's List by this time and I am not kidding. I think you NOW know how to attack the school situation, and this is an enormous achievement. This summer you should do well at Northwestern . . . and . . . next year should be your best at Brandeis.

I'll keep you posted . . . and please have some goodies in my mailbox at the

Statler. I love your letters. Remember, I'll be there Tuesday . . . the 18th thru Saturday . . . then I go on to New York . . . from the 18th thru the 23rd . . . St. Regis, natch.

Love,
Mother

———————⟨∞⟩———————

APRIL 25, 1961
[THE ST. REGIS
NEW YORK, NY]

Dear Margo:

I saw Herb Tepper [new general manager of the St. Regis] here today (for the first time this trip)—He didn't even say "hello"—just blurted out "How is your gorgeous daughter?" Well!!!!

I just had my morning juice and coffee ($3.85 plus tip)—and I must say it was delicious. I have #1604 which adjoins a magnificent suite. They left the door open to the suite unlocked—so I am wandering around in a $200 accommodation for <u>only</u> $23 a day!

Daddy phoned last night and he is on

Cloud #19. He just signed a new group [for a Budget franchise] who want Honolulu—which means—all in one month he has signed Denver, Portland, Seattle, San Francisco and Honolulu. Need I say he is elated.

Be a good kitten and write, even if I don't deserve it.

Love,
Mother

May 12, 1961

Dear Margo:

Absolutely marvelous Mother's Day card. Simply great . . . and, I must say . . . the highest compliment. I think you are more like me than you think. I see myself in you in so many ways. And I think you will do better than I did, if you work at it.

I am thrilled about the Brandeis offer to let the child graduate with her classmates if she buckles down. You can't imagine what an achievement this will be. I am certain that you can do it.

The only thing <u>you</u> have to do is decide that you can and the rest is duck soup. If anyone had told you four years ago that you would get a degree from Brandeis, would you have believed it? Well . . . there you are.

I am enormously proud that you are so close . . . because I KNOW you'll hack it. I can't think of anything that will do more for your general feeling of well-being. Also, Lolly, Baby, it's nice . . . just for the record to have this behind you . . . in case you marry up with a guy who has a dee-plomer in <u>his</u> hip pocket.

Daddy will be back from Honolulu tonight. He called from there yesterday and it was as if he were phoning from the Pure Oil Bldg.

This is no letter—just a note.

Love, and all that jazz
Mother

"The Boston guy" was John Coleman, an investment banker, who would become Mr. Right Number One.

SEPTEMBER 29, 1961

(1) Field's is putting a tracer on your linens.
(2) Glad you like the new heating pad. It's better than a fire in the bed.
(3) I love you.

Dear Margo:

It was good to hear your voice yesterday. And . . . hoo ha . . . the call was entitled "I think I've found him." This was not the first such, but it had a ring of conviction. Too bad I was rushing to the beauty shop. You know how <u>THAT</u> is.

Since unsolicited advice is a drug on the market, I won't give you any. After all the kaup-far-drayeness* you've had, you are well equipped to think things through to a logical and rewarding conclusion. I

---

*"Kaup-far-drayeness" (often "kop") was Mother's personalized version of repeating myself, literally, bothering your head.

hope that you will reach back into the mental file called "experience" . . . (look under E) . . . and give yourself plenty of time to let the situation unfold naturally. Don't go pulling the petals apart in an attempt to get the flower to bloom faster than it should.

You've told me very little about the guy except that he has "a fine face" and the external trappings. Now . . . the big question is . . . does he have the real stuff. Only time will tell. Bob Stolar has decided you can have anybody you want. The important thing now is to make a solid selection.

I hope you'll keep the neuro-surgeon on ice . . . and have him come to see you if he wants to. It will be good for the Boston situation as well, to know there are others around. Don't make the mistake of spending every waking hour with the Boston guy "because he's leaving soon" . . . this would be a mistake.

And of course you know the importance of making this a banner year in school. <u>Nothing</u> should be allowed to stand in the way of a first class school year. This is your major project and as a matter of self-respect you must have this feeling of achievement. You musn't go through life feeling that you have charmed everyone into giving you things. You have ability and you must produce something on your own. Now is your last chance. Don't fail yourself.

Daddy and I are both home till next week. Then I do my Ohio trip, which is six days long. I'll keep you posted. Daddy goes east but then he calls you from the road when he can.

Write when you're able.

Mother

———————— ⦿ ————————

Mother made a big deal out of "seven ayem," which denotes the horror we both had of rising early. Our joke was that if we had to catch an early plane, we'd be better off staying up all night, or buying a house near the airport. I, somewhat, outgrew sleeping late; she never did.

OCTOBER 17, 1961
[HOTEL UTAH
SALT LAKE CITY, UTAH]
BANK DAY IN YOUR SIOUX CITY THEATRES

Dear Margo:

Your mother is in Salt Lake City—and loving it. The bath-water here is divine.

I speak today at the Rotary Club . . . a sweetheart luncheon. The men bring their wives. If they brought their girlfriends the hall couldn't hold 'em. Tonight I speak at Weber College in Ogden . . . which is about 20 miles away. Tomorrow I get a <u>seven ayem</u> plane (you heard me) . . . and go to St. Louis. I speak at the Missouri state PTA convention tomorrow night. Then on to Mexico, Missouri, to Bob White [the local publisher]. Outside of the above schedule, I'm not doing a thing . . . just sitting around and playing canasta.

Daddy will be home until Thursday when he goes to Indianapolis. Then we reintroduce ourselves on Friday (we ask a mutual friend to do the formalities) and the weekend we spend home together. I leave for New York (one day trip . . . for radio and TV . . .) and Daddy goes to Atlanta. He says he has business there but I know he is really going to see Scarlet O'Hara.

The book [her first, *Since You Ask Me*] seems to be doing fine and everyone is happy. If it stays on the list from now until Christmas they figure they have a real smash. I'm keeping my eyes crossed because it could go off next Sunday. I hope you will send me the <u>N.Y. Times</u> list and watch it for me. We don't get the paper here you know. Can't afford it.

Write when you have the time and if you can let me know your Thanksgiving-Christmas and Easter schedule it would help us make our travel plans. Are you coming to Vegas with us on the 13th? You are welcome to come live it up if the idea appeals to you. I think everyone ought to see Vegas ONCE.

This is it for now . . . more later.

Love,
Mother

OCTOBER 22, 1961

Dear Margo:

Mother has just returned from Salt Lake City, Ogden, St. Louis and Mexico, Missouri. She had a ball . . . (cotton ball in Missouri . . . and Salt ball in Utah). I am fast becoming known as the darling of the book stores on accounta I go in and introduce myself . . . they faint and swoon and I sign books and make nice on all the sales people and they tell me that when Christmas comes and shoppers don't know what to buy for Cousin Minnie or Aunt Gus . . . they will shove S.Y.A.M. into their hands and that will be that. (How to create a best-seller in three easy lessons . . . or four hard ones.)

I'm almost afraid to look at the N.Y. Times best-seller list tomorrow. I just hope I have not bounced off. I WON'T LOOK. You, please look for me.

. . .

I leave Monday for New York, and several TV and radio shots. Don't ask me what, because I have a mind like a sieve and can't remember anything. It is all written down, however. I may give you a phone call from New York if I have time, but as I recall the schedule, it is a beast.

Daddy is leaving for the east soon and maybe he will get to Boston. He is waiting on a phone call from the Boston crowd. They will probably reach him in Washington, D.C. which is where he is going after Dallas.

. . .

Be well and write when you have time. My regards to John [Coleman], and have some your own self.

L and K,
Mother

The gap between Mother's earlier mention of John Coleman and the following letter was because the courtship was whirlwind, and discussions with my parents were in person or on the phone. Both parents were opposed to my marrying him. A personality they found chilly and damaged I found fascinating and challenging. I also did not share my mother's

*enthusiasm for graduating, so that became—to me—
a non-issue. With all of us in New York for a weekend,
I made it plain I could not be dissuaded. Out of my
father's presence, Mother cried, begged, and threatened
me—totally losing control—something most unusual
in our relationship. This letter of apology, and support,
was to be her position for seven years, until the marriage
was no longer viable. And because she thought it was
the proper thing to do, they planned a lavish wedding,
with no hint to their friends that they thought the
whole thing was a huge mistake.*

[NOVEMBER 1961]
[THE ST. REGIS
NEW YORK, NY]

Dear Margo—

Please forgive me. I was unfair, not
only to you, but to Daddy. I had no right
to let you know.

Daddy has tried so hard to be strong,
and knowing how he adores you, makes
his efforts even more noble. He has
been magnificent—and I have let him
down.

I can't tell you how sorry I am about this morning. It was the last thing in the world I wanted to do, but I lost control, and all judgment left me. You, on the other hand, were wonderful. I was ashamed of myself—and proud of you.

Please strike this morning from the record. Whatever you decide to do with your life will be acceptable to us. We have no right to interfere. Your choice must be based on what <u>you</u> think and what <u>you</u> feel. You must choose the way to go. And whatever the direction, and whoever the partner, Daddy and I will give you our blessings and we will love you as always.

Mother

Part Two:
Letters from
the Road

INTRODUCTION

The question, "Will she, or won't she?" (graduate, that is) was settled by my engagement to John Coleman. After the first semester of senior year, I returned to Chicago to plan the wedding. Leaving school in the middle of my fourth year was not the calamity it appeared to be; I was still shy a boatload of credits, having been a "special student" with a reduced course load for two and a half years.

Mother threw herself enthusiastically into mother-of-the-bride mode because she believed that to do otherwise would damage our relationship, something she felt was more important than a possibly ill-fated marriage. As she told me—years later—the bit of "philosophy" that kept her going through this time was a remark attributed to Mrs. Diego Suarez, an in-law of the Marshall Field family. Regarding the marriage of a younger relative, Mrs. Suarez had said, "Well, he will be a suitable first husband." My father followed Mother's lead, as he often did on family matters, and tried to put his misgivings aside. (This would, years later, prove exceedingly costly for him, financially and emotionally.)

Although a great deal was going on in our family during these years—Mother was now majorly famous . . . Father had built Budget into a multinational corporation . . . I'd become the mother of three, with a subsequent divorce, single motherhood, a newspaper career, then remarriage—part two is comparatively slender because, during this time, Mother and I both lived in Chicago. This allowed us to see each other frequently and have numerous daily phone calls—

ergo, there was no need for heavy-duty correspondence. The following letters, spanning fourteen years, were sent from her business and pleasure trips—letters from the road, as it were.

———————— ❧ ————————

The following letter is interesting because, in retrospect, and maybe even at the time, I knew that what Mother had written was not what she felt. Her letter was simply a game effort to be positive and hopeful. Her decision was no doubt colored by the fact that she had not been able to change my mind, and therefore found no upside to putting a chill on our relationship . . . so the pretense was that she and my father had allayed their misgivings. They hadn't. Which is not to say that there weren't genuine times of warmth and amity between my parents and my first husband during the years we did live together. Had Freud seen the original of this letter, he would have had a field day with the exceptionally high number of mistakes, misspellings, and crossed-out words—most likely manifestations of her NOT leveling.

MAY 13, 1962

Margo Darling:

This is your wedding day. It is my last chance to talk to you as Margo Lederer. From this day on you will be Margo Coleman. Still a part of us, you can be sure, but you will be a member of another family. Your own.

I know I have talked to you thousands of hours through the past 22 years—too many perhaps. But you have listened, patiently, sometimes you've been bored I am sure, but you have been patient with me for the most part. And you <u>have</u> listened. So often I have seen evidence that you HAVE listened.

You have been blessed, Margo dear, with gifts too numerous to mention. You are beautiful, and bright, and good. You have had the devotion of parents who adore you. You have had a remarkable father. He is really an angel whose only fault was indulging you too much. And you selected a man who is very much like your father in many ways. John will be good to you always I am sure—he will cherish you and take care of you . . . as your father has cherished and taken care of me. John is a listener—and a learner and he is a fine person and a good human being. You have chosen wisely and well.

And now the advice. I guess this is my neurosis . . . giving advice. I seem always to be giving advice. So please be patient and bear with me because I won't be advising you in the future.

Remember your good fortune. Believe in God and thank him often for those blessings. Remember that we are here for a reason. We are here to make this world just a little bit better because we were in it. We are not here to take, to please only ourselves. Be kind, Margo, be giving. This world needs love and kindness and giving. So many hearts cry out for just a little love. You have so much to give. Be generous. Warmth and kindness is never wasted. For those rare commodities there is always a demand. Remember that cold, cruel, unresponsive people are suffering people who don't know how to give. Be of strong heart, Margo dear, because life can be disappointing, and punishing, and sometimes cruel. I have always said that you are a "shtarker."* And you are. You have great strength and a strong character and your principles are high. You know the way to go.

You have been a wonderful daughter. We have enjoyed you to the full. You have brought us much joy and happiness. We have always had a rare relationship . . . solid,   honest, sometimes stormy, but always we have leveled with each other. And now our hope and our prayer is that you will make a good life for John and for yourself.

Love,
Mother

---

*"Shtarker," a slang expression, means, literally, tough guy. "Shtark" means strong.

MAY 17, 1962
THURSDAY

Dear Margo and John:

Well—it's over. And according to the reports, no one ever saw a more beautiful wedding. Everything went off without a hitch. Even S. George [Abrams] who was wandering around the lobby in tennis shoes at 4:45 was perfect!

I've had all sorts of letters and phone calls and will send some of the notes on to you. The consensus was . . . elegant . . . exquisite. . . . The senior Colemans were most distinguished and aristocratic. . . . The Lederers gracious hosts. And everyone had a marvelous time. Not a single drunk or a moment's unpleasantness.

You will have so many things to do when you get home I decided to send on some of the stuff en route. There will be time for enjoying these telegrams together on the honeymoon. At home, you'd just rush thru them. We opened all the telegrams since some were addressed to the Lederers. It is not essential, but I think it would be lovely if you acknowledged them by postcard while on the honeymoon. It will take an hour or two, but it would be well worth it. You and John were so lovely to stay and visit with the guests and most unusual. Acknowledging wires would be a really lovely extra flourish which would be a thrill for the receivers.

. . .

Your wedding picture made the AP wire. We phoned the Colemans yesterday, Daddy and I, and they said their telephone hasn't stopped ringing. Alfred didn't go to business until 2:PM! We had a helluva time figuring out how an AP photographer got into the Guildhall. After all, kiddo, there were two cops stationed at the door. Well—it seems that Jimmie Guthrie [publisher of the *Sacramento Bee*] paid the AP for this. (Trez tracked this info down for us) . . . and he said "It cost him a nice piece of change." He ordered seven shots to make sure they got a real good one.

The gifts are still coming in truck loads. Willie and I are opening everything to save you a helluva job. We are labeling everything. Saving all the slips and stickers and putting a big sign NOT ACKNOWLEDGED, so you'll know. Also, we are putting the not acknowledged ones on your bed, separate from the rest. I am personally dropping a note to the people to let them know their gift DID arrive, that you are abroad and will send a personal note on your return. I don't want them to think you are a slob 'er something.

Be well . . . enjoy . . . and let us know when you will be coming home . . . no hurry. Also, please let me know you received this stuff.

Love,
Mother

May 22, 1962

Dear Margo:

To date we received one terrific letter from you—which was wonderful. This is no complaint. I think it was thoughtful of you to come through with even one. I would worry about a girl who wrote several letters to her parents while on a honeymoon.

Please let me know soonest if you received the large manila envelope I sent to you in Barcelona. According to your letter you may have changed your travel plans and loused me up.

At any rate, if the envelope missed you in Barcelona, I have air-mailed the hotel manager to forward it to you at Majorka.

Today I'm sending another envelope to you at Majorka—so—you should have two envelopes in all.

Daddy and I leave for Mexico Saturday. Call us from New York when you land. We are still aglow from the loveliest wedding anyone ever saw.

Love,
Mother

Even forty years ago Mother was Jack La Lanne in her spare time. Though admittedly not athletic, she was faithful to her own routine of stretching, floor work, and "jogging" around her apartment. And for many years, Mother walked to and from the paper, roughly twelve or fourteen blocks. Coincidentally, the Sun-Times *and the* Tribune *were only a few blocks apart. She really did love to walk, and had a group of "walking buddies," with whom she could both walk and gossip.*

[APRIL 1963]

Dear Margo:

I've written you some strange little notes in these past 23 years, and this one may well be the strangest. First, it was such fun being up in the woods with you and John. I think maybe I was a little too critical of unimportant things—but you take me very nicely, and that's not easy, because I do come on pretty strong.

I am not concerned about your mental health . . . you are doing progressively better. And we'll let Bob [Stolar] be your general manager in that department, but your physical condition is what shakes me up. When I saw how you struggled to get two legs off the floor at the same time, and just couldn't even begin to keep up with this 45 year old bag on the most elementary of exercise I was really shook. Here you are, only 23 and in unbelievably poor condition. If this is the way you are <u>now</u> I hate to think of what two more kids and 10 years will do to you.

I'm sure now that your off-again-on-again stomach discomfort is related to your sedentary state. How can you expect to feel good when you eat eight or nine times a day (and junky stuff like donuts, at that) and then sit sit sit and not move? Your stomach muscles get absolutely no exercise. No wonder they are weak and non-functioning.

I am not suggesting that you go in for tennis or golf or any such stuff as that. But there are some very useful and constructive things you CAN do. Being a completely un-athletic person myself I know what you can do because I am in exactly the same boat, never having had any talent for, or interest in sports. I will suggest two things, and you should, I hope be able to do them without much trouble. You can WALK . . . WALK WALK . . . either with the baby in the afternoon or with John after dinner. Walking is wonderful because it uses almost all the major muscles and gives you good circulation. Then you can work up gradually—a little program of daily exercises. . . . Do it to music. It's easier. But this must be consistent . . . every day . . . at about the same time if possible. Remember to start modestly, at first just one or two at a time, and build up. This will take no more time than 10 minutes out of your entire day, and it could make a world of difference in your general condition.

Last, but certainly not least, you must stop eating all day long—and you should not eat hozzerie,* which means greasy, fatty foods . . . rich stuff, and beer is about as fattening a drink as you can lay your hands on. You should not have any fried stuff, and spaghetti once

---

*"Hozzerie," previously written by Mother as "chaserie," means junk.

a week is enough. Also, pizza is like eating garbage. It is full of spices and crap beyond description. In short . . . remember you ARE what you eat, and if you will be honest about it, you must admit that you ought to take off about 10 pounds, and you should do it before you get busy on your next little red-head.

. . .

There is a lot more of me in you than you think, Margo. . . . If you once make up your mind that you are going to do something, hell and high water can't stop you.

Just tell yourself that life is ten times as much fun when you feel good. To feel good you have to be in good condition. This takes WORK. . . . It is not going to be a gift from out of the blue. You were born with a really good body and a good mind. You inherited good material from the "factory." Your father and I are a couple of oxes . . . and you are, too. So please appreciate your gifts and don't abuse them. I can't think of a better investment in all the world than a few minutes a day, and a little will-power toward feeling better and adding years to your life.

Love,
Mother

───────── ⌾ ─────────

SEPTEMBER 4, 1964

Dear Margo:

Daddy and I want to thank you for the beautiful collage. It is truly a labor of love.

The thought and the effort that you devoted to our 25th anniversary gift is further evidence that you are a wonderful child.

It's a source of great satisfaction to see you learning and growing—a little every day—winning some of the small battles and some big battles as well. I see so much of myself in you, because I, too, have tried through the years always to <u>do</u> better and to <u>be</u> better, and I'm still trying.

I have always said you are my greatest achievement and I say it again.

Love to you and your John,
Mother and Daddy

―――――――― ⟨∞⟩ ――――――――

The Jeannie referred to is Popo's daughter, two years junior to me. She now writes "Dear Abby."

DECEMBER 15, 1966
THURSDAY

Dear Margo:

I'm under the dryer at Mauna Kea Hotel—and while the girl is clipping away at my toenails I will use these few moments to say "hid-o-dere, tochter."*

Daddy and I have had a lot of fun—the L.A. leg of the trip was great—I told you about Pamela's [Mrs. James Mason] party and the Roder [relatives] bash. Pam did it up in style and it was a beautiful job of organization, selection, and execution, which for her— (according to her own admission) is unheard of. "Usually, I'm such a slob"

―――――――――
*"Tochter" means daughter.

she says—but she really wanted to make this party tops. And it was.

J. Paul Getty Jr. was there and his marriage is recently on the rocks, so Zsa Zsa was making a play for him, because her marriage isn't doing terribly well either. It seems she found out something *terrible* about her husband (Josh Cosden). He has no money. Also, something dreadful happened to him right after they were married. He was thrown out of the Blue Book! So—since he is neither social nor rich, what does she need him for? Daddy talked to Josh for about 5 minutes and declared him the dumbest person he has met in years.

The family bash was fun—considering the heavy concentration of relatives. Morey Rubin and Dub [the family name for Mother's sister Dorothy]—and Esther Mirkin [Mother's cousin] were generous in their praise of you. Jeannie was also very pleasant—said you were so beautiful—and that she had always worshipped you. We met her steady fella who is quite attractive, bright, and has a very warm personality. It would not surprise me if they married. Popo says she hopes Jeannie will get married before her hormones dry up and she is too old to have a family.

Popo and Mort [Popo's husband] looked very good and were extremely friendly to Daddy and me. There was no tension or uneasiness. We had a nice visit, sat together at the dinner and it worked out fine.

. . .

Daddy and I spent the night at the Kahala Hilton when we flew over from Los Angeles. We decided it would be better than trying to go from L.A. to the Mauna Kea in one fell swoop. When we were leaving the Kahala to come over here, we encountered Cassius Clay in front of the place. He was in training clothes and had his buddies along. He recognized me at once and spoke to me in a very courteous and friendly manner. He said he had seen me on the <u>Mike Douglas</u> show and that I was very good. "I expected you to be taller" he said—"About 5'6 maybe—you're awfully little" he complained. I apologized, of course, and said I hoped he wasn't too disappointed. "Oh no," he replied, "You are a very nice looking woman."

I have to leave the dryer now—so I'll sign off with love and kisses. I'll be home on the 22nd—late and will call at some civilized hour on the 23rd.

Love—
Mother

MAY 14, 1968

Dear Margo:

The Mother's Day gift [a robe] was just right. I thank you, in behalf of the Room Service waiters of the Washington Hilton, Ritz Carlton, St. Regis and assorted motels from coast to coast— including the Tidelands in Wichita Falls, Texas.

You are a wonderful daughter and I love you very much.

Nonno

AUGUST 6, 1969

Margo:

Here is the recipe for compote:

Buy a cellophane package of the largest prunes you can find. (Note, I said largest <u>prunes</u>, not largest package.) Also buy a package of dried apricots. Also buy a package of frozen peaches.

Put all the prunes and half the apricots in an aluminum or glass bowl. Also half the peaches. Pour boiling water, a fair amount, over the fruit. Put a silver knife in the bowl if you are using a glass bowl so that it will not crack. Add half a lemon. Cover with aluminum foil and place in refrigerator. I happened to have some old bing cherries kicking around so I added a couple dozen—took the pits out first, and it made a delicious mix. The lemon should come out after the second day as it makes the mix too sour.

This is better than candy for the kids and it should be standard equipment in your refrigerator at all times.

L & K

Betty Crocker

In the following letter, the first piece Mother mentions was from my twice-weekly column in the Chicago Tribune, called "Margo"; the second was a long piece I'd written for their Sunday magazine. I had stumbled into the newspaper business . . . just as Mother had, only my version of her winning a contest had been a suggestion by the late Gene Siskel, whom I first met when he was nine years old! In 1969 he was the Tribune's very young movie critic. We were seated together at a wedding, and he told his editor he had a hunch I could write. (My burgeoning newspaper career began at a propitious time; I was divorcing my starter husband, making my parents' unspoken prophecy a reality.) And from the very beginning, my mother was my biggest booster. The "Dr. Rubin" she refers to (and of course misspells) was Dr. David Reuben, the author of the book with the famous title: Everything You Always Wanted to Know About Sex, But Were Afraid to Ask. *I wrote a snide piece about him (well, actually, more than one) and he threatened to sue.*

Harold Hughes was the colorful senator from Iowa. I met him at a Democratic fund-raiser at the farm of Adlai Stevenson (the father) and we had become friends. During his very brief run for the presidential nomination I joined a small contingent of political reporters and went on the campaign trail with him to write a profile. That Mother uses the name "Pack" bespeaks a social approach of hers that some people found overly familiar. In this instance, "Pack" was Hughes's nickname to his closest friends from World War II. This would not have been me . . . nor would it have been her. Because his war service was a major memory and an important influence in his life, I mentioned that name in my piece. Interestingly, Mother made it her business to get to know him . . . I suspect because he was one of the few important political people I knew and she didn't. This is one of the few instances where I sensed any competitive instinct. Ed Campbell was Hughes's administrative aide and loyal friend. He went on to become a political power, in his own right, in Iowa.

[JUNE 1970]
FRIDAY (BENSH-LICHT)
PLAZA ATHENEE/CHI.

Dear Margo—

I'll probably beat this letter home—but it's worth the try. Just wanted you to know Daddy brought your Fat Cat piece over to Paris—and it is <u>hilarious</u>! I loved it! More!! More!! I'm convinced your best pieces can come from reading the papers and magazines. The second best source—people to interview—provided they are jerks—Like Dr. Rubin.

My office sent your Howard—uh Harold Hughes piece. It came this morning. I thought it was first rate. It held my attention to the finish. Pack should love it. Also Ed Campbell. You were most generous. The art was great. That fellow Fink [editor of the *Tribune Sunday* magazine] is primera class. You should pay attention to whatever suggestions he has regarding magazine pieces.

Daddy and I are having a ball. The weather is gorgeous. The food is divine. The prices are outrageous. Paris shopping is submission to financial rape.

Ran into Gabe [*Sun-Times* executive] and Janet Joseph here. Also—fans from Detroit—Las Vegas—Chicago—ho hum—no place to hide.

Gotta run. Love to your little folks.

Mother

"George" was the chauffeur of the moment. He was from Yugoslavia, a good driver, but barely spoke English. I have no idea how they communicated.

Bob Hall was head of a newspaper syndicate, as were Arthur La Roe and John McMeel. Mother's advice, in this letter, was about how to deal with the different syndicates trying to sign me. My twice-a-week column had caught on and the syndicate guys apparently noticed.

"Papa Bear" was Walter Simmons, the Chicago Tribune's *feature editor whom Gene Siskel had pestered to meet with me. Simmons hired me, and would become my great patron. A gruff, crusty, former foreign correspondent in his sixties, he was a few years from retirement. Everyone was terrified of him . . . but I could make him laugh, and quite soon after our initial meeting I named him "Papa Bear." I always felt that his wife, who liked my writing, was influential in his decision to help me advance. With his help, as well as that of the late J. Anthony Lukas (my beau at the time, and the* New York Times *bureau chief in Chicago), I learned the technical aspects of newspaper writing.*

[DECEMBER 1970]

Dear Margo:

I'm back from La Crosse today and heading for Topeka tomorrow. I'll have George hand deliver this so it doesn't get bogged down in the post office and arrive after your visit with Bob Hall. I thought I'd jot down a few things you might keep in mind while Hall is talking. Of course you won't be giving him a definite answer until after you've seen Arthur La Roe and possibly John McMeel.

(1) Don't go for a ten-year contract. Tell them you'll go for a five-year contract with a three-year renewal clause. The clause should give either party the right not to renew.

(2) A 50-50 split in revenue with the syndicate paying all expenses. (Promotion . . . mimeographing—your long-distance calls and whatever traveling you have to do to interview or attend special events.)

(3) If your out-of-state mail gets heavy, you might need a full-time secretary. The syndicate should pay for this.

(4) Have an understanding with Papa

Bear that the <u>Tribune</u> will house such a secretary without cost and give her a typewriter, stationery—etc . . . stamps.

(5) Be sure to get it in writing that the <u>Tribune</u> is NOT their client . . . that your contract with the <u>Tribune</u> is separate and has nothing to do with them. Tell Hall if he behaves himself, you might occasionally urge Papa Bear to look at a great new Pub. Hall feature for the <u>Tribune</u>! This is a subtle suggestion that you just might be a good person to cooperate with.

(6) I hope you'll pass on the CBS thing for now. I don't see how you could put enough substance into a radio show so that it would be a plus for you. You mustn't do anything that might detract from your column. If they are willing to use re-heated material, which I doubt . . . it just might be too much exposure. If they want you to produce fresh material for radio you'll be in trouble with your papers. I have passed up many radio and TV offers over the years and I have never regretted it. Art Buckwald [*sic*] hurt himself with papers by signing up for a radio show which

died like a dog. He also wrote a Broadway Show that layed eggs the size of basketballs. Be a winner . . . not a loser.

L and K
Mother

———⌘———

I have included the following letter—one of the very few in this book not written to me—because it is revelatory of Mother's belief in non-avoidance, as well as her practice of responding even to things that were meant to sting. I omit the writer's name but the gist of her letter describes that she had some journalistic credentials and couldn't get a job in Chicago . . . while the famous columnist's novice daughter had no such difficulty. My fast start in the news business was, indeed, much discussed and not universally applauded. Many people, offended by my debut as a heavily promoted feature writer, then a columnist, ignored that I was hired not by my mother's paper, but the opposition paper "across the street." People just assumed that Mother made it happen, or she'd "bought" it for me, or that I was having a romance with someone in a position of power. Apparently, many people found it difficult to imagine that I could be who I was as well as capable. Because I drove a Rolls-Royce and never had a job before, I was a logical target. In time, I think, the quality of my writing tamped down my detractors, but I always understood the resentment of people who felt that, were my mother not Ann Landers, I would be nowhere. In any case, that is the background informing the following letter.

JANUARY 22, 1971

Dear [J.E.]:

Thank you for your letter of January 20. You raise some valid questions and deserve a thoughtful answer. The fact that you signed your name is evidence that you are a person of integrity.

I agree, it's pretty darned discouraging when a girl with your credentials and experience can't get a job, then some rank amateur comes along, gets scooped up—suddenly her face appears on trucks, in full-page ads, on TV—everywhere you look. I can understand your feelings of resentment and I'm sure other bona fide newspaper girls in town feel as you do.

Unfair? Of course it is. But who ever said life was fair? Getting a break is a matter of who you know, more than what you know, and just being at the right place at the right time. I'm a good example of just that. Like Margo, I had no background, no training, no experience and no credentials. I was lucky enough to know an executive at the <u>Sun-Times</u> and I just happened to wander into the newspaper three days after the original Ann Landers had died. If I had shown up a week earlier the answer would have been "No"—and if I had come a week later the job would have been filled.

Luck is an important factor in every aspect of life and I would be the last one to deny it, but having gotten the break a person must know what to do with it. I've discovered that the harder I worked the luckier I got. I've been on the firing line every day—365 days a year for 15 years. If I had become lazy, or lethargic, or out-dated or boring I would have been replaced by someone who could do the job better.

And so will it be with Margo. She has indeed lucked out and is the first one to admit it. Having had the break it's up to her to do something with it. In the final analysis it's talent that counts. The readers don't care about relatives or pull or charm or good looks. They want to be amused, or educated, provoked or turned on. If Margo has the stuff she'll survive. If she hasn't—nobody can save her.

You mention that as a last resort you might go to Columbus for the AP. The Dispatch is my paper there and I know the top people. If you would like me to put in a call or write a letter for you, send up a shout and I'll be happy to do it. Obviously you haven't had a break and if I can help you get one I'll do it. After all, I've had more than my share.

Sincerely,
[Eppie Lederer]

Dinners at "Gram's" were, indeed, company affairs . . . served in the dining room with gold flatware, Limoges china, Baccarat crystal, and discussions of current events. The "company," however, was all under ten years old. In 1972, my children were nine, seven, and five. They thought it all quite odd—which Mother knew—but she felt something of value would seep in. She also found me lax in the "intellectual enrichment" department, and said to me, on more than one occasion, that children could be trained to think about serious things. Her concession to the young ages of the guests was a coloring contest after dinner, for which there were prizes of toys and books.

AUGUST 25, 1972

Dear Mugsie:

Here's the bi-annual G note. Buy your ragamuffins some nice fall clothes.

From now on, dinner at Gram's is going to be a company affair. I will try to make the dinners more guest-like and I would like to have them feel they are being invited out to dinner. I want them to show up with clean hands and faces, combed hair and dressed like they were dinner guests and not like they were going to the ball park.

If you think I am nutty, I gotta right. I've been turning out 365 columns a year for 17 years and have been married to a Rumanian for 33.

Love you,
Mother

Casual about names she was unfamiliar with, Pimento of course was Pentimento. Mother would readily admit that there were gaps in her knowledge of literature.

[1973]
SUNDAY NIGHT

Dear Margo:

. . .

Enclosed is a piece that touched me. I know you admire Lillian Hellman's writing. Once you gave me a copy of her book, <u>Pimento</u> . . . or something like that.

I was moved by what she feels about her Jewishness. Maybe it's because I feel the same way. If I could give my grandchildren that feeling it would make me very happy. I have tried, but I'm afraid I've failed . . . and it is a painful failure. But then it was not up to me. It was up to you. Maybe this means I failed somehow to transmit the feeling to you?

It's past midnight and time I got off the guilt trip, but I wanted to get this in the mail before I turned out the light. . . . And changed my mind in the morning.

Love you,
Nonno

"Jules" (Furth) was Mr. Right Number Two, about whom my mother asked, "Did you search the world for a man with your father's first name?" This was a relatively brief marriage.

Father Theodore Hesburgh, the longest-serving

president of Notre Dame University, met my folks when both my dad and Father Ted were YPO'ers. Fr. Ted and Mother forged a friendship that lasted more than forty years. My youngest child, "Cricket," is actually named Andrea Ted—in honor of him. He was one of the few people allowed to come say good-bye when Mother was at home, knowing that her illness was terminal.

"Mary" (Lasker) was Mrs. Albert Lasker. She was not only a close friend of Mother's, but an older role model, as well. Mary is credited, through her philanthropy and clout, with essentially creating NIH, the National Institutes of Health. Her intense interest in treatment and research is what clearly influenced Mother to become involved, herself, with the world of medicine and to serve on boards of various medical institutions. Mary's principal home was in Manhattan, with a summer estate first in Amenia, New York, then later in Greenwich, Connecticut. Mother was a frequent houseguest.

"Tosh" was our Yorkie, McIntosh. I gave him to Furth when we were divorced because he felt so sad about everything. I told the children I did this to be kind, and they said, "But Mother, he was OUR dog!"

MARCH 29, 1974

Dear Margo and Jules:

I will undoubtedly beat this letter home—but I am writing in the hope that you will call Jordan Block [her dentist] and ask him if he will wire my mouth shut when I return. Please plead my case. I've been averaging two desserts a meal and am utterly hopeless when left to my own devices.

This has been a marvelous crossing. The sea is smooth and I know an awful lot of people on board. Ted Hesburgh's nephew is in tourist and I invited him up for lunch yesterday. He and 50 Notre Dame students studied a year in Rome and they are all U.S. bound. I've been invited to come down to their "party" in tourist tonight, and it should be a real blast.

My one evening in Paris was a delight. Sam and Judith Pisar [Sam Pisar, an international lawyer] entertained for me and it was a marvelous night. As you know, I passed up Mary Lasker's Amenia "vacation," met Daddy instead and we had a great evening—just the two of us—Had dinner at Romeo Salta—

ran into some friends from
Minneapolis—also Freddie Wacker
[prominent Chicagoan] and his sister—
who, it turns out, was <u>really</u> his sister.

I did see Mary [Lasker] the second
night, however, in New York—she had a
small dinner for me (very gracious after
I really loused up her plans at the last
minute). But she understood and I'll go
to Amenia in June—just before the
Vineyard. I hope all is well with you and
the little people. Lots of flu in Europe
and many people sick on the boat—

One couple from Canada were
discussing that "new approach" to child
rearing and said it damn near wrecked
their four children. When I told them of
<u>your</u> experience they damn near died
laughing. They had very little success
with their "messages"—and decided
their parental instincts worked a lot
better than the theory put forth by the
doctor—who it turns out is a four-time
loser and a bit of a boozer, t'boot.

Cornelius [*sic*] Otis Skinner [prolific
playwright] is on board—and she is
positively charming. Also some
psychiatrists from Pittsburgh and N.Y.

Senator Byrd's assistant is at our table, so we argue a lot, but he's a <u>marvelous</u> dancer so I haven't given him too much hell.

I plan to be home on March 31st since I have to make a speech tomorrow night at the Plaza—the day we dock!!! Also on the program is Marya Mannes, Rollo May & Eugene McCarthy—We each get to talk 1½ minutes! Nofoolin'—Or should I say "Oi?!!!"

Much love to all—including Tosh
Nonno

———————— ⌘ ————————

[JUNE 1974]

[Included is a note, by hand, accompanying an interview with Popo in which her numbers are enormously inflated, such as receiving 18,000 to 20,000 letters a week.]

Dear Margo:
This is an example of what goes on. It came today.

I swear she is two different people. When people ask her how she got into this work—never a mention that I was in it. In fact she has actually told some reporters that she was in the field first and I followed.

I receive about 7,000 a week—(in a <u>busy</u> week, that is). Usually it's about 5,500. But look at this figure! It's crazy.

I'd love to meet Nora [Ephron], but no joint interviews, dear.

L & K—
Mother

—————————— ∝∞∞ ——————————

Mother was the only "civilian" invited on this AMA (American Medical Association) trip . . . one of the early groups allowed in after "Red China" opened for tourists. She was (obviously) a good friend to the group. Mother said the country was, at that time, so restrictive, and the people so afraid of being charged with criminality, that a pair of torn panty hose she threw into her hotel wastebasket kept showing up in the next town—lest anyone be accused of theft.

Edgar Snow was a China scholar allowed into the country in the 1930s. His Red Star Over China *is considered a historical masterpiece.*

JULY 12, 1974
PEKING HOTEL
CHINA

Dear Margo and Jules:

Long on envelopes—short on stationery—at least that's the way it is in our Hotel today—So I am making do—

This is a once-in-a-lifetime trip. Simply <u>fabulous</u>—a word I hate, but the best one I can think of to describe what we are seeing.

The weather is very hot and humid—but I have just the right clothes and am having a marvelous time. Can you imagine <u>me</u> getting up at 6:30 AM—raring to go? Well—that's exactly what I'm doing.

Today I'm having lunch with Dr. George Hatam—that remarkable doctor from Buffalo, NY who came here in

1933—stayed—married a Chinese— and cleaned up the V.D.

I was very lucky to get to see him. Mrs. Edgar P. Snow wrote in my behalf—and apparently they are close friends. He was "expecting me."

I'm enjoying the Chinese food immensely—too much, in fact. Eating three large meals a day—and drinking gallons of orange pop—(It seems to be the national drink—even for Breakfast.)

Love to the little people and to you,
Nonno

Mother, either in the column or en passant in an interview, mentioned Norman Mailer's assault on Lady Jeanne Campbell, his wife at the time. As with Pimento, she was a bit Gracie-esque in her retention of things that did not particularly interest her.

Senator Percy, from Illinois, wore a hearing aid, as I recall.

MARCH 7, 1975

Dear Margo:

You were <u>right!</u> The thing <u>was</u> on the wire and Norman Mailer will probably get out a contract on me shortly.

Wasn't he the guy who hit one of his wives with a bottle? (Lady Campbell, I believe!) Better I shouldn't have these nuts mad at me.

OH!!! WELL!!!!

Nonno

MARCH 12, 1975

Dear Margo:

So it was a letter opener—<u>not</u> a bottle. You know <u>everything</u>—which is nice, since my memory is going the way of my hearing, apparently.

Shall we ask Chuck Percy what he's doing about <u>his</u> hearing?

L & K
Nonno

I have enjoyed needle-pointing for almost forty years. Mother so loved my work (feeling she was incapable of doing something of that nature with her hands) that most of my pillows, eyeglass cases, and so forth went to her, and she displayed them all over her apartment.

The reference to my father, here, has to do with their agreement to divorce . . . the reason being my father's wish to marry an Englishwoman. From the beginning, Mother was extremely gracious and generous to him, given the situation.

MARCH 15, 1975

Dear Margo:

This is your 35th birthday and I am writing to thank you for the magnificent Imari needlepoint pillow you made for <u>my</u> 56th and 57th!

What a beautiful work of art it is! But more than that, it represents thousands of hours of effort—your lovely little hands on the needle, the yarn and the canvas. A true labor of love it is and I will cherish it always as a very special gift.

Not only is it special because <u>you</u> made it for me, but during the year that pillow was taking shape—you were, too. You've come a long way, Baby—and you've helped me come along, too. In spite of what you've believed for too many years, I am <u>not</u> perfect. I have made mistakes, and I'm sure I will continue to make them. But so much of the old hostility you felt for me is gone— really gone—and the fact that you are able to accept and love Daddy is a great measure of your maturity. He needs your love and acceptance desperately and he'll need it even more later. I know you'll always be there for him.

This is a peculiar way to say thank you for a needlepoint pillow—and I didn't mean to lay all this on you—but it's all a part of me—and how I do things. A little compulsive—excessive maybe—but with much love—

Nonno

MAY 8, 1975

Mugsie, my baby:

Thank you for just exactly the <u>right</u> gift for Mother's Day. I <u>love</u> it!!!

This is as good a time as any—and maybe better than most, to say I love you very much and that you have been a tremendous help to me at the lowest point in my life.

I am not accustomed to being unhappy and these last months have been very rough. There will be better days ahead I'm sure, and it's good to know you are there for me. Please, dear, keep in touch with Daddy. He needs you, too.

Much love,
Nonno

Following is one of the most talked-about columns Mother ever wrote. People still mention it to me, all these years later. I have included it because the back story is an exemplar of our relationship. Mother asked me to come to her apartment one afternoon, and we sat in her office—she at her desk, I in the "visitor" chair.

She read her final draft to me. I wept. She asked whether I thought it should run. I said yes. Mother then told me it was her and Father's plan that if they could get it by me—their only child—it would run.

JUNE 30, 1975

Dear Mugsie:

Here it is—the saddest column I ever wrote.

Love,
Nonno

For Immediate Release

Dear Readers:

In my 20 years as Ann Landers this is the most difficult column I have ever tried to put together.

I do so after many hours of soul searching. Should it be written at all? Would it be appropriate? Would it be fair? I have decided yes—because you, my readers, are also my friends. I owe it to you to say something. There should be some word directly from me.

The sad, incredible fact is that after 36 years of marriage, Jules and I are being divorced. As I write these words, it is as if I am referring to a letter from a reader. It seems unreal that I am writing about my own marriage.

Many of you may remember the column that appeared in 1969. It was in honor of our 30th wedding anniversary. You may also recall the column I wrote when my beloved mother-in-law, Gustie Lederer, passed away. On both occasions I gave you some intimate glimpses of our own life together. Thousands of readers were kind enough to write and say you considered these columns my best.

Every word that appeared in those columns was true when I wrote them, and very little that was said then could not be said today, in complete honesty.

Jules is an extraordinary man. His nickname for me was "The Queen." He was loving, supportive and generous. He is still all those things—and I will always cherish our many wonderful years together.

That we are going our separate ways is one of life's strangest ironies. How did it happen that something so good for so long didn't last forever? The lady with all the answers does not know the answer to this one.

Perhaps there is a lesson there for all of us. At least it is there for me. "Never say—'It couldn't happen to us.'"

Please, don't write or call and ask for details. The response would be—"Sorry, this is a personal matter." Just wish us both well. Time will not alter my position. I shall continue to say, "No comment." There will be no compromising—no exceptions.

Not only has this been the most difficult column I have ever written but it is also the shortest. I apologize to my editors for not giving you your money's worth today. I ask that you not fill this space with old letters. Please leave it blank—as a memorial to one of the world's best marriages that didn't make it to the finish line.

Ann Landers

Note to all editors: No booklet plug, please. Leave a white space of 2 inches or more—if possible. Thank you A.L.

Mother was a speaker at the YPO convention in Greece around the time her divorce was granted. Mention of not having been members for seven years refers to the fact that YPOers are mustered out at the age of fifty.

"The maven" was Mother's nickname for my second husband, Jules Furth. It was short for "hockey maven," a sport he was devoted to . . . though not something we enjoyed as a couple. As a matter of fact, when he took me to see the Chicago Blackhawks—my first game—I watched for a while, then said to him, "My God, they're on skates!" I was excused from attending any more games.

NOVEMBER 16, 1975
ATHENS HILTON
ATHENS, GREECE

Dear Mugsie:

I am having a lovely time—and my speeches went over beautifully. The weather is gorgeous and the people are great—But there are too many "memories" I hadn't counted on. Daddy and I were here with Popo and Mort 2 years ago—and the doorman remembered—and asked "How is the mister?" Also—the little shop where he bought me those two lovely opaline vases is right across the street. The first night here—two couples took me to dinner at the Plaka—the "in" place— and I remembered it so well. The four of us had a marvelous time dancing the Greek dances and breaking plates. Seems like a million years ago.

Being without a mate is not easy for me. It's like trying to clap with one hand, but I will get accustomed to it because I <u>must</u>. I'm sure the sadness will pass soon.

The best part of this convention for me was meeting the Ambassador and his wife. Jack and Connie Kubisch. He's a career diplomat—first class—and they had me to cocktails after we met at the opening session. (He gave the official greeting.) They invited me to join them at an official dinner tonight—and I'm going. It's an honor! I'm delighted. The group will not miss me since they have scheduled a <u>cruise</u> which I don't care for—never did—and will probably turn out to be a drunken orgy on the Aegean Sea.

I am having fun. The hardest part is when they ask me about Daddy. He is amazingly well remembered—even though we haven't been YPO'ers for seven years. And he's highly thought of too.

Wm. F. Buckley bombed and left. Sam and Judy Pisar didn't come. (He has intestinal flu.) Roy Menninger was good—and Walter Heller, the Economist from Minnesota, was <u>excellent</u>. Arnaud De Borgrave [*sic*]—(<u>Newsweek</u>) a hawk, right-winger—was articulate and still Pro Viet-Nam. Phyllis Schlafly murdered her opposition. (Sorry about that.)

I'm off to Rome Sunday—but not staying. It's too dangerous. I have reservations to Capri—& that's where I'll be for 5 days. I'll call you when I get home. Love to the Maven & the 3 little folks.

And special love to you.

Nonno

NOVEMBER 28, 1975

Dear Margo and Jules:

Tonight is Thanksgiving—and I have much to be thankful for.

The dinner today was such a pleasure. It's so good to know I have <u>real family</u>, and you're <u>it</u>! What a blessing that you came along, Jules—and took that ugly kid off my hands—like I said, it's not easy to unload a divorced woman with three kids. And now if you know of anyone who might be interested in a divorced woman with <u>no</u> kids (at home, that is)—please let me know.

Love you both—
Nonno

⸺⸺⸺⸺⸺

JANUARY 26, 1976

Mugsie dear:

You have the unbeatable combination when it comes to buying exactly the right gift—ESP—a reckless abandon for money, and a husband with a nice bank balance.

You couldn't have brought me two lovelier (or more practical) presents. How Rochas perfume falls into the category of "practical" I haven't yet figured out, but I'm sure you know what I mean. I always loved that perfume but could never bring myself to buy it.

Bless your pretty head for selecting that elegant schlep bag. I've been almost in mourning since those louses at Gucci's quit making the felt number. My last two remaining—a red—has a hole in it the size of a sewer lid and the green one was returned from Goodwill last week.

So—thank you, sweetheart for bringing joy to my heart and *now* I know what a daughter is for.

Your
Nonno

Part Three: California

JUNE 1977–JULY 1990

INTRODUCTION

The California correspondence surpasses, in volume, the other three parts combined. The letters in this group are so copious because I left Chicago . . . and Mother and I were no longer in the same town. With my new husband, the actor Ken Howard, I moved to Los Angeles, ergo, the drop-ins for coffee and the weekly dinners were no longer possible. Not wanting our customary communication to lag simply because we were now half a country apart, the letters flew. Mother's were exceptionally rich during this time because these years encompass the peak of her influence, her social and romantic life after my father, significant political and cultural changes, and the ongoing public difficulties with her twin sister.

When this period begins, in 1977, she is fifty-nine and I am thirty-seven. I have left the newspaper business, my children go off to boarding school, my new husband—a stage star—builds a television career, and my whole life is recast. Mother is nothing if not supportive, both because she is extremely fond of Ken—and because in her own life, with my father, her philosophy had always been, "You go where the grapes grow." Because Mr. Howard's grapes were growing on sound stages in Los Angeles, we were off to La La land . . . and Mother's letter writing begins, again, in earnest.

"Mr. X" was Mother's first serious suitor after her divorce. This man was at the top rung of a Fortune 500 company, which meant that, like my father, his major interest was business. He was introduced to Mother by her friend Mary Lasker, who often had them as houseguests together. Mr. X was in a second

marriage that was not going well. Another way of putting this would be to say that he was married. This caused a very problematic situation for Mother, because, from her work, if nothing else, she knew well the pitfalls of these kinds of liaisons. Mr. X vowed to exit the marriage in order to carry on the romance more openly. This, in turn, became problematic for him because he felt some reluctance about divorcing for the second time.

JUNE 30 [1977]
THURSDAY

Dear Mugsie:

This will probably be waiting for you . . . your first piece of mail in the California home.

. . .

Tomorrow you will be leaving to start a new life. I envy you. What a doll your husband is. How did you get so lucky, anyway? The beauty of it is that he thinks HE'S the lucky one. I love the way each of you thinks the other saved your life!

Saturday I go to Mary's for four days. I know I'll have a marvelous time. She is such a classy lady. I spoke with her last night and she just returned from MacArthur's <u>Fantasia</u>—whatever that is . . . I don't know, but Ken would.

[Mr. X] called me this noon to tell me he was elected Chairman of the Board at the morning Board Meeting. The former chairman was dragged kicking and screaming from his throne. The guy is alcoholic, diabetic, had a lung removed six months ago— malignant . . . and is also crazy. Outside of that he's in fine shape. The last two months he has been so loath to resign (age 65—a must in that company) that he accused [Mr. X] and others of conspiring to "get rid of him." In the meantime he will have a car and a chauffeur, a secretary . . . all paid for by the company . . . and an office (in another bldg.) . . . plus 165 grand a year. . . . He will also be a "consultant" but [Mr. X] has to decide what to consult him on . . . and so far he's sure he can't think of a thing.

Write when you can, and please get a typewriter. And don't be surprised if you wind up loving California. It has happened to lots of folks I know.

Kiss Ken for me . . . when you are through kissing him for yourself, which, I suspect, will be never.

Love you,
Mama

―――――――――― ⌖ ――――――――――

The drama of the moment was Mother's ambivalence about whether Mr. X should see a psychiatrist in New York suggested by my husband, Ken. The doctor was the late Sam Safirstein.

[JULY 1977]

Dear Margo and Ken:

Too bad we haven't talked much these past two days. As I said during our last conversation—I am more of a pest now than I was when you lived a mile and a half from here.

Since things seem to be squared

away—at the moment I don't think I will be bothering you like that again, at least not for a while. I would like your travel itinerary. . . . Where I can reach you, tho'. A mother hen has to know where her little chickens are at all times.

I am still unclear as to whether or not I would be doing the right thing by putting [Mr. X] with Sam. Any more thoughts from you on this subject will be welcome. I feel I have things well under control and just what Sam might do to his head is a big question mark. You know my motto . . . "If it ain't broke, don't fix it."

. . .

Gotta finish my piece for <u>Family Circle</u> today and get it in the mail tomorrow. They are screaming for it. I hope it's good. You know me, I'm always flying blind . . . never know for sure what I'm doing.

Much love to you both. Boy how I wish I could get that lucky.

Mama

"Treadway and Main Street" are the names of the inn and the address of our residence for most of that summer. Ken was doing summer theater at the Williamstown Theater Festival where he was directing Equus, *the play in which he starred in Chicago.*

Marian Falk was from the Searle drug family. Mother had, by then, been appointed to the Harvard Medical School Visiting Committee and was involved with fund-raising.

"Red" was one of Mother's names for my first husband, John Coleman. Even though he was, by now, two husbands ago, she kept him in her orbit to try to control the situation as it related to my children. As ex-husbands go, I found him difficult.

[JULY 1977]
SATURDAY

(I know I shouldn't be writing today but I hope God will forgive me.)
Dear   Margo . . . and   Ken . . . of course . . .

I loved your letter today . . . and see it carried a more complete address. I hope you have received all the letters I have written. From now on I'll use Treadway and the Main Street shtick.

Yes . . . you are both so right about my brown-eyed-long-lashed love. If Dr. Safirstein doesn't help him get his head together it is better that I don't get hit by that "speeding bullet." WE GET ALONG SO WELL TOGETHER when we <u>are</u> together, it would seem a shame. I don't think I have ever felt this way about anybody else . . . at least not as far back as I can remember. In the meantime I am keeping all my options open and am not about to check myself in as a cloistered nun.

Jack Valenti called yesterday to tell me Kirk and Anne Douglas will be in town for four or five weeks and will I call them? He is doing a picture called <u>Fury</u>. I did call this afternoon and she sounds like a very nice, smart, lady. I told her I am a serious walker . . . I don't give parties . . . I don't waste my time on bores and from what I hear she doesn't either. (They are very close friends of Mary Lasker's.) Anne said . . . "Wonderful . . . I know we are going to have a lot in common and Jack Valenti said the one person in Chicago worth knowing was Eppie."

Soooo . . . when I get back from Washington and Boston I will get together with her—or them. She said "Kirk would love to come, too . . . if he isn't working. Would it be all right?" From everything I hear they are a sane and sensible couple. Incidentally, I did meet them years ago at a party Pamela Mason gave for me . . . and we had some pictures taken . . . Kirk and Daddy . . . with me in the middle. People used to think Daddy looked like Kirk . . . and I guess he did . . . quite a lot before his boozing days. Last week, incidentally, I spoke to Sam Fawley at the Harris Bank and he tells me he hears "Jules is on the booze again." This is very bad news.

John Merrill the Harvard doc [nephrology authority] is coming next week to tie up the three million dollar deal he THOUGHT he had with Marian Falk. Well . . . I saw her on the street walking the dog yesterday and she nonchalantly tells me she just found out there is <u>no money in the Foundation</u> . . .

(all lawyers are crooks and thieves, according to her) . . . and she can't go through with the plan. I almost dropped my buckets. The old girl is very tricky. She has about 40 million and uses it to dangle in front of people so they will wine and dine her. She is afraid if she gives anything away the fun will be over. Well—I gave her a good earful . . . and made it clear that she had better figure something out or her name would be M-U-D with three of the most prominent doctors in the world . . . not to mention ME. . . . It will be interesting to see what happens. I'm betting she will come through.

. . .

Hello there. Here I am on page two and haven't said a damned thing . . . but I do type SO well I think I'll just keep going to parade my skill.

I am looking forward to seeing the grandmonkies. I really miss them. SO far nothing new from Red. He hasn't phoned for a few days. It used to be like every night . . . and he was always good for at least 40 minutes. He asked me to get him a luncheon date with [—] . . . which I have done but he doesn't know it yet because I haven't heard from him to pass the message. I'm sure he will be thrilled because he has been trying to connect with him for quite some time and couldn't quite hack it.

I called [—] and he was out of town. I left my name and number. When he returned my call he said . . . "I hope whatever was on your mind is still on it. I was very excited when I saw you had called." He should calm down there. You are more his style I am sure. I am at least 25 years too old for what he is interested in. In addition to which I am not playing those games.

[—] told me his dad and mother and wife are ALL in the hospital . . . no longer critical but they were—with encephalitis, undiagnosed fevers from a trip . . . etc. I didn't say it but I was thinking . . . "If your wife dies, call me . . . but not until."

Well . . . enough foolishness from me for you. I am looking forward to lunch with Stu Eisenstadt [future adviser to

Jimmy Carter], thanks to you. . . . I'll give him your love. You have mine—

Nonno to you
Mama to Ken—

[Cut out from an airmail envelope and enclosed was a picture of a gorilla's arm and hand, along with this note from Mother: "THIS CAME ON THE <u>OUTSIDE</u> OF THE ENVELOPE . . . A LETTER FROM POPO . . . WHO ELSE??????? THE DOORMEN WHO SORT THE MAIL IN THIS BUILDING PROBABLY THINK MY SISTER IS IN A MENTAL HOSPITAL AND THAT MAYBE I BELONG IN ONE, TOO."]

―――――――――― ⟨∞⟩ ――――――――――

In the following letter, the obligation referred to was my suggestion to her that she be the speaker, gratis, at the international meeting of Gamblers Anonymous. I had written about the group and found them fascinating and worthwhile.

As for her seeing Safirstein regarding Mr. X's situation, such a maneuver is highly irregular, but she was somehow often able to have entrée to doctors who were treating friends. For such situations as surgery or transplants, I had heard her on the phone with the treating doctor, having a medical conversation!

[JULY 25, 1977]
SUNDAY

Dear Margo:

I am off to New York . . . again . . . just got back Friday . . . and would have stayed the weekend with Mary Lasker at Amenia . . . which is about as close as you can get to heaven without dying. BUT . . . I had to return to Chicago to settle a little "obligation" . . . thanks to you. I am not complaining because it was an enormously rewarding experience, but it sure did knock hell out of my weekend.

Remember Gamblers Anonymous???? Well . . . I spoke at the International Convention this afternoon at lunch . . . and <u>EVERYBODY</u> sends love to Margo. You went to interview them and that's how they got on the map. You then got me interested . . . and well . . . don't ask. We are their patron saints. What a great group of dedicated people they are . . . truly amazing. And when they come up and say "You saved my life" . . . you just want to bawl.

I had to laugh. . . . Jimmie the Greek is also a pal of theirs and they asked him to speak at their convention. He said his fee is $3,000 but he'd cut it in half for them. Well . . . they couldn't afford $1,500 . . . so he said he couldn't come out this year—maybe next year. I told them <u>my</u> fee is now $4,000 and I came back from New York to speak for nothing.

Thanks for your last letter. Yes . . . you are right. I am not going to "orchestrate" anything. Tuesday I will see Safirstein and see if I can get things going between him and [Mr. X]. It's such a hell of a situation I can't tell you. I know he is really crazy about me . . . and I sure am nuts about him. Maybe I have to tell him good-bye and see if he can live without me . . . and if he CAN . . . I'd better know it. At the same time . . . TIMING is so important. It may be just a little too soon for that move . . .

and such a thing just might wreck it. If you have any ideas on this subject please enlighten me.

Our last trip was heaven. He is adorable and we had such a marvelous time. And I'll see him again tomorrow. Oh hell . . . why does life have to be so complicated?

. . .

Again doll . . . enjoy life. When you're in love the whole world is Jewish . . . even when your husband ain't.

L and K,
Mama

Hubert Humphrey, who would not recover, was suffering from bladder cancer. Mother and Mary Lasker used their influence to have Interferon, then an experimental drug in trials, made available to him. They really thought they might be able to "save" him.

[AUGUST 1977]
MONDAY

Dear Mugsie:

I am under the dryer—and taking off for New York in a few hours. La de da!

. . .

I spoke to Muriel Humphrey last night for about an hour. She is a remarkable dame. Nixon tried THREE times to get through to Hubert and they wouldn't accept the call. HE WAS FURIOUS. . . . "Don't you <u>understand</u>" he yelled . . . "This is RICHARD NIXON??" They understood all right. . . . Muriel said [President] Carter has called three times . . . and of course Hubert spoke to him . . . also all the cabinet members have phoned. . . . Actually it would be better if they left him alone. He has my number and I figure he'll call me when he feels like it. . . . He called me several times from Sloan-Kettering and we had some nice chats. Remember Mary and I got him to go to Sloan-Kettering? The idiot wanted to go to Bethesda!

. . .

Keep in touch . . . and so will I . . . In fact—see you soon, Baby.

Kiss the beautiful fella . . . and have one for yourself.

———————————— ⁘ ————————————

Father Paul was a priest from the Eau Claire days with whom she maintained her friendship.

"Louisiana Fats" was the moniker that some Chicagoans used for John, Cardinal Cody. It is self-explanatory.

[AUGUST 1977]
THURSDAY . . .

Dear Mugsie:

[Mr. X] called this A.M. and read me your letter. He was thrilled that you would think to write to him. Naturally— so was I. You are a thoughtful child.

I received your cute letter today that began . . . "[Mr. X] took you <u>WHERE</u> . . . To buy you <u>what</u>???" It wasn't exactly that way. He actually bought the ring in

Tiffany's Chicago store. . . . And it needed to be sized so we decided to do it in New York. He paid CASH for it in Chicago. They have no idea who he is. If I had the ring sized in Chicago they would know a gentleman had purchased it for me and I didn't want that. But—I must say it wasn't very smart of us to romp into N.Y. Tiffany's together . . . but we did have great fun and I wanted him to help me pick out the gold earrings that Mary gave me for my birthday. He did . . . And they are lovely.

It was a gorgeous day and we had such a good time. We were also shot full of luck that nobody we knew saw us. [Mr. X] LOVES Safirstein and is taking double sessions. . . . He will have two tomorrow . . . and on Monday I meet him in Washington. He is so enthusiastic about the doc I am really thrilled. Whether or not this will end up the way I want it to or not I cannot say . . . but it's also the way HE wants to end up or he wouldn't be going . . . unless I am nuts. However . . . it will do him a world of good. It's time he got to know himself.

I went up to La Cross, Wis. today for Father Paul's ordination. He was made a bishop . . . and it was beautiful. . . . I almost wanted to get converted. The pageantry is gorgeous . . . and Louisiana Fats was there . . . also every Bishop in the State. Many Eau Claire people including all the serious Catholics like the Frank Wilcoxes. (I think he's a knight of Malta or some damned thing.) The hats had plumes and they carried silver sabers . . . and you should have seen the Gold Chalices and Shepherds' staffs . . . and gold and crimson robes.

Father Paul's mother was sitting right across from me. Again I got aced in with A-1 credentials . . . you'd think I was a returning dignitary. . . . Along with "Mother" were 200 relatives and I am not kidding. I think there are 13 kids in the family . . . and they multiply like rabbits. Mrs. Paul told me she has 58 grandchildren and 10 or 11 great-grandchildren . . . she doesn't know which. I felt like a piker . . . me with my three!

It was a great day and I am beat . . . so

off to bed and write to me soon again and I'll reply in kind. I LOVE your letters. Kiss your beautiful guy for me and I'll kiss mine for you.

Nonno

"Mort" (Phillips) is Popo's husband. Mother's relationship with him was hot and cold, most probably mirroring her relationship with Popo.

AUGUST 25, [1977] . . .
MORT'S 59TH BIRTHDAY . . .
AND I CAN'T BELIEVE IT!

Dear Margo:

If I start one more letter with . . . "Sorry no time for a decent letter today" . . . I think you will kill me . . . but I am so cockeyed busy I don't know up from down. Everything seems to have caved in on me at once and I am running like a theif with the money. Also I think I misspelled thief up there. Well . . . lock me up is all I can say. <u>Now I need to know the name of the</u>

shop that finishes needlepoint pillows. Please reply to this. I remember you had a special spot and they did lovely work. Enclosed for your convenience is a self-addressed stamped envelope. And while you are at it you can write me a few lines . . . even if only to tell me how much you like that guy you are married to.

Popo is coming to visit on September 2nd. [Mr. X] will be here the day before . . . NO . . . I am not tipping my mit. Ya' think I am nuts? Until there is something specific to say I am keeping my tater trap shut. And it ain't easy. I'm sure she is wondering what I am doing for excitement but mum is the word. I use Everett and Houston and a few New York friends as decoys and they will have to do.

. . .

Oh—Roder [her nickname for Rhoda, a close friend] Pritzker and I are going to Temple (hers, not mine. I resigned from Shalom) on the night before Yom Kippur. It's Wednesday, Sept. 21st in case you are interested. It's the Kol Nidre and the only holiday that means a great deal to me. The rest of 'em I can forget . . . but not this one.

. . .

Much L and K . . .
Mama

———————— cᴁo ————————

The ring Mother refers to in the following letter was a rather large lavender star sapphire surrounded by diamonds. The color was unusual and I named it "Elizabeth Taylor's eye." She always admired it, and I offered it to her. Some years later, she finally accepted it, and I think she loved both the look of it and that it was a gift from me. She was not particularly interested in jewelry.

AUGUST 27, 1977
SATURDAY

Dear Margo:

We spoke a few hours ago—and you should have your phone checked or the telephone company should junk some of its equipment. I did indeed call you at 213— a few hours earlier and no response. I don't like to phone before at least 11:30 AM where you are because I know what your sleeping routine is—so I always wait. Can it be that you are outside and don't hear the phone ring? Now if it was the other way 'round we could understand it a lot better because everyone knows I am deaf. (If they didn't get the idea on their own, you told 'em.) Can a mother sue a daughter for ruining her image? I loved that last letter where you wrote ... "for a straight-laced Jewish girl from Sioux City you are sure managing to lead one hell of a complicated life."

I would like nothing better than to "uncomplicate" my life as soon as possible and am working along those lines. As the holidays draw near I become increasingly apprehensive—for <u>him</u> not me. He is such a decent guy I don't know how he can handle the duplicity and conflict. It must be murder. If it's hard on ME I can imagine what it does to him ... the son of a minister yet.

I have been thinking very hard and

long about that ring and have decided I should not do it. It's a real beauty and you should keep it and enjoy it. One day you will be happy to have it. There will be times when you might want it to "make a statement" and that is the piece that will do it. What's more you did design it. I want you to keep it and wear it when you are in the mood. I will find one. Actually it's the only stone I like. Huge diamonds are for Miami and blue star sapphires are as common as stray cats. Rubies and emeralds don't send me . . . and a pearl I have.

. . .

Love to your beautiful mate . . . and keep in touch with your deaf mother,

Nonno

[Enclosed was the following shorter letter:]

SATURDAY

Dear Margo:

Today is Saturday. The enclosed goes in an envelope which will be handled by my office tomorrow. I didn't want this page to get away from me.

PLEASE notice BOTH sides. There's a great Royko column on one side and of course the Arvy obit on the other. (This is one of ten obits . . . the papers have been full of it.)

I will phone you today or tomorrow and we will have a nice gab fest. I really miss you. But soon you'll be home—only if for a little while. This is the first time you have actually lived away from me . . . except for camp and Brandeis. I realize it is both good—and bad. (Probably good for you and bad for me!)

Love your letters . . . and can't get over your typing. It is damn near flawless! Did you ever take typing in school? My guess is that you are a quick study and can master just about anything you make up your mind you want to.

Monday the man arrives—he changed it from Tuesday—The way he runs off and virtually "disappears" you'd think he was running a bagel wagon on 3rd avenue instead of a three billion dollar business. But he says he's <u>got</u> to see me and I'm not arguing. We are very good for each other and adore every minute together but we must get things a lot straighter pretty soon or they'll have to put me away.

No letter????? Well . . . here I am running off at the mouth—which means I'll have to put this in a sealed envelope. . . . Much love,

Mama to him
Nonno to you—

The book that is making Mother crazy is The Ann Landers Encyclopedia, *published in 1978. The idea for the book had been Mary Lasker's: to alphabetize every problem known to man (or woman), then ask an expert for the answer . . . sometimes adding Mother's own. The finished work comprised a hefty 1,182 pages, not counting a 30-page index. The book included some very arcane concerns. The last entry, for example, was "Zoonoses," diseases humans get from animals.*

[SEPTEMBER 1977]
WEDNESDAY

Dear Margo and . . . well . . . I know you are reading this so I might as well say—Dear Ken.

We have had two long conversations . . . (and one short one when I interrupted your dinner) . . . all in the last three days.

. . .

I am really happy that you are seeing something of the mishpocha.* Family can be a pain in the ankle but it can also bring you a lot of joy and the feeling that you have somebody close. We know some of our relatives are nutty—tricky—irresponsible—unpredictable and downright double-crossers, but then we take 'em . . . warts and all because there is no way to make them different. They are what they are. (Mugsie, as I have often said the only two people in the world who are perfect are you and me . . . and sometimes you aren't so hot.) As for me . . . I am always

---

*"Mishpocha" means family, or relatives.

adorable, charming, witty, wise and I am also a brilliant typist.

. . .

My book is driving me over the brink. This is the last major project I am doing as long as I live. There are times when I could pull the hair out of my head by the roots . . . like when a piece comes in from a brilliant doctor and there are no verbs in his sentences. I am convinced that 90 percent of the doctors in this country couldn't pass an eighth grade grammar test. Germs they know about . . . syntax—nothing.

I had Ted Hesburgh's two nieces for dinner the other night. They are working this summer to make money to put themselves through next year. (Notre Dame, of course.) Really lovely girls. They are waiting tables, tutoring and washing dishes . . . and will make about $7,000 these summer months . . . working two jobs! It can be a very good thing but I wasn't brought up that way and neither were you. We both missed something.

Rather than go to a second page and

risk the need for a second 13c stamp, I am using the other side of a sheet and signing off. This letter is enough nonsense for one day . . . in addition to which I may add something . . . like a clipping or two.

Oh . . . did you know Barbara Eden and Chuck Fegert are getting married? Yes—at long last. Barbara Rush is coming back after the show closes (<u>Same Time Next Year</u>) and she is opening a Boutique or some such . . . to be near Mort Kaplan . . . or so the columns say.

Take care. Buy a scale. . . . Read a newspaper. . . . California could sink into the Pacific and you wouldn't even know it.

L and K,
Mama

It was just Mother's style to be interested in and supportive of Ken's career . . . though she always had reservations about what her father called "the show business."

"Sam G." was from Gamblers Anonymous and we kept in touch. Apparently he thanked me for getting Mother to be their speaker, but he neglected to thank her. As my children can attest, Mother was a stickler about thank-you notes.

"Ilana" (Ilana Diamond Rovner) is a dear girlfriend of mine in Chicago who became close to my mother.

Ken was never really a smoker. He smoked to play Dr. Dysart in Equus *and kept it up only for a short period after that. I, on the other hand, could not stop until years later.*

SEPTEMBER 8, 1977
WEDNESDAY NIGHT

Dear Margo:

It was wonderful to get your Good News Call today. I was certain all sorts of good things would pop and they did— all at once. Now—to make the best choices, and he will.

I'm glad he didn't go for <u>Soap</u>. It's supposed to be the raunchiest thing to come down the pike on TV and ... while it might be successful, it wouldn't do for our lovely fellow to get type-cast in something that smells like a barrel of lost herring.

Thank you for sending on the note about Sam G. It's more than I got. Would you believe not a soul from that outfit dropped a line to say thanks??? I did that number for free, as you know, and it was a huge audience ... also a most responsive one, but not so much as a line did I receive from ANYBODY. I did enjoy doing it because I'm sure it was the highlight of the convention ... and the only "name" they had. I was told it drew a lot of people who otherwise might not have come— especially the wives ... well anyway, one good thing (besides the personal satisfaction) ... did result. Their patron saint ... Dr. Culver who sat next to me at the speakers' table wrote a beautiful piece on The Compulsive Gambler for my Encyclopedia.

I loved Ilana's card from Eau Claire!

Glad to see what Main Street looks like!
Can you believe we lived there for
almost ten years? I think we got out just
in time.

. . .

Dear Ken:

Remember you made me a promise . . .
no cigarettes . . . not you and not the
child . . . by Labor Day. Well . . . it's next
week, love. Are you going to be able to
keep that promise? Let me know.

Your ever-lovin'
Mama

Margo again:

I'm signing off . . . got so much work
to do I am cockeyed. . . . Write when
you can and call me when you hit
Chicago and settle down. I'll be back
from Washington on Wednesday . . .
night. I'm busy as the devil but you
know that you can always count on me.

Nonno

In my coming and going from Chicago, closing one place and organizing another, my mother wound up supervising the children preparing for new schools. "2450" (Lakeview) was my last residence in Chicago. Lulu was my housekeeper at the time. I was traveling with Ken, who was filming Superdome, *a TV movie.*

My mother had everyone join hands and say grace when we all had dinner together. My kids found this eccentric.

"Joe" replaced the Slav as chauffeur. He stayed for several years.

Mother's mentioning The Catcher in the Rye *brought to mind a wonderful gaffe having to do with her dead spot where literature was concerned. She was at an institutional dinner in a Chicago ballroom, sitting at one of those big round tables, opposite a man who was chain-smoking. Getting his eye, she pantomimed putting out the cigarette. He ignored her. Perhaps ten minutes later, when everyone introduced themselves, he said he was Kurt Vonnegut. She recognized the name . . . and paid him this compliment: "My grandchildren LOVED* The Catcher in the Rye." *He very wisely said, "Thank you," and left it at that.*

A few years later, I was struck by the thought that

maybe this instinct for the gaffe—literary division—was genetic. I was at a fund-raiser in Connecticut at the home of a woman I'd been told was very proud of being the daughter of Lewis Mumford. When I was introduced to her, wanting to be friendly, I said, "We all really loved Alice in Wonderland." *That author having been Lewis* Carroll, *not Mumford, she gave me the fish-eye and said, "Weeell . . . yeeess." When we moved away from her, my husband told me I had confused the social critic and philosopher with the famous storyteller.*

"Making with the mouth," or alternately, "the mouth circuit," was Mother's way of referring to her speeches.

SEPTEMBER 12, 1977
CHI./NEW ORLEANS
SATURDAY

Dear Margo:

It's been only 24 hours that you have been gone from Chicago and it seems like a year! SO much is going on.

First . . . I had dinner at 2450 last night and it was lovely. Lulu had a wonderful meal. . . . Cricket was at the

Sussmans. . . . Abra had two very lovely girls as guests. . . . Adam was home and then there was me. . . . Abra asked me before dinner not to say a prayer . . . because . . . "I wasn't brought up like that." I told her, fine . . . it was her house and her problem. Actually I think she was looking for an argument and was disappointed that she didn't get it.

The afternoon was something of a scream as I told you on the phone. The prices of everything are mind-boggling . . . but of course your kids never look at the price tags . . . and they always manage to find the most expensive everything. Three bucks for a pair of white sox with a couple of lousy stripes. Abra got a dozen pairs . . . plus a handful of extra shoe laces and a tennis racket case (only $2) and Adam got two pairs of shoes . . . he needs another pair which he will get Monday with his father . . . plus some belts . . . and so on. I also told you they have no charge accounts at Mage's but now they have . . . and John [their father] is going to pay for it or I will. He said HE would . . . "No problem." We'll see.

Last night at 11:00 PM I get a call from Adam. He wanted to know if <u>Catcher in the Rye</u> was an autobiography. I told him no. This morning he called with an emergency. He needs to read one more book on the required list and maybe another book on the unrequired. Could I get them and help him pick? I said . . . yes . . . "start reading. . . ." So . . . he read a whole list of books and I helped him pick several. <u>Diary of Anne Frank</u> . . . <u>The Miracle Worker</u> . . . <u>Robinson Carusoe</u> [*sic*] . . . <u>The Count of Monte Christo</u> [*sic*] and <u>The Persidium Adventure</u> [*sic*]. Also . . . <u>Treasure Island</u>. Next question . . . "Where's Joe?" I told him Joe wasn't working and we'd have to figure out something else . . . but first I had to find out where I could get these books. Well Carol Stoll had only one, so I called Krock's. They had them all at the downtown store . . . but I told them I could not get downtown and I needed them today . . . SOOO-ooo as a personal favor they are

sending all the books to the Water
Tower store . . . which is the one closest
to me . . . and I am going to get them
this afternoon and they will be my gifts
to Adam. (P.S. He tried to make me for a
football when we were at Mage's . . . I
said "nothing doing . . .")

To go on . . . I decided not to serve
Adam these books on a silver platter . . .
your kids are accustomed to chauffeurs
doing chores and getting things done for
them . . . so I phoned him and told him
to be <u>here</u> . . . my apt at 4:00 and we
would go together to get the books. So
that is what we are doing. I think I am
going to have a closer relationship with
him than any of the others. He is by far
the most reasonable and the most
responsible. Also he has more initiative
and does what he is supposed to do
when he is supposed to do it. He will
have all his books read . . . and a few
extras when he arrives at Eaglebrook.
And he IS a DARLING little guy. I just
love him.

. . .

I am so busy I can't see straight . . .

and Monday I leave for Texas to make with the mouth . . . (and the $$$$). . . . [Mr. X] is meeting me there and we will have a little time together. He phoned yesterday . . . just before leaving for the wedding of the son of a very close friend.

[Mr. X] also told me he just got the bills from Safirstein. Are you ready for this? It is costing him $800 <u>a week</u>! You read right . . . two double sessions a week . . . $200 a session!!! Have you ever heard of such a thing?

I'm rushing to get ready to meet Adam . . . so this is it for now. It was good to talk to you and all the kids were thrilled. . . . I hope you won't be hurt if I tell you they sounded more eager to talk to Ken than to you. These are what I call high-class worries, honey. Damned few step-fathers get that kind of genuine adoration. All I can say is he must deserve it. Boy are you lucky! Now . . . get back into first class physical condition and enjoy yourself. With Red [John Coleman] out of your life it should be a cinch. The kids love you . . . you've got a magnificent husband and you got me.

Love,
Nonno

───────────── ⸎ ─────────────

"Dr. Gene Kennedy" (Eugene Kennedy) is a former priest who married a nun. Mother's surmise about a possible book title was purely her own, no doubt indicative of what SHE would have named such a book.

SEPTEMBER 13, 1977
CHI./NEW ORLEANS
SUNDAY

Dear Margo:
   This won't be a letter ... (a letter is when my arm falls off ... a note is when I lose only two fingers).
   NEWS: I talked to Popo today and she tells me Jeannie got a call from your second husband. He is coming out to California ... also   he   sounded

"terrific" . . . very up . . . up . . . up. . . . HE IS IN LOVE. It's a girl in the building. Well—that's what he said. Popo went on to explain . . . "I know Margo will be happy for him. It's always nice, when you make a wonderful marriage, to know that the ditched party isn't laying dead in the road." So . . . whether or not he is making up a neat story or not I don't know but let's hope it is the truth.

In the meantime . . . Kup carried an item today that Dr. Gene Kennedy is trying to get permission from Rome to leave the priesthood and marry a nun . . . . . . etc. . . . etc. I did know about this several months ago but now that it's in Kup's column it's open season at the Church. Gene told me they treated him rotten in Rome. He went over twice and it was a stinking deal he got. Others have been "excused" . . . but it seems, not him. In the meantime he is "taking copious notes" and I think the church is going to get an earful like never before when his book comes out. He may call it <u>Screw You, Pope Paul</u> . . . or something equally respectful.

I talked with all your kids today and they are just fine. Adam is reading and writing like crazy . . . and Lulu says "They're just fine." I did enjoy taking the little guy to the bookstore yesterday. He is a real mensch.

. . .

Hubert phoned me yesterday and we had a marvelous talk. He sounded wonderful and had some hopeful reports from the doctors. Really believes he has it beat. Pray a little. . . . Maybe a heathen like you has more clout up there than a semi-Ortho-ox [*sic*] lady who is seeing an outa-bounds fella. At least you are married.

Love to you
Nonno
[Kiss print]

In the following letter, the person trying to send Mother a message under the table was a well-known man recognized in both business and government.

SEPTEMBER 18, 1977
CHI./NEW ORLEANS
SATURDAY

Dear Mugs:

I am up to my hocks in work—like never before. BUT—if you can write me three letters in one day I can chuck everything and write to my one and only child.

. . .

Latest dirt: [—] is recovering nicely from his illness . . . but his marriage isn't doing very well. It seems [Mrs. —] is having a sizzling affair with a newsman . . . and he caught them coming out of a hotel quite early one morning recently. Of course he has been monkeying around for years, but that is another story. He once made such an overt pass at me (at one of those Bar Assn. Dinners where they have the musical comedy). . . . He was sitting next to me and all of a sudden I feel something running up my leg. . . . I thought maybe an animal had got loose under the table (It was an animal alright . . . a skunk . . .) and I just couldn't believe it! I have had a few passes in my life but never anything as

A Life in Photos

The twins in their yard in Sioux City, perhaps the oldest kids in town to still have baby bottles.

Family Archive

My society page debut.

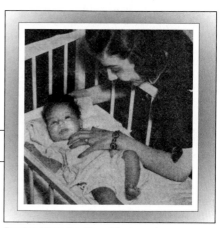

Mother, Popo, and their daughters — my cousin Jeanne and me.

Reprinted from the *Sioux City Journal*

Reprinted from the *Sioux City Journal*

In Eau Claire, at the local radio station, some Democratic party workers plugging voter registration. I'm in the second row, third from right and Mother is right next to me. The tall blonde to Mother's right is her close friend "Blondie" Brigham, and to my left, my childhood best friend, Sandra Caffee.

Our somewhat unusual high school used a theatrical photographer for senior yearbook pictures.

This is my favorite picture of Mother. She was at the podium acknowledging an award.

Family Archive

My father, Jules Lederer.

Family Archive

Me at Brandeis, 1960.

Photo by Henry Grossman

My engagement picture, the first time around, in 1962.

Me with my first child, Abra, age 3.

A publicity photo of Mother with some of her owl collection.

Mother in Honolulu, 1957.

Mother and I with my kids, Abra, Cricket, and Adam, whom she called her "grandmonkies."

Same photo session. (Same kids.)

Mother and I at the very small wedding dinner she gave for me and Mr. Right Number Two in the early '70s.

Mother and I, 1982, at a book party for my first book, a family memoir.

Another from the book party.

At my fiftieth birthday, right before we fainted from the heat.

Photo by Steve Shay

Family Archive

Perhaps Mother's best-known photo, used by many papers with her column.

At the small dinner I gave for Mother's eightieth, in Chicago. She didn't want a party, but relented if it would be just family.

Reprinted with the permission of the *Chicago Tribune*

Another picture I love: Mother and her constant companions—letters from her readers.

Popo, Helen, and Mother—three of the four sisters celebrating Helen's eightieth birthday in 1991.

Mother and one of her "girlfriends," Helen Hayes, in the mid-1980s.

cheap as that. And your father was sitting at the table yet . . . next to his wife! I pretended not to notice . . . and kept inching away . . . but he persisted and finally I gave him such a kick I am sure I gave him a blood clot. Ever since that incident I haven't been able to look at him.

Last night was the Horatio Alger Dinner at the Continental Plaza. The food was divine but the program was endless. Arthur Rubloff [real estate mogul in Chicago] was the chairman and I was his guest. Many former Awardees were there from all over the country—Kemmons Wilson [Holiday Inn] . . . and Dorothy . . . also Johnny Johnson [Johnson Publishing Company, parent of *Ebony* and *Jet*, among others] . . . and Pat Patterson [United]. This year's awardees were Ira Harris [investment banking], Dave Mahoney from Norton Simon . . . etc. etc. The M.C. was Arthur Godfrey . . . (such tired jokes . . . oi vay . . . he shaved 'em and told 'em.). . . . Danny Thomas was very good . . . from there it was down hill all the way. Would you believe that one of the awardees brought <u>38</u> guests (at $100 a head) . . . and INTRODUCED each one and told what they did. The best part of the dinner for me was the fact that Vernon Jordan was there (guest of Norton Simon) and we sat together and had a lot of laughs. They introduced a singer . . . who was to sing God Bless America . . . "and a few other patriotic numbers." Well she could sing like my leenka foos . . . (which means left foot). . . . The old babe may have been able to skreetch out a note 40 years ago but nothing lately. You could see traces of faded beauty. I'm sure at one time she was a real looker. So—— after she started to croak out a few bars I leaned over to Vernon and said, "She must have something on the chairman of the committee. . . ." After she finished her <u>THIRD</u> number . . . and started to play the harpsichord (along with her rendition of The Star Spangled Banner) Vernon nudged me and said . . . "She must be screwing the whole committee."

Anyway—I LEFT at 11:30 while they

were still making speeches . . . and that was enough for me.

Things are very good with [Mr. X] and me. We had a glorious time in Texas. The only trouble is the more we are together the tougher it is to be apart. I know he adores me . . . as I do him . . . and I must be patient—although I admit there are times when I want to pull all the hair out of his head and scream . . . "What in the hell are you waiting for??" He calls every day . . . often twice a day and we do get together as often as we can. He is <u>so</u> busy and I am, too . . . (this book is driving me bananas) . . . but we make time for each other somehow and it is miraculous. No one would believe it. Right now I am completely swamped—but I will work out from under this weekend <u>if</u> I put in 12 hours today and 12 tomorrow. Also, it would help if I got off this typewriter and got going already.

. . .

I love you, a whole lot.

Nonno

The Greenspuns, then, as now, owned the Las Vegas Sun *newspaper.*

The dustup referred to between Jeannie and me had to do with a remark I made about Eldridge Cleaver, a client of her then-husband, an appeals lawyer. She took exception to the remark.

"The G.G." was Mother's not very politically correct name for Ken Howard: it stood for "the gorgeous goy." Mother was never p.c.—either before or after it came into vogue.

SEPTEMBER 29, 1977
CHI./NEW ORLEANS

Today is Sunday . . . and I'm off to N.Y. tomorrow . . . but trying to stagger my letters to you so you won't get them all in one day. This one is supposed to be mailed Thursday. Them's the instructions.

Dear Margo:

As I said up there . . . off to N.Y. on Monday . . . just a quick trip . . . must spend 10 hours with my editor . . . the rest with my friend . . . and am staying at Mary Lasker's. She is just back from Ireland . . . Paris . . . etc. . . .

On Wednesday night I come home from N.Y. very late . . . and am off to Las Vegas on Thursday—for a money talk. . . . Dinner with Hank and Barbara Greenspun . . . Thursday nite. I make with the mouth on Friday and noon and am home that night. If I knew where you were today I would phone. Florida? But WHERE?

The enclosed is from Popo. Also from Eda LeShan [a writer friend of mine]. . . . I hope you will accept Jeannie's apology. It would be better if you could be friends. Too bad she has such a mouth on her. I'll bet she could bite her tongue off.

Tonight (Sunday) I get the Jane Addams award, otherwise known as the Hull House Medal. Bill Simon called Friday and wanted me to have dinner with him Sunday. I told him I couldn't because I had to go to a dinner where I was receiving the Hull House medal . . . and he thought I said <u>Whorehouse</u>. . . . He really cracked up.

You can call this a letter if you want to. I don't, but it's the best I can do. So . . . let's see you do better . . . and soon.

Love to you and the G.G.

———————— ⌒⊗⌒ ————————

"Mr. X" was taking too long to reorganize his life, and Father Ted was strongly advising Mother against sticking with the situation—so ended the first serious romance following her thirty-six-year marriage. There would be other "gentleman friends," as she called them, but no one she ever felt that much for again.

OCTOBER 11, 1977
WEDNESDAY

Dear J. Fred:

It was pure joy to see you and Ken and spend a night in your very own love nest. It's such a "homey" home and you did a remarkable job of getting things in order. I expected to see barrels and boxes and piles of things . . . but nary a thing out of place. The only thing left to do is hang the mirror in the living room. It's a big mother—so make sure you've got hooks strong enough to hold it. (By this time it is probably up . . . so what am I bothering you for?)

. . .

I came home to an unbelievable pile of work. I won't know what to do with myself when this book is off my back. Oh yes I will. . . . I'll have fun—or will I??????? I am having a hard time facing the fact that the guy is really out of my life. I try to tell myself it's all for the best but it's a hard package to sell. He was the center of my existence for 18 months. Everything I did revolved around him. I miss his calls . . . sometimes twice a day he'd phone . . . and the wonderful anticipation of meetings . . . and then the reality of being with him. It was such joy. And now it's gone. In my gut I know there was something really off with him . . . and maybe I am lucky. It would be wonderful if someone new would come along to fill in the empty spaces. There has got to be somebody out there. I think I'll pull the old wooden motto out of my desk drawer and prop it up . . . "And this, too, shall pass."

A really bright spot in my life is your happiness. It is so beautiful to see you calm and at peace with Ken. Never before has your life been so solid and settled and really in perfect harmony with all the good things. He is a gem. Now don't forget to let me know when his movies air so I can alert the intimate world.

. . .

Here I am on page two with more drivel . . . haven't said a thing and there is no news really. I'll have to think of <u>something</u> to make this worth the 13c it will take to mail.

. . .

November 8th I am opening the apartment for an Andy Young do at $50 a head. I have never done this before and am curious to see how it goes. I shall learn from others who have done this number . . . and put away (locked up someplace) my fine small pieces which people find so easy to slip into their pockets. It's hard to believe that guests in a home would take things, but they do—all the time, I am told.

Would you believe . . . a page and a half of typewritten nothing? Well—here it is and now I button my lip and go to work. But not before I tell you what a lovely feeling it was (again) . . . to be in your home and sleep in YOUR guest room . . . and see the towels . . . monogrammed KMH. . . . !!!!

Please write to me when you can. Your letters mean a lot to me—especially when I can read them. So use the typewriter, kiddo. Kiss the G.G. for me and I'll be watching the mails.

Much love,
Nonno

—————————— ⌀ ——————————

"The Nobel Laureate" was Saul Bellow. Mrs. Bellow Number Three, the late Susan Glassman, was my dear friend. They had had a difficult divorce, which ultimately went to the Illinois Supreme Court.

[OCTOBER 20, 1977]

THURSDAY

Dear Margo——and Ken, of course:

It was such a joy to get your call last night. You have no idea how it cheered me up. Not that I was depressed. . . . I am well over the sadness, but just hearing you two—and knowing that you were thinking about me and wanted to call was a real upper.

J. Fred, . . . Ken reports that you are getting thin as a rail. Don't overdo it. We don't want you to look tubercular, heaven forbid. No hip bones should stick out. Just get the tochas* under control. By this time I'm sure you've already done it so I'll shut up my mouth already.

I'm busy as a one-armed paper hanger with a severe case of crabs. This book is driving me bananas. When I get finished I'll have so much free time I may take in laundry or sewing. It will be six months from the time I hand in the script until they get the book off the presses—so that will be playtime for

---

*"Tochas" means rear end.

Mama. THEN . . . comes the promotion. I will be on the TV circuit making with the mouth like crazy. It's the only way to sell books. I have said "NO" to all autograph parties . . . even though Stanley Marcus and Lady Bird Johnson and others have done them. When I talked to Carol Stoll [independent book store owner] the other day she asked me about having an autograph party at Oak Street and I said I wasn't doing that number. "Oh . . ." she yelled . . . "Dick Himmel [interior decorator] had one here and he sold 600 books." When I heard <u>that</u> my mouth began to water. Maybe I'll make an exception in HER case . . . but to go around the country waiting for people to come in and buy your book . . . well, it's downright degrading. Actually, I think if I am going to do an autographing party in Chicago it ought to be at Krock's . . . downtown. . . . What do YOU think?

Enclosed is the clipping of the year. I refer to the case of the Nobel Laureate. He really got it in the neck this time. If you haven't heard by the time you get this letter I'm sure it will make your day. I wish I had Susan Glassman's phone number. I would call her up and say "Mazel tov. You've nailed the S.O.B." This is going to make him look like such dreck from coast to coast. Just look at the picture the <u>Sun-Times</u> used. He looks like a chicken whose neck has been wrung. I must say I am getting a special delight out of this because he has been really rotten to her. Time wounds all heels and he's finally getting what he deserves.

On Sunday I leave for the Bankrupt Apple . . . mainly to work on my book. I'll be seeing Mary Lasker for cocktails . . . (she drinks tomato juice and I'll have tea) . . . and that lawyer John Doar cannot make it, dammit . . . so we'll just have to get him another time. He is especially appealing to Mary because he has a summer place about a mile from Mary's in Amenia. She wants me to be a summer <u>and</u> winter neighbor. In fact, she'd like for me to move into the U.N. Plaza bldg. but I am not nuts about that place. A few months ago I did look at some apartments there . . . as well as [Mr. X]'s apartment which he wanted me to see because if I liked it he would not have sold it. Did you ever? The more I think about it the more I have come to believe he really misled me plenty. Dumb, I am not—and I would never have made such serious assumptions on my own.

Well, Little Chickens, I gotta get to work. So this is it for Thursday . . . October 20th. . . . Damn near my anniversary. I was divorced on October 17th . . . two years ago. Can you believe it? And let me tell you—these last two years haven't been bad. Nobody should ever have worse ones.

Much love to the world's nicest lovers . . . from

"Nonno" or "Mama"

NOVEMBER 11, 1977

Mugsie:

I'm leaving for Charlevoix . . . Traverse City and Battlecreek on Thursday . . . boonies, sure, but the $$$ is there . . . lots of it . . . and I'm going to have a ball. NOBODY goes to those tank towns so, of course, I am treated like royalty. I'm also going to see Will Munnecke . . . haven't laid eyes on the old gray fox in three years. I hope I beat the snowstorms. November 3rd can be a blizzard in upper Michigan yet. But today it was like spring.

Tomorrow Marella and Johnny Angelli [Gianni Agnelli, owner of Fiat] will be in town. She called me and asked to have lunch but I can't. My Doubleday editor, Ferris Mack, is coming in at noon to spend the day . . . and evening. So—I won't be able to hear John speak at the Council of Foreign Relations . . . and I had to decline their invitation for dinner at the Casino. Marella was very disappointed and said that she and Johnny might come by for cocktails and "be a little late" for the Casino party. I said "fine." You would adore her. She's very Italian and a real swingin' lady. (From what I hear HE swings plenty.) But Italians don't believe in divorce, so the men run hog wild and the women go crazy in stores to get even. This is how Bulgari stays alive.

My book is coming along very well . . . at long last . . . I can see the end in sight. I have some wonderful pieces in there . . . along with my kishkehs* . . . I have really worked like a damned dog on this thing. If it's a turkey I will only kill myself.

If you see a <u>Reader's Digest</u> in the doctor's waiting room . . . November issue . . . pick it up. I gotta piece in there.

Love to the G.G. and have some yourself. PLEASE let me know what the plans are as <u>soon</u> as you do. If you wind up here for Thanksgiving I HOPE Ilana invites us <u>all</u> for dinner since you have already told me the food here stinks.

Your Very Own . . .
Nonno

---

*"Kishkehs" means, literally, intestines, but in common usage means gut, guts, or "stomach."

DECEMBER 4, 1978

Dear Margo:
<u>NOW</u> will you listen to me?

L&K—
Nonno

[Enclosure, from the *Sun-Times,* November 29, 1978. Headline: "Most Influential U.S. Woman: Ann Landers." From Fourth Annual Selection of the *World Almanac.*]

———————— ⚬⚭⚬ ————————

The "Perfect" referred to in the following letter was a gold drop on a chain I had sent to Mother. The word "perfect" was spelled out—but with the "T" lower than the rest of the letters . . . and lopsided.

Najeeb Halaby was the former chairman of Pan-American Airways and father of the future Queen Noor. Mary Lasker was introducing Mother to everyone eligible she knew, feeling unhappy that it had been her introduction that brought "Mr. X" into the picture.

DECEMBER 20, 1978
FRIDAY NIGHT . . .
SQUID AND WHALE—BY THE CATHOLICS . . .
BY ME—GEFILTA.

Dear Mugsie:

First—I love the PERFECt . . . I really had not seen it before and tried, gently, to bend the T so it would be in line. Then it dawned on me that it was supposed to be like that. It's a darling gift and I adore it. Especially so because I <u>really am perfect</u>. Actually, instead of having been named most influential I should have been named the most perfect.

If the truth were known I think I am a little screwy. Why would I think twice about staying at the Beverly Wilshire when I gave the Institute of Psychoanalysis $5,000 last week . . . and Meharry Medical College $25,000 and Notre Dame $12,500 this year and $12,500 last year to complete my pledge of $25,000. Yet, I balk at a lousy few hundred bucks at a good hotel. Margo, your mother is really loony. Please don't tell anybody. It's bad enough that Ken knows I asked you to find a little motel in Brentwood. So what would I save??? $200????? That's what I give to 30 Congressmen I don't even know. Please, I'm ashamed of myself. Forget it. I can't hold my head up.

. . .

So . . . today I taped the Kup show and ran into a great admirer of yours—Rita Moreno. She is a darling lady . . . and thinks you are GORGEOUS . . . and SO SMART. . . . When she asked where you were and what you were doing, Essee Kup asked . . . "Did you know Margo married KEN HOWARD?" Well . . . Rita screamed! . . . "My God . . . he's so GORGEOUS. . . . I am so thrilled for them both. What a beautiful couple!" And she meant every word of it. We had a great show. . . . Maurice Stans was on the panel . . . and a guy named Friedman [Bruce Jay Friedman] who has written a book about Loneliness and a play about a Steambath. Anyway Maurice Stans was Sec. of Commerce under Nixon . . . and he has written a book trying to justify WATERGATE. Well . . . I really gave it to him very nicely . . . and so did Rita. She's a very articulate and bright Lady ... and Maurice got more than he bargained for on that show.

. . .

Tomorrow I go to New York ... Mary Lasker's annual party at La Grenouille. It should be a gasser. I am eager to meet Najeeb Halaby ... although I have an idea he ain't my kind of guy. He's Lebonese [*sic*] ... and my age ... but I think a bit of an international swinger. But ... I shouldn't pre-judge. The fellow supposed to be on the other side of me is VERY handsome and never married ... But I think he's a side saddle tenor ... He also goes with Countesses and Princesses and all that crap. Royalty leaves me cold. Lee Radzwell [*sic*] ... altogether a princess. She's about as interesting as a dead herring. I had my fill of that wench at Bill Hewett's party in Moline when he sent his plane for me and she joined the fun ... having come commercial from New York. What a phony. Snobbish beyond belief. Feh.

I must get to bed because tomorrow is a big day and I want to be bright eyed and bushy-tailed. I'll be seeing you soon and it will be marvelous to get to see the kids again. They sounded great on the phone. Yes—everything turned out for the best. Somebody up there likes you.

Much love to you and the G.G.

Nonno . . . or Mama

JANUARY 16, 1979
TUESDAY

Dear Mugsie:

We spoke last night—interminably but it was a good conversation. The enclosed was supposed to be mailed by my office, but it was inadvertently mixed in with my "mail for Washington" folder and I'm adding this note and it will be posted from Wash. DC.

. . .

I must confess I feel very guilty about tipping my mitt on what I suspect is the real reason for Popo's attacks on you—and me. I had no business telling you. She confided in me and I betrayed her trust. I slept very poorly last night and am still bothered by it. I'm ashamed of myself.

Basically, she <u>is</u> a good person and we should remember that. She's been good to you in recent years—and good to me, as well. When things go wrong in her life she needs to lash out at someone and I have always been her prime target. You, I'm sure, are an extension of me—in her thinking—so, you got it, too. Try to understand what motivated her attack. (Who was it that said—"To understand is to forgive"??)

Part of her problem is that she has never been able to lash out at Morton. <u>Ever</u>—He would never tolerate it—and this I know full well. So—don't be too hard on her.

Enough of this—On to better things— like life is <u>good</u>. I am <u>HAVING A MARVELOUS TIME</u>—going to London Feb 5—for a week—and until something better comes along I plan to live it up and enjoy!

Love you Baby—
Nonno

Regarding my father: he fought an alcohol problem on and off for much of his later adult life. We were very close until not long after Father and Mother's divorce . . . though ironically, the fact of their parting had nothing to do with our subsequent estrangement. It just seemed healthier to have no relationship with him as he became angrier and more bitter about "life." He was having a midlife crisis so severe it altered his behavior. He was very far from the man I had known for thirty-five years, a man who had been a wonderful father. Coleman refers to John Coleman, my starter husband.

MARCH 27, 1979

Dear Margo—

First—the picture of you and Ken arrived today and I love it!! The photographer really caught you both and it couldn't be more like you if it had been painted by Gilbert Charles Stuart.

You sent 2 pictures and I'm wondering if you wanted me to send one to somebody else. Please let me know.

Speaking of "somebody else" I spoke to Daddy today for quite a while and

believe it or not, he is completely dry—
has been for two months and says he
will never take another drink as long as
he lives. He also said he has lost 15
pounds and is looking forward to a new
life and a new start in California. He
and Elizabeth will be leaving in mid-
April and are renting a house in
Brentwood. He always asks about you
and the children, and I have told him
that everything is simply wonderful—
which, thank God, it is. Now that he is
sober, he makes a lot more sense and I
am keeping my fingers crossed that the
deal he and Morey Mirkin [Mother's
cousin and Father's associate at Budget]
are working on will pan out. If it doesn't
he says, "I'll get a job and at least my
self-respect back." He also said, "I can't
believe what a schmuck I've been and
how I loused up my life." Yes, he does
know you are married to Ken Howard
and thinks Ken is a terrific actor and
"must be a hell of a guy." I hope one day
you will be able to pick up the threads
somehow—but this, of course, is strictly
your decision and until you come to it

yourself, there is no sense in talking about it. I just thought you might want to know that Daddy is off the booze and this might mean a different ballgame. He still hates Coleman with a passion, however. In that regard, nothing has changed except maybe he hates him more. When I talk to you on the phone remind me to tell you what he heard about John. I'd never put it in a letter no matter what.

I'll call you soon—in fact, I may call you tonight, which means we'll talk before you receive this letter.

Again, thank you for the marvelous picture. Much love to you and the G.G.

Nonno

The following letter describes a dinner in South Bend, Indiana, at Notre Dame.

MAY 13, 1979

Dear Margo:

. . .

Phil Donahue was the winner of the entertainer of the year award. (He also went to Notre Dame.) Marlo was there and we had a very good time. I had a great visit with Ted [Hesburgh]. He is a solid citizen if ever there was one—really a jewel of a guy. Such a tower of strength. He told me to tell [Mr. X] to quit phoning—"He wants the omelet but doesn't have the guts to crack the eggs"—is the way Ted put it.

I miss the guy—a lot—but I am determined <u>not</u> to see him again. If only there was someone else I could have some fun with—someone to dress up for—and look forward to being with. I've sure been out with a lot of men these past 6 months—and not one has been really promising. But—I'm not giving up. He's out there someplace.

It's late—and I'm calling it a night—this is not a letter—just a note.

Love to you and the G.G.
Nonno

The Sumatra reference is that, for whatever reason, I was late sending Mother's Day flowers, so the card said, "It's Mother's Day in Sumatra."

The man referred to in the P.S. was an industrialist who lived in Chicago. I realized, long after this letter was written, that he must have been sweet on Mother, because not long before his death he wrote her a letter saying he "had just read Margo's book, for the second time . . . for obvious reasons." He was appreciably older—but Mother clearly had electricity for geezers, for he was not the only man interested in her whom she felt was simply too old.

MAY 16, 1979
TUESDAY

Dear J. Fred:

I am so glad it's Mother's Day in Sumatra because I received a dozen beautiful red roses from my daughter—and they are now occupying the place of honor . . . (center of coffee table) . . . and will be paraded before all my visitors . . . starting with Jane Dick [a social doyenne in Chicago] who will be here for coffee in ten minutes. Later two shrinks and their wives will be here for cocktails . . . and the third shift . . . Nate Kline (the guy who was the first to use anti-depressant drugs). Thank you for sending these truly beautiful flowers. You have class, child.

Anyone who needs psychiatric help is out of luck this week unless they happen to live in Chicago. Every wig-picker in the country is here—with his hostile, angry, crazy wife. I never saw so many screwed up marriages. Last night [an office-holder from an Eastern state] was here for cocktails with his wife. I was meeting them for the first time . . . (Another couple brought them.) She looks like a moose in heat. You never saw such a tochas on a person . . . and she puts an electric blue plaid on it yet. Her husband is a mousy little man who is seething with hate. She finishes his sentences, corrects his syntax . . . and leaves the room in the middle of his stories because "I've heard all his garbage already." One day you will read of an axe murder in [their city]. "Assailant Still at Large."

The above was written <u>YESTERDAY</u>. I got side-tracked by the telephone and before I knew it Jane Dick was here . . . and the day was gone. Also the evening. Sorry about that.

I have your beautiful roses ON THE DESK as I type this. Thank you again. It is lovely here in Sumatra. Too bad it took me so long to get here. Had I known how gorgeous it was I would have come sooner.

This morning's mail brought the clipping about the lady doc who had to go into the cosmetic business because she has had a lot of luck these past two years. All bad. It seems she did breast implants and a face-lift—all at once . . . on an 81-year-old woman who died on the table. The woman's daughter sued and the publicity wasn't exactly what every plastic surgeon dreams about. THEN . . . she operated on her own husband. She was attempting to eliminate the wrinkles in his forehead by raising his eyebrows. The operation was a flop and the guy will go around looking surprised for the rest of his life.

. . .

I loved the last line in your letter about "being good at waiting . . . because I taught you." It would be easier to wait if I thought that eventually I would be as lucky as you were. Maybe I am nuts but I hate to waste my time just to go out. If I don't see anything really interesting in a man I won't accept a second date. In many cases I won't even accept the first. And then I say to myself . . . "Give the guy a chance" . . . and wind up going out a second time with a jerk like [—] . . . for which I could kick myself.

Did you ever see such typing? I wish I could blame it on the machine but actually the machine is fine. It's me.

Did I tell you I saw [—] at the Congressional dinner in Washington? I had heard she had a face lift and that it was a disaster. Well . . . would you believe I did **<u>NOT</u>** recognize the girl? The doctor screwed up her eyes and she looks like [an Asian friend of Mother's]. Also there seems to be a new fad . . . which is illegal . . . silicone in the cheeks. It looks to me like Betty Ford did this and it looks very fakey. [—]'s silicone is slipping and she looks like she has a couple of impacted wisdom teeth.

Gotta run, doll. So this is it for now. Write more often. I love your letters.

Nonno

P.S. The information on [—] reminded me of a neat one-liner I heard a while back . . . when she married [—] the person said, "She loves him for what he is. RICH."

―――――― ⟨∞⟩ ――――――

The set of glasses, from whence the broken one came, had been a wedding present from Mr. X.

"John" was John Coleman. The travel to Chicago Mother speaks of had to do with his suing Ken and me for custody of the children. There were many emergency motions and so forth for which we all had to trek to Chicago. The final outcome was that nothing changed . . . except the children were given more freedom than they previously had about whether or not they wished to spend time with their father.

Joan Braden was an extremely well-connected public relations maven in Washington.

MAY 29, 1979
TUESDAY . . . AYEM

Dear J. Fred:

Loved talking to you last night—and to the G.G. who had just broken one of [Mr. X]'s glasses. Symbolic maybe? Anyway, I am sorry I was on the horn so long. . . . It's maddening to keep trying a number and get that damn busy signal for over an hour. And it WAS over an hour I'm sure. But I hadn't talked to Bob [Stolar] in a long time and he called when I was just getting into the tub and we mee-ah-shed* about everything and everybody. We talked a lot about you and Ken and the kids and John . . . who, it seems, is getting a lot of bad press these days— plus personal gossip. In addition to the 25 grand lawsuit for non-payment by

---

*"Mee-ah-shed," Mother's phonetic spelling—and maybe even her own *word*—meant a long, gabby visit. This usage was past tense . . . if a made-up word can have tenses.

Hill and Knowlton, he hasn't paid Joan Braden a dime for all her work. She does, however, have the "right" to have lunch at the Jockey Club (where I hear the food is poisonous) . . . and she can bring friends . . . if they are of the Kissinger quality. Enough about him. But I was delighted to know he is paying for all the travel to Chicago. By all means stay at the Ritz under those conditions. Back to the Drake, however, when the jerk quits with the lawyers and depositions. But will he EVER quit? I think he is obsessed with that sort of excitement, for a lot of reasons, all of them sick. It's one way to have something going with you. Then, too, he enjoys harassing people. It gives him a feeling of importance—also visibility. I really think the pathological bastard would rather have BAD press than no press at all.

I will leave it to you to tell me if you want to be met . . . also will you have any time for me. If not, I will surely understand. Of course I would love to see the kids but will wait until you call and tell me when or if it is possible. My schedule is as follows: I am home on June 10–11 and 12 . . . I leave to speak in Indianapolis on the 13th.

Ric Soll [*Chicago Tribune*] is coming to interview me tomorrow. His wife, Pamela Zekman, came to ask me if I would give him the time. It will be a cover story for a magazine called Chicagoland which I never heard of. I said yes because she said you were a special friend of Ric's . . . had admired his work and sent him notes of praise when you were both at the Tribune. He treasures your little memos and still has them. I thought . . . "Well . . . I'll do this if my kid thinks so well of his writing. He's got to be good."

Sorry I was so downbeat about my "aloneness" when you called. I should have my mouth washed out with lye for complaining—about ANYTHING. If ever a person has had it good it's this one. Even when Daddy and I were living in that dump in Milwaukee and you were sleeping on the cot in the kitchen . . . it was GOOD. There was a war on and it was the only place we could find near Gimbel's (he was the millinery buyer . . . for BOTH upstairs French room and the basement . . . big deal!) . . . and I never felt sorry for myself. I think maybe the only really sad days of my life were your last two or three years with John. I knew you were having a terrible time but you never once complained to me and I never said a word to you. Most mothers suffer when their children get a divorce but believe me I felt no pain . . . either time . . . just relief and thankfulness that you had the courage to do it. And of course now that you have this beautiful mensch . . . this golden guy . . . my heart leaps with joy.

No, I should not have said anything and I hope you will forgive me. Today is brighter . . . much . . . and there is a lot out there ahead of me.

I'm sure you had a ball in Seattle. It's a lovely city. And any city would be lovely with The Mensch. Just let me know where you are so I can tell God to look to bless you both. Although I'm sure he knows.

. . .

This letter is getting to be a copy of the Dead Sea Scrolls already. Enough . . . are you still reading or did you fall asleep (or put it away for "later"??). . . . In any case I wouldn't blame you. No one should have to read anything this long unless they are preparing for finals.

One more thing . . . I had a marvelous two days with Ted Hesburgh. He's some terrific guy . . . and a real source of strength. He knew before I did that [Mr. X] wouldn't have the guts—and he told me, as best he could. But when you don't want to accept something you don't hear it.

Call or write when you can. Kiss the G.G. I'll be traveling a little between now and when you come . . . but not much.

Love you lots,
Nonno

My work Mother refers to in the following letter is my book, Eppie: The Story of Ann Landers, *hence, the "historical" information she is passing on in this, and other letters. I took three years to write that book, which was published in 1982. It was mostly about Mother and her work, but, perforce, somewhat about her parents, sisters, my father, and me.*

JUNE 4, 1979

MONDAY . . . RUNNING BUT GOTTA GET THIS OFF TODAY.

Dear Margo:

I just spoke with Cricket [my youngest]. You are working. You may call me back . . . later. If not, I wanted you to have the information. My Daddy's nickname was Skippy. Everyone called him that. WHY . . . I don't know. . . . It had to do with the movie. . . . I think Jackie Cooper was Skippy. . . . Anyway . . . he loved it. AND as recently as last weekend when I spoke at Notre Dame someone reminded me. A lovely man in his 70's came up after my speech and said, "I'm from Sioux City. I knew your father. . . . We all loved 'Skippy.' Wherever he went he spread sunshine. He always made people feel better about themselves—and the world." The man was a C.P.A. . . . first a Notre Dame Graduate (it was Alumnae weekend . . .) . . . and he did work for Daddy in Kansas City. In addition to being President of The Affiliated Theaters, Inc. Daddy owned part of some Ice Factories in Kansas City and Omaha. (This was BEFORE refrigerators!) He also had the exclusive distributorships of Millers High Life Beer in Sioux City. He had his fingers in lots of pies. He also was part owner of the Windsor Terrace in Des Moines . . . which is still considered one of the finest apartments in that city. When he died he left each of his four daughters a very respectable inheritance <u>evenly</u> . . . with no regard for "need." As a matter of integrity he felt he should treat all of us the same . . . in his will . . . and he did.

More info . . . this for the book. Daddy (yours, not mine) quit high school . . .

Northwestern in Detroit at 16. His father was killed in a train accident . . . (his car hit the train in Jackson, Mich . . .) . . . Daddy was then 13. He quit school at the earliest legal minute . . . to go to work. His first job was in Kern's basement . . . (a dept. store in Detroit). . . . He was hired to unpack and tag ladies millinery. Someone noticed how attractive and aggressive he was and he was hired by Goldstein O'Conner Millinery (they were then a chain) to be assnt. mgr. in their dept. at Herpolsheimer's Dept. store in Grand Rapids. He made $18 a week . . . lived at the YMCA and sent $6 a week to his mother. From there he went to Lansing . . . a big promotion . . . mgr. of the Ladies Millinery Dept in the J.W. Knapp Co. . . . From Lansing . . . to Sioux City . . . T.S. Martin Co.

If you want some shmaltzy stuff on Daddy . . . call Morey Mirkin. He knows it all.

I am running . . . but not before I tell you I love you.

Kiss the kids and the Mensch . . . and I hope I see you soon.

Nonno

———————— ⌾≪◇≫⌾ ————————

Ken Howard created and starred in the television series The White Shadow. *It was based on his own years as a high school basketball star in Manhasset—where he was, in fact, called "The White Shadow" for being the only white starter on an all-black team. This was a trailblazing series, both for its form as an early comedy/drama and the realistic episodes that didn't always have a pat ending—like life.*

Mother's birthday parties, post divorce, were always given by Mary Lasker . . . until Mary became too ill to entertain. Mary, knowing the history of the birthday-anniversary trips, told Mother that until she remarried, the birthday celebrations would be Chez Lasker. And her way of giving gifts was either to select something from her own homes, or to send the recipient into a store to make her own selection!

"Dancing for disease" was a phrase I dreamt up for my first column in the Chicago Tribune . . . *a*

very distant thirty-three years ago. It had dawned on me that most of the charity balls in town were given to benefit . . . diseases.

Marvin Davis is the mogul from Denver and L.A. who at one time owned a number of entertainment companies.

JULY 7, 1979
SATURDAY

Dear Margo:

I LOVE the vase . . . which, as I said on the phone, is really a VOZ on account of it is so elegant. I noticed it is By The Haldon [*sic*] Group. Is this maybe like the Walton family? I can just see the whole mishpocha sitting in a circle making pottery. Really, dear girl, you couldn't have sent me anything prettier . . . or more practical. As you know, I get lots of flowers and most of the florists send fairly tacky vases. So, I do thank you. Also, the fact that you went out and shopped for something means a lot. Bless you.

Last night was my quad-annual dinner with the Minows. (We take turns hosting, and when it's mine we go to the International Club. When it's theirs . . . it's the Standard Club.) Last night . . . mine. This has been going on for a long time. We just enjoy being together and there is always so much to talk about. Jo brought along your darling letter. (It WAS dear—and she loved it.) Jo said she doesn't know of anyone in your generation who knows such great Yiddish. When I told her and Newt that you have been tutoring Ken in the mother tongue they cracked up. Jo thinks <u>The White Shadow</u> is terrific— and has great social significance. Newt said the residuals should make a fortune. I am enjoying the re-runs— some I'm seeing for the first time.

Gossip department: Coleman had a party to launch "the New Whitehall" . . . or some such and was drunk as a skunk. So now it is common knowledge that he is back on the booze. As you know, Newt loathes John, in fact he was one of the first ones in Chicago to catch on to him. I hope you don't mind, but I told them about the Father's Day card to Ken and they almost wept. I don't know if you have thought of this, but that card, in the hands of the judge could be the strongest evidence yet. It says it all—and in a way no attorney or witness could possibly say it.

I had a ball in Athens. The Athens Hilton holds a lot of memories for me. About six years ago we were there . . . the four of us on our annual birthday-anniversary trip . . . and we were having dinner in the dining room. Next to us was Nelson Rockefeller and Happy (in Happier days) with their darling sons. Time sure changes things. If anyone had told us that six years later I would be divorced and Nelson would die in bed with a dame . . . who would have believed it? Say la vee. (That's French, kid.)

My birthday was fun . . . and I had the usual very good time in New York with Mary. She asked me to pick out a gold rope or anything I wanted at Tiffany or Cartier (AGAIN) . . . I didn't see anything I liked in New York but I did see a very pretty gold ring in Farber's on Michigan Avenue. So—that's Mary's birthday present. I also got many flowers (the ice box is full) . . . and [Mr. X] sent a huge bottle of Marcel Rochas. Helen Copley (the newspaper publisher) sent the ugliest Boehm piece I have ever seen . . . and they are all pretty terrible . . . but THIS one . . . a water lily is the absolute pits. Mary Lasker said, "Insure it and break it, dear." I think I just might. Arthur Rubloff sent three gifts . . . a Chinese paperweight (monstrosity) . . . an alligator wallet and a very lovely Chinese ashtray or candy dish. He is a very sweet and thoughtful guy but his taste is in his mouth. And speaking of taste I am saving the wedding invitation from the Marvin Davises. You will NOT believe this. I have decided to go to the wedding. It's in Denver on August 4 and I'm sure there will never be anything like it again on the planet. The Diabetes Ball (Dancing for Disease . . . remember?) was INCREDIBLE.

Turn the page . . . or have you fallen asleep????

This magilla is running on and on and I haven't said much. In fact, as I re-read it to ink out the errors I wondered if it was worth mailing. But I SHALL mail it since something is better than nothing. (This time, just barely.) But I did want to write and thank you for the lovely birthday gift even though you said the phone thank you was enough. Not in my book it isn't. If you found the time to schlepp to the Haddon Group and pick out a gorgeous gift, I can find the time to say a proper thank you.

We'll talk on the Ameche and keep in touch. I send love to you and the Mensch and Abra.

Nonno

"The enclosed" Mother speaks of had to have been a complaint from a reader that the Herald-Examiner *was cutting the Ann Landers column. Local editing drove Mother berserk. Though it usually had to do with page layout or space, regular readers knew that there were three letters a day, and fewer than that got their dander up.*

Marcy Sugar, as the Brits would say, was one of

the "top girls" in the office. She was there for twenty-four years, and with Mother's number one, Kathy Mitchell, is now writing "Annie's Mailbox," one of several new advice columns meant to fill the void after Mother's death.

Regarding her relationship to my first husband, Mother was ambivalent. Periods of time lapsed when she would have nothing to do with him and totally cut him off—but then she would ease back into communicating because she felt she was like a mother to him, she felt sorry for him, and she thought she might be helpful in mediating between him and the children. She was actually never able to improve the situation.

JULY 19, 1979

Dear Margo:

Don'tcha love the enclosed! I have responded to her via the Confidential . . . <u>L.A. Herald Examiner</u>. Keep watching and see if they print it. That paper is not one of my favorites. They cut the column like crazy and I am forever fighting with the editor, Jim Bellows.

I loved talking to you . . . you are dear to call, but we don't have to talk THAT long. I'll bet it was 40 minutes.

. . .

Keep me posted on the kids and the schools. I have a feeling this is going to be the turning point. Incidentally I am making it known among my friends that I have written John off completely and want nothing to do with him.

Kiss the G.G.

Nonno

It would be an understatement to say that Mother didn't get it with cats and dogs. Also, her political fortune telling—not for the first time—was all wrong.

Mother first got to know Bill and Rose Styron, close friends of the Buchwalds, when she would make her summer visits to Martha's Vineyard.

AUGUST 9, 1979

Dear Daughter:

. . .

I've been traveling a lot. . . . First the
Vineyard with the Cronkites. . . . They
had a party for me and Jules Feiffer
sends his warm regards, also, Anne
Buchwald . . . and Betsy and
Walter . . . add to the list, Rose and Bill
Styron and the Vern Aldens. They
always ask about you. In fact so many
people do . . . but you don't believe it.
Like Dick Christensen never fails to
stop and ask me about Margo. He
really is very fond of you . . . but when
I tell you, you think I am making
it up.

The Cronkites' dog, Buzzie, age 17—
which is like 119 in a person . . . went to
the great kennel in the sky. It happened
on the day after my arrival. They were
heartbroken. When we returned from a
party they went into the kitchen to
check Buzzie because he had been
failing. Well . . . poor thing was like half
gone. . . . They called the vet in New
York and asked what could be done.
"Bring him here as soon as possible,"

the vet said. So—they immediately tried to <u>charter</u> a plane. Betsy was actually going to take that hound to New York in a blanket! No plane was available. All the charters were out, so they called the local vet and he said to bring Buzzie in, in the morning. (It was after midnight when they did this phoning.) Then Betsy and Walter, teary-eyed, went upstairs, changed into shorts and sneakers and came downstairs, laid on the kitchen floor all night, holding Buzzie's paw. When I came to breakfast the next morning they were beat, naturally . . . no sleep. Buzzie was in better shape than they were. They took him to the vet's and well . . . what can I tell you— that night he paygerred.* They got the call in the middle of the party, but carried on without telling anyone. Later they broke up. If I sound cruel and stonehearted it's because I don't think it makes a whole lot of sense to keep an animal around who has no control of his bladder, can't see . . . keeps bumping into furniture . . . has liver trouble, a 90

---

*"Paygerred" means died.

percent hearing loss and craps on the rugs.

The day after I returned from the Vineyard I went to the wedding in Denver. It was so Jewish you wouldn't believe it. Paper mache [*sic*] swans with orchid leis . . . in the swimming pool—yet. Ten pound tins of caviar wherever you looked (and I looked everywhere). The dinner for 400 . . . was catered from Los Angeles. The dance band came from New York. . . . The guests came from all over the globe. . . . With a special contingent from Istanbul. Yeh . . . Turkey . . . the groom is a Turk. The bride got a 42 carat diamond (from her father, you can be sure) . . . hand carried by Dick Winston. Her gown was by Scassi. . . . gorgeous, but the excesses were so flagrant you would have thrown up.

I sat behind Betty and Jerry Ford. He looked terrific . . . and is running like crazy. I do like her a lot . . . can't stand him. The word is that he will come in on the home stretch and take the nomination away from Reagan. Also, it looks like Kennedy will take over when Jimmy falls on his face.

Suddenly it's six bells and I gotta run . . . so this is it for now. Love to Abra, Adam and Cricket, the GG, and you—as always,

Nonno

———————— ⌒∞⌒ ————————

Mother's riff on drinking at home, alone, is a send-up of her being a famous teetotaler.

Meaning "Keebler elves," but spelling it "Kubler," must have been an unconscious reference to Elisabeth Kübler-Ross, the stages-of-death expert, whom she knew.

The "debtor's cell" was an example of her putting her money where her mouth was. Mother had co-signed notes, for between three and four million dollars, with my father, who had not been able to make good on them. She paid all the debts . . . after their divorce.

SEPTEMBER 4, 1979

Dear Thigs:

. . .

I am busy . . . happy . . . energetic and
<u>THIN</u>. I decided to knock off five pounds
so I would look smashing in my new St.
John knits. So—I have been walking a
lot . . . exercising . . . cutting down to a
single-dip of Rocky Road and of course
cutting out <u>all booze</u> . . . which, as you
know, was always my biggest calorie
problem. I decline drinks at parties but
when I get home at night I get bombed.
Needless to say I cannot work in that
condition so I have hired five elves who
have been laid off by Kubler [*sic*] . . . the
cookie business is bad these days . . .
and this is how I keep going.

. . .

I'll be doing a lot of traveling in the
Fall. . . . I've promised to do Le Grand
Tour   for   Ballantine   when   the
Encyclopedia comes out in paperback.
Bless that book. It bailed me out of
debtor's cell. Before I come to California
I will give you plenty of notice—so you
can be in New York.

Write   a   note . . . or   pick   up   the

phone . . . or send up smoke signals. I'll do the same. In the meantime, kiss everybody for me. . . .

Your ever-lovin'—
Nonno

[Enclosures: (1) a newsclip of a man named Regis Vey. She typed on it: "We call him 'Oi' for short." (2) a business card from a friend of hers: "Henri J. Lewin, millionaire." Her note on the card: "This is <u>real class</u>—He's Western Regional Director of Hilton Hotels."]

"The Popo jewelry" Mother referred to was made with iron, diamonds, and pearls. I first saw it when Popo was wearing a matte black metal ring with a large Mobe pearl at the center, surrounded by small diamonds. I loved the idea of a common metal with precious gems and admired the ring. She took it off her finger and gave it to me. Popo could be very generous and warm.

SEPTEMBER 14, 1979
THURSDAY NITE . . . LATE.

Dear Margo:

I apologize for writing another letter so soon . . . but I just got <u>another</u> dear one from you and wanted to respond because I will be on the road . . . Rockford . . . then New York for several days. This is a Ballantine trip . . . lots of T.V. . . . radio . . . interviews . . . etc. . . . and I will be breaking my keister. After such trips, when I get home, it takes me at least three days to get my head off the deck and clean up the desk mail.

Your Jewish mother was very happy to hear the description of the outfit you wore at the Emmy affair. You look terrific in that black knit. I must say I don't recall the big diamond ladybug pin. I <u>DO</u> remember the Popo jewelry . . . and that <u>IS</u> gorgeous. If I bought you a black sequin evening jacket would you wear it? Or a rather muted multi-colored one with some navy, purples . . . etc. . . . instead of all black? Let me know. I have seen a few and I think they are stunning. They should be worn over a very simple black dress with a low neckline. . . . Please be sure to answer this.

I cannot believe that neither you nor Ken knew Abu Ben Adam . . . unless I am misspelling it which is entirely possible. . . . But anyway . . . in school I recall a poem about Abu Ben Adam . . . may his tribe increase . . . awoke one night from a deep dream of peace and there within the quiet of his room . . . there appeared an image . . . and it went on to say something about the great heroes of the time and . . . Abu Ben Adam . . . <u>HIS</u> name led all the rest. . . . So, the point I was making was simply this. I told Roy Menninger if he wanted to take a vote on those who wanted to throw John off the board . . . I wanted to be Abu Ben Adam . . . in other words . . . my name should lead all the rest. GOT IT?

. . .

So Adam is working on his book reports and the girls are buying hair conditioner! Well . . . that figures. If any school offers a class in hair care your daughters are sure to get the highest marks in the entire state.

I am running. . . . This isn't much of a letter but it lets you know I love you . . . and it's always a joy to get a line from the Palisades.

. . .

L and K,
Nonno

———————————— ⌘ ————————————

"Iz-Do Rosenfeld" (Dr. Isadore Rosenfeld) is a cardiologist in New York. He wrote popular medical books, Mother plugged them, and they achieved best-seller status. He was a close friend of Danny Kaye. I can second Mother's opinion of Mr. Kaye as an egomaniac. The one time I met him was in her living room, with no more than eight people present. When the attention was not focused on Mr. Kaye, he actually put a brandy glass on top of his head, waiting to be noticed. I struck up a conversation with the man sitting next to me and Kaye took umbrage, thinking I should listen to him. When the gathering was over and everyone was saying their good-byes, he said to me,

"It's a shame you don't listen better. You have beautiful skin." One does not meet egos like that every day. He was letting me know that I had ruined my chance to be propositioned by Danny Kaye!

SEPTEMBER 22, 1979
SATURDAY

Dear Thigs:

. . .

I have heard about Popo's commercial . . . in fact she told me when she was here that she was going to do it. I asked "<u>WHY?</u>" She said, "because they pay a hell of a lot of money and I want to give it to charity." I told her she already HAS a hell of a lot of money . . . and if she wants to give something to charity she doesn't have to do a commercial. Actually I think she is competing a little with Rhonda Fleming who does a commercial. Maybe I'm way off—but I suspect that's it. Incidentally, it ain't even a bank . . . it's a Savings and Loan.

About the Match game . . . well . . . <u>when</u> will she learn?? She was on

Hollywood Squares and made a jackass out of herself a few times with wrong answers. I really wish she wouldn't go in for that sort of stuff . . . it downgrades what she is trying to project—and hurts me, too, because people DO get us mixed up. But, there is nothing I can do about her decisions in these areas. I cannot understand why she is so crazy for that kind of exposure. It really doesn't add a thing to her.

. . .

Just before I went to Orlando I spent three days in New York. Had a ball. No, I did not see [Mr. X] and have no plans to. When I say I did not see him, I should have said "privately." I DID run into him at a dinner at the Four Seasons for Iz-Do Rosenfeld. Danny Kaye sat between me and Mary Lasker and he is clearly off his nut. The service wasn't fast enough for him so he got up and brought in several plates from the kitchen. The waiters damn near died. He kept this up until everyone was served. He really is very funny when he is not depressed (every fourth day) . . .

but I don't care for him because he is not only egomaniacal but very combative and if he isn't the center of the conversation he sulks and pouts and clams up.

Book of Deuteronomy . . . Page 111 . . .

. . .

I had lunch with Baba Walters. She is unsettled about [—] . . . can't make up her mind, but realizes she must. I also went to a party for Beverly Sills and had lunch with Marietta Tree. <u>Everyone</u> saw YOU on TV the night of the Emmy's BUT ME! They said you looked <u>gorgeous</u>. Also . . . I heard you were on a TV show wearing a scarf on your head and didn't look at all like yourself. Kiddo . . . what happened? They called you at the last minute?

. . .

Love,
Mother

Harriet Welling, a high priestess of Chicago society, and surprisingly a Democrat, was a close pal of Adlai Stevenson, the father.

OCTOBER 22, 1979
SATURDAY

Dear Margo:

Just got back from a trip . . . Boston-Akron-Cleveland . . . and my desk looks as if I have been away for six months. I don't know where all this drek is coming from. BUT—there was a letter from you in this pile and I'm putting everything else aside to respond at once. It's important.

First—it was heaven to see you and Ken in Boston. Kevin [White, Boston's mayor] loved every minute of the four-way visit—and he's not an easy guy to get a compliment out of. But he RAVED about you—and Ken . . . thinks you are just about the handsomest couple he has ever met . . . and so-oooo—ooooo interesting, informed, with-it and wired in. Nu, what can I tell you?

I enjoyed it immensely . . . and I am

glad you feel our get-togethers are more "at ease" and comfortable. I hope you won't reach out and hit me if I say I don't think I am any different. I think YOU are much more loving and much nicer now that you are loved by a wonderful guy. People who are loved and happy (both understatements, in your case) tend to be less critical—and everything takes on a lovely hue. Our worst times were when you were between lousy marriages. But why am I telling you all this? You have figured it out by now—having lived thru a small sampling from your eldest. Mothers always catch it from their daughters when things don't go right. She's the natural target.

Now about the part of the letter you were afraid might be a "downer." It was anything but. It certainly was realistic . . . and a subject that has crossed my mind more than once. Chances of something happening to you and Ken together are a million to one, but it's worth thinking about. You can be sure I would put on a hell of a fight to "take over." Coleman wouldn't stand a chance in a court of law against me. After 25 years, I <u>am</u> an institution and HE has already been <u>in</u> one.

I hope you have a will. If not, make one right away. A letter to me saying you want me to "take over" wouldn't hold up. Neither would one saying you DO want me to be the guardian. . . . But, if it is stated in your will it might help . . . especially, if you said why. Your will should clearly define what you want done with everything you own—especially the jewelry . . . car . . . cash . . . stocks . . . whatever. A good lawyer can advise you if it would be best to turn everything into cash and spent for the kids' education and inheritance. You know I would put all the kids through school if education had not been provided for. I'd also marry off the girls or get them settled in careers. So, now that we've got this closet issue out in the open I'm sure you and Ken will feel better. I do. Thanks for bringing it up.

The mail brought loads of letters from

all over about the <u>Phil Donahue Show</u>. Mostly raves. A few people complained because they thought Phil didn't spend enough time with me . . . too much audience participation.

I was glad to get the feedback because I felt this was the case—then wondered if maybe I wasn't being objective. One thing I am sure of . . . he didn't do a hell of a lot for the book. I am not about to complain, however. People KILL to get on that show—and there I was with a paperback yet. Incidentally, I was on the <u>N.Y. Times</u> bestseller list last week . . . off THIS week . . . and am back on next week . . .

The mail also brought a couple of letters that made me wonder . . . how odd that they arrived the same day. A letter from Merle Strauch from Memphis . . . telling me he just sold his Budget franchise for a million and a half dollars CASH. . . . He added . . . "Jules sold me that franchise for $30,000 ten years ago . . . almost to the day . . . . what a deal!" And the next envelope I rip open is a legal notice informing me that Jules is filing bankruptcy this week. His lawyer is Thomas N. Thompson. The reason I received this notice is that I am the principal "creditor" . . . I think. Why in the hell Jules Lederer didn't have the foresight to keep a few Budget franchises for himself is the mystery of the decade. All it would have taken, actually . . . is ONE. Well—enough of that.

. . .

Just got a call from Harriet Welling. She loves <u>The White Shadow</u>. I'm running now . . . like a thief with the money . . . and miles to go before I sleep. I gotta be nuts to work like this. Actually, I'm not nuts. I like paying bills and having something left over to sock away. After all, a girl's looks don't last forever.

Love to you and Ken,
Nonno

The Gridiron Club dinner is the journalists' annual fiesta in Washington, at which the President and First Lady are traditionally present. Well-known news people put on an original musical sketch show in which they skewer the pols. It's a hot ticket, and news organizations receive a limited number of seats— making it a very good place to network. Members are encouraged not to bring spouses, but rather industry-connected or celebrity guests. Mother liked this event so much that she had two guaranteed tickets written into her contracts. She did not pass up many Gridirons.

FEBRUARY 20, 1980
WEDNESDAY

Dear Margo:
Your call was heaven-sent this afternoon. Yes, I was on the down side . . . my fat fanny was dragging . . . and you came along at just the right minute with all the right words. You will never know how much you helped. You are so perceptive and sensitive . . . and even though you had to go tinkle you weren't ready to hang up. You knew I

needed more. So back you came . . . on the mound . . . to pitch again. Bless you.

. . .

Yes, I will pass up the Gridiron and be at your party on the 15th. It was not a hard decision to make, believe me. There will be other Gridirons but you will never be 40 again—and I don't think I will be having any other children.

Love to Ken . . . and again, thanks, angel,

Nonno

―――――――――――― ∽∞∾ ――――――――――――

The governor in this letter was Jim Thompson, Illinois (Christian) governor. For some reason, he loved Passover! And it was also a way to honor his Jewish supporters and associates.

Ilana Rovner, my close friend, was Jim Thompson's deputy governor, an early stop on her way to becoming the first woman to sit on the Seventh Circuit Appellate bench.

APRIL 2, 1980
WEDNESDAY

Thigs, Honey:

I just returned from Springfield where I had a ball at the Governor's second annual Passover Seyder [*sic*]. Dick Rovner and I went together and Ilana took the <u>train</u>. He is such a sweet guy— and funn . . . . . nnnny. We laughed a lot.

The Governor's secretary had a copy of the Boston write-up on Ken . . . right by my bed . . . in the Lincoln Room. How thoughtful of her. Would you believe I now have ten copies of the piece? After yours arrived, I received NINE more. The readers send them because they know of the relationship.

. . .

Your note was very dear to my heart. You wrote . . . "See . . . I <u>AM</u> Jewish." Yes, baby—you are . . . and as Eric Sevareid said so many years ago . . . "You have timeless Jewish eyes." But your children are going to miss that special feeling that you and I have, I fear. I am afraid that since they left

Chicago no one has said one word to them about their heritage. And they will miss the marvelous fun you have with the Yiddish words and phrases that set you apart from your peers. I would not trade my Jewishness for anything. As I write this I think of the poverty of spirit of John Coleman who took it upon himself to tell your children that his real name is "Darling" . . . and that he is Irish. He has GOT to be one of the most screwed up and miserable people in this whole world. So help me, I feel sorry for him.

. . .

Gotta run. . . . This letter turned out to be more than a little note. Write when you can. I love to hear from you.

Kiss the kids. . . .

Your,
Nonno

Mother's questions about a new house, and "Is it near Greenwich?" had to do with a farm we bought in the northwest corner of Connecticut. Ken, being an easterner, wanted a place to run away to when he wasn't working in California.

[MAY 12, 1980]
MOTHER'S DAY EVEN.

Dear Margo . . . and Ken . . .

Thank you for the simply beautiful basket of flowers that arrived in time for Mother's Day. They are lovely . . . and I shall keep them on my coffee table until they are so dried out and gone there's not a single sign of life. If you had not sent anything . . . it would have been all right. I would have put my head in the oven.

The picture of the two apes knocked me out. Yes, it was YOU . . . when you were little. Definitely. The resemblance is there. And you are right on my head. That's where you were THEN . . . and that's where you are now. A mother is never through with her kids.

I have seen a lot of Ilana these last two

days. . . . The ERA rally was in Chicago . . . and we marched together . . . and sat together . . . and it was a lot of work, but well worth doing. Poor Ilana had to get up and announce that the Governor couldn't make it. She got booed . . . and . . . it was terrible. . . . But she knew it would happen and like a good soldier she faced it and went on to speak about the way he was at the Republican state convention fighting for ERA . . . and ended on a note of triumph and cheers. That girl has really taken it on the chin for him and I phoned him today to let him know it. He promised me he would see Ellie Smeal and Norman Lear tomorrow . . . privately, and he also promised me he would personally phone the five borderline representatives and try to get them to swing over. So—I did more than enough for the cause. Best of all, I was able to give Ilana the build up she deserves. I know he appreciates her, but I thought he should hear it from someone who was there and witnessed how she went to bat for him.

Ilana phoned to tell me that you called her at <u>just</u> the right minute. . . . She said, "it was like mental telepathy . . . the girl is an angel . . ." She then went on to say that you said all the right things and made her feel so much better. It was a real mitzvah, your call to her. She was so down in the dumps and you really cheered her up. Bless you. She is such a darling girl and a golden friend. I received, this morning, some beautiful tulips from her for Mother's Day. Two dozen beauties in ivory and purple. When I called to tell her how lovely they were she said, "You are like a second mother to me . . . even if I'm a little too old to be your daughter . . . that's the way I feel about you." I asked her how old she was and she said, "Forty-one." I reminded her that <u>YOU</u> are 40 . . . and that she could easily be my daughter. For some reason she said it just didn't seem possible. Ilana does seem a lot older than you. I guess it's because I think of you as my baby monkey, on my head . . . like in the picture.

Norman and Frances Lear are a lovely couple. We spent a lot of time together these last two days. Phil Donahue and Marlo had a dinner party at Chez Paul and we were all there . . . including Bella and Martin Abzug . . . (who else) . . . and Gloria Steinem and Ellie Smeal and Muriel Fox and all the people who put the rally together. . . . Betty Friedan still gives me a pain in the ass. Such guts. She wanted me to ask Jane Thompson to give a luncheon or a tea for the Democratic senate wives in Illinois. I told her "Sorry . . . ask her yourself." [Jayne Thompson was the wife of the Republican governor!]

I did get Jane Burn [Jane Byrne, mayor of Chicago] to show up at the ERA Rally, however, and they couldn't get over it. Ilana introduced me to Jane's number one advisor who is a classy, smart black lady. I asked her if the Mayor was coming and she said . . . "No . . . she is sick in bed with the flu." I told her to go call her and tell her if she doesn't show up she is going to be a hell of a lot sicker. . . . Jane has not done one damned thing for ERA. . . . Never has shown up for a single event . . . and there were nearly 100,000 people there. . . . They came in buses from Louisiana and Alabama and Texas and California . . . from every state . . . at their own expense. So the dame went and called Jane and told her I had sent that message. Well . . . in half an hour she turned up . . . looking very well indeed . . . in a lovely outfit and far from sick. (Tired, maybe, but no flu.) She got a tremendous ovation and I can tell you she did herself a lot of good that day. Her popularity is zero these days and she needed something to give her a lift. Her appearance at the rally did it. She needed us a hell of a lot more than we needed her.

I sat a few seats away from Jane on the platform and when she arrived I said . . . "I'm glad you made it." She turned to me and said . . . "On account of you, <u>NOW</u> I have to go to that <u>goddamn</u> Greek parade!"

Tell me more about the house . . . and when you will be furnishing it . . . and moving. . . . And what is the nearest large city? Is it near Greenwich? or Hartford? How does a person get there? Also, what will the kids be doing this summer?

Get off your pratt, honey, and send up a few smoke signals. I adore the clippings . . . especially that hilarious one about Carter . . . but I'd rather hear about my kids.

I'm running . . . tomorrow is another day and it's almost here.

Much love to Ken and the kids and to you . . . as always,

Mama

With this letter Mother begins, or perhaps continues, her long reconsideration of the Reagans.

[JULY 15, 1980]
MONDAY NIGHT. . . . THE CONVENTION IS ON
AND I'M WATCHING WITH ONE EYE AND
LISTENING WITH ONE EAR. REAGAN . . . OUR
NEXT PRESIDENT. AH KLOG!

Dear Thigs:

I am at home at last . . . and the desk looks as if I have been away a year. But I am chucking everything and writing to my daughter.

. . .

[—] met me in Chicago and we went together to Mary's beautiful home in Connecticut. I never thought she could improve on her estate in New York, but she has done it. And it's only 50 minutes from Manhattan . . . OR La Guardia . . . a real pleasure. She doesn't have 50,000 rose bushes . . . yet. But give her until September and she will have the place looking like Versailles.

From Mary's place, [—] and I returned to New York and spent a couple days seeing Barnum (a really marvelous piece of entertainment . . .) and we also took in the Picasso Exhibit. With normal feet the Exhibit would have been too much. It was like a cattle scene . . . but worth an hour which is about what we spent there. There was lots of time to talk and get acquainted because most of the time at Mary's we were surrounded by other people. Mary had guests in for lunch and dinner every afternoon and evening.

This trip has convinced me that [—] is not for marriage. I feel a little sad because I know he had high hopes that our friendship would ripen into something much closer. And Lord knows I gave it every chance. I really wanted it to work because he is so decent. But—after all the time I have spent with him, I confess nothing ignited as far as I was concerned. I couldn't let him past the smooching a little stage. And for people our age this is pretty damned ridiculous. Not only was there the physical deficiency . . . but there was an intellectual missing link. His responses were so slow— almost leaden. I didn't really mind the grammar after a while. It actually wasn't THAT bad. Once in a while I would hear ... "between you and I" ... and it would be like a messer in holdz (that means a knife in the neck). ... But he was quite well read ... and well informed, tho' inarticulate. The more I listened to him the more I realized that he is a depressed personality—and it would be up to me to amuse him and prop him up and soothe him and reassure him ... and oh well ... I'm sure you get the picture. Heavy furniture, dear. So—I made the decision that I would not settle for being a bird in a gilded cage ... with no song in my heart.

As I look back at our relationship ... there wasn't a lot to talk about after we finished with <u>his</u> divorce and <u>my</u> divorce and his children and mine ... and I discovered before long that all he had ever done in his entire life was pile up money.

. . .

So this is it for now ... on to other things ...

Kevin White's son, Mark, is in town and I will see him tomorrow ... and the

Republican convention is on. Every now and then I turn on the tube and catch Walter Cronkite who is trying desperately to make something exciting out of nothing. What a drag! I heard Bill Simon's speech . . . a real sleeping pill . . . rhetoric . . . empty phrases . . . making a last ditch stand to get on the ticket as V.P. And Don Rumsfeld . . . ditto. If Reagan has any sense he will take Bush. That would give him a sure win. (I think he'd win with Mortimer Snerd . . . everyone is so fed up on Carter. Including me. But I just can't bring myself to vote for Ronnie Baby and Nancy . . . no matter what.)

I'm signing off. . . . Write when you can. Love to the G.G. and the kidlets . . . of course.

It's your ever-lovin' . . .
Nonno

Eunice Johnson is the wife of John H. Johnson, founder and publisher of Ebony, Jet, *and other publications for a black audience. Eunice was active in the business, and both Johnsons had been friends of Mother's for many years.*

AUGUST 10, 1980
SATURDAY . . .

Dear Mugsie:

Gotcher letter today . . . with the Shelley Winters review. I saw her on the <u>Phil Donahue Show</u> and she was terrific. Her head doesn't know what her mouth is saying. She is really off the wall. But somehow a streak of honesty (or insanity) or vulnerability runs through that dame that is very appealing. She told about the men she has had affairs with—named names . . . and the audience peed in their pants. I thought it was going to turn into a mass flood. Donahue's ladies are rather middle America . . . though brighter than the average dame who is up to her elbows in dishwater. When Shelley told about her two (or three) abortions there was such a silence ... and then she said ... "I have never regretted anything so much in all my life. I'd give an eye and an arm and a leg to have had those kids. What a terrible thing I did ... and I am paying for it plenty." That brought the house down. She really made a hit and I know the book is doing well ... never mind that she looks a little bit like a hooker.

Anne Buchwald has written a book ... with a little (or a lot) of help from her husband. The cover has him on the jacket with her ... and I did read a few chapters. I found it interesting because we know many of the same people. Also, it was a very honest book—especially when she gets into the Catholic girl-Jewish boy thing ... and how they were sleeping together plenty—and the guilt and the shame. I have two copies. If you want one I will send it. ... She really had a lot of guts to go to Paris in the middle of the depression—no job, just a letter from Stanley Marcus [of the Neiman-Marcus family].

. . .

I am going to the Democratic Convention to catch up with some of my old buddies. It's always fun. I haven't missed one in years. I still think Carter will get elected in spite of the rotten job he has done. I can't believe that Reagan will make it. Today I walked with Eunice Johnson and he [Reagan] was in town Friday . . . and was interviewed at the <u>Ebony</u> offices. Eunice said Nancy was <u>very</u> uncomfortable . . . like she never saw black people up close before. And he wasn't much better. Also, Jesse (Big Mouth) Jackson sat behind me on the plane from Washington yesterday and I heard him talking about how Reagan blew it at the Urban League Convention.

. . .

If I write any more I won't have anything to tell you in person . . . so this is it for now.

. . .

See you soon. I can hardly wait.

Nonno

Richard V. Allen, a Republican operative, eventually served as Ronald Reagan's chief foreign policy adviser and first national security adviser. The reason for my mother's antipathy towards him is unknown to me.

The story with Abra (my eldest) and the dog was this: When Ken and I were safely out of town, Abra "adopted" a stray from the pound. Next, she quickly called my mother to round up an ally. To show gratitude for familial support regarding the unauthorized "adoption," Abra named the animal "Ali," for Ann Landers. We believed the dog was part shepherd, part coyote—if such a thing is possible. I have never loved a dog as much as that one. Tony was Abra's beau at the time. She was then finishing high school in California, to be with us.

[AUGUST 21, 1980]
MONDAY NIGHT

Dear Mugs, R.N.:

By now Abra's gums have stopped aching and life is good again. We just talked on the phone and I will be at your door at 7 bells on Thursday.

. . .

I was amazed to hear you say Dick Allen is a key figure in the Reagan camp. He is really from hunger. And if Ronnie Baby's opening volly is "hurray for that noble war in Vietnam" . . . the jerk from Georgia may just get re-elected. I could throw up from the whole scene.

You are right about the Mondale speech and Teddy's finale. They were both excellent. If Kennedy had started off the way he ended up he just might have captured the nomination. And how did you like the icy appearance he made to offer his "congratulations"? There are several versions of what really happened. Actually, if he had been TOO cordial he would have looked like a phony. Someone sent a wire to Kennedy saying . . . "Carter said he would whip your ass. Please don't kiss his."

I have a ton of work to do, but wanted to get this in the mail tonight. With a little luck this letter will reach California before I do.

Please tell Abra I am thrilled that she named the dog after me. I have never

had a dog named after me before that I
know of. Two horses, however, one in
Wisconsin who came in third at
Saratoga. The other was a candidate for
the glue factory.

Gotta run . . . the work is piled up like
I was gone a year. Actually it was nine
days . . . and you know me . . . I gotta
get to work tonight! So—miles to go
before I sleep.

Love you,
Nonno

AUGUST 24, 1980
SATURDAY—(DID YOU BENS LICHT [LIGHT
CANDLES] LAST NIGHT?)

Dear Margo:
I'm in the Red Carpet Room of
United—in Los Angeles—waiting for the
plane to Chicago. It's a gorgeous day
and I feel as if I have been here for a
week—I did so many things and saw so
many people.

The dinner at Dante's was just <u>lovely</u>.

I enjoyed meeting "Salami" [a character on *The White Shadow* played by Timothy Van Patten] and was amazed at how pretty Cricket is. She's going to be a stunner. I phoned yesterday to see how she was—and Abra said—"100 percent better—" The doctor's diagnosis was the same as mine, which means his years at Stanford Medical School were not wasted. The kid has some allergies. She can thank her mother—who got it from the Lederer side (not the Friedmans, thank you)—Also, I am beginning to doubt the paternity of all your children. I see <u>no</u> trace of Coleman <u>anywhere</u>. Are you sure he fathered those kids? Were you seeing someone else on the side??

I had a good time at Popo's. We went into her swimming pool and enjoyed it. Of course we both swim like a "hock in vassair—" This means like a rock in the water—and has nothing whatever to do with Vassar, Radcliffe or Sarah Lawrence. She found a couple of cork boards (in her garage) and decided to try one out. Well, it kept her afloat and she didn't get her hair wet . . . she goes in <u>naked</u>! I would <u>not</u> do that number, no way, even tho' she swears the neighbors cannot see over the hedges. Actually she has only one neighbor and she says they are "gone a lot—" but we both wore suits and had a ball. She insisted that I take the cork board home—and I did.

Abra and Tony are a great couple. I love them. The ride to Popo's was fun and Popo graciously invited them in for a 7-Up. They stayed for quite a while and are <u>very</u> good company. Finally I said, "Go home already so I can go to sleep. It's two hours later in Chicago!" Popo and I were flattered they wanted to stay that long. The highest compliment of all is to feel that somebody really enjoys having you around. And that's why I had such a <u>wonderful</u> time Thursday night. I felt loved, and it was beautiful.

xxxxx to you and the mensch & the kids

Nonno

Some temporary tumult obviously existed between us, but I have no way, now, of remembering the issue.

SEPTEMBER 20, 1980
SATURDAY

Mugsie:

Thank you for sending the pictures of "Shadow Farms" . . . it is truly a gorgeous place . . . completely charming. And the ACREAGE is like wow. . . . You are <u>landowners</u>. The brochure says "stone walls, pines, a series of pools . . . and circa 1700's." Did you ever think you would wind up on an estate in Connecticut?

I am going to do everything I can to make the New Year a very good one for you and me. No, I don't think I am perfect . . . far from it, and I am working hard to do better. No one is ever too old to learn—and improve. It is harder to change when you're older, but it is not impossible.

Happy New Year, Tochter,
Nonno

XXX For Ken, Abra and Tony
X For Ali—my namesake.

SEPTEMBER 21, 1980
SUNDAY NITE

Dear Thigs:

I meant to enclose this in last night's mailing but it got away from me.

I should tell you (better from your mother than hearing it on the street) that I am seriously considering moving to California. I have talked only to Popo about this and the more we talk and the longer I think . . . the better it seems.

I have a wonderful life in Chicago but I am ready for a complete change in scenery. I can afford to live anywhere I want . . . and for the last two years I've been thinking of New York or California. I like the California lifestyle . . . and would buy NOT a home, but a condo. I realize the prices out there are crazy, but they are slightly nuts all over and I expect it. Also, I can probably get an equally insane price for this apartment.

I know your principal home will be in Connecticut but then we never did live in each other's pockets—and never would, so this won't make a whole lot of difference. As for my office, Popo tells me it can be managed very nicely from afar—as long as the mail works. She kept her offices in St. Paul for two years after she moved west. Also, my syndicate moved to California two years ago so I will be closer to <u>them</u>.

What do you think, Mugsie?

I should also tell you that I am going to try my darndest to behave better. Yes, I DID put you on the spot with Popo and Thanksgiving, and I should NOT have done it. I guess I was so delighted that you had suggested it, I couldn't keep my big trap shut. Also, Popo is a wonderful person in many ways . . . and she <u>does</u> love you dearly. She has also been one helluva friend to me. Love to the G.G. . . . Abra, Tony and Ali.

Your
Nonno

What pleased Mother so much was that Popo had written her that I had invited her, Uncle Mort, and Jeannie to join us for Thanksgiving dinner. In a letter to Mother she wrote that she had mentioned to me, on the phone, that the last encounter Jeannie and I had had "wasn't a very happy one," but that I told her, "Oh, Popesy, that was a long time ago." Like my mother, and most probably because of my mother, I had an on-and-off relationship with Popo. I did find some of her lashing out at Mother shameful, but there was a warm and sweet side of her that I did love. And when I lived in California, which was her home, there were many times of shared warmth and laughter.

SEPTEMBER 29, 1980

MONDAY. I JUST DID THE WASHING AND MY
BACK IS KILLING ME.

Dear Margo:

Because your letter today was such a day-brightener, I am using my best stationery.

It began . . . "Hoho, this is just me being snotty." Actually, you have been a lot snottier. I loved this little number.

I did not realize that Jerry Lewis has

such a lousy reputation. All I can go by is <u>my</u> relationship with him and it has been sparse but good. He is a close friend of Mike DeBakey's [renowned heart surgeon] . . . and we have met at those DeBakey affairs where Mike is being honored.

The last dinner for Mike was very elegant (Houston Petroleum Club) and extremely formal. . . . The tables were U-shaped and I was seated so that I could look straight across at Jerry. Well . . . during the most solumn [*sic*] moment . . . a clergyman was speaking . . . extolling Mike's virtues, for a change . . . and I look over at Jerry who is as bored as I am with all the accolades . . . and there he is, making a simply <u>MARVELOUS</u> monkey-face . . . and he has a silver teaspoon covering one eye like a lorgnette . . . and I just cracked up. Then <u>he</u> did, too, and we were both with our heads <u>UNDER</u> the table . . . plotzing.*

He is a psychiatric case if I ever saw

---

*"Plotzing" means dying, not in the literal sense. Literally, it means exploding.

one. Very moody . . . very talented . . .
impetuous and I am sure he suffers a
lot. I have always loved seeing him and
he has been very sweet to me. So—I find
him loving and lovable. Many people
have told me he is not easy to work
with . . . which I do indeed believe. . . .
And now I hear he is trying to divorce
Patti after 34 years and six sons . . .
because he has fallen for a flight
attendant or some such number. Patti is
10,000% Catholic and Jerry is going to
have a hard time with this hurdle.
. . .

Sister Ken [Helen's nickname] wrote
and told me she thought you were in
very high class company to get the
cover of that magazine . . . and "she
surely must deserve it." Speaking of
sisters. . . . This came in the mail a few
days ago, from Popo, of course. . . .
Need I say, it made me feel awfully
good . . . especially the part about "that
was a long time ago. . . ." which does
mean you have grown a lot, baby.

Popo may have her faults . . . (of
course I have none. I am perfect . . .

which you put into language, via a gold
necklace) . . . but she has been
wonderful to me and proven herself in a
thousand different ways. Considering
the way we were raised . . . as a single
unit . . . it's a damned miracle we don't
despise each other. You can't imagine
how screwed up we were with each
other. And for 22 years there was <u>total
denial</u> on both sides. I can thank Bob
Stolar for opening my eyes . . . and in
turn . . . opening hers. We both resisted
the notion that there was any
competitiveness . . . that we didn't love
each other 24 hours a day . . . every day
of the year . . . which, of course was a
lot of crap. It took a long time to get
those wires uncrossed . . . and we are
STILL uncrossing them. But life is a
moving, dynamic thing . . . ever
changing . . . and hopefully, I will
become wiser and continue to grow in
the right directions. That's what it's all
about.

I didn't mean to get so
philosophical . . . but you know me . . .
when I get wound up, there is no

stopping me. I gotta run . . . a load of work awaits me at the paper . . .

And now. . . . I sign off with love to EVERYBODY . . .

Nonno

DMSO, a fad at the time, was a veterinary medicine that for some reason could be purchased in hobby shops. People were using it for bruises and injuries alike. This was just one instance proving our family joke that Mother thought she was a physician, but we *knew she was a pharmacist.*

OCTOBER 29, 1980

Dear Thigs:

It was lovely mee-oshing on the phone with you last night. I love to hear about the wee ones . . . who ain't so wee anymore.

The news that Cricket has found a place she truly loves [Buxton, her prep school in Williamstown, Massachusetts] . . . and that she is coming into her own, is the best yet. She has good stuff . . . a real survivor . . .

and I have always said she has more of my genes than any of the group. (I can just hear you saying . . . "This is GOOD?" So watch your mouth already.)

. . .

I'm running . . . to Jordan Block . . . chipped a front tooth . . . oi! So who is your dentist? I may need him.

Hugs and kisses all around . . .

—Ken . . . Abra, Tony and Ali

Nonno

P.S. Please go get DMSO at the hobby shop . . . and no foolin'. Keep it on hand for bruises. Leave on twenty minutes, then wash off with soap and water. Apply no more than once every 24 hours, I can vouch for it!

———————— ⌘ ————————

Mother's change of heart regarding Jimmy Carter is explained more fully later on.

[NOVEMBER 5, 1980]
TUESDAY . . .

Dear Mugsie:

We just had a brief talk . . . ONE
SOLID HOUR . . . and I loved it. I hope
you voted for Reagan. It will be a good
feeling to know that you helped defeat
that Georgia jerk. I have become so
hostile to him in the last five days I can
hardly believe it. He really is a fake.
What's more he has done a LOUSY job.
With everything in his favor he still
couldn't pull it off. Well . . . goodbye,
Jimmy. I am predicting that Carter will
lose by a landslide. . . . Unfortunately a
lot of good Democrats are going down
the tubes with him . . . that's the sad
part. But maybe this country is ready
for some conservatism. When I see
what goes on in Washington with the
crazy spending . . . it's a damned
shame. They literally throw money
away. And taxes are out of sight.
Reagan WILL cut taxes . . . and
business WANTS HIM IN . . . so the
market will go up up up.

I received your mailings . . . for which

I thank you. The Wilshire House is indeed the place. I received, in the same mail, a brochure and you were right on the money. It does look elegant . . . and for one million five it should be nice. So—I will leave less . . . I do want a lovely place. And what's more I deserve it. I work hard . . . and am a self-supporting woman who has made good investments. So . . . now I am able to dance because I have already paid the fiddler. In advance.

I have not had time to read the DMSO article but I do thank you for sending it to me. From a glance I see they are making it look like snake oil. Well . . . as a person who has used DMSO I can tell you it worked for me. The only "side-effects" are the garlic smell which it sometimes produces . . . (but it didn't do that to me). Also . . . it should be washed off with soap or it might create small blisters if left on for too long a period of time. The only reason the drug manufacturers didn't push for an FDA O.K. is that it is so cheap to make . . . no money in it. Eventually, they will o.k. it, however.

Well . . . this ain't much of a letter, baby . . . but we did talk a long time today . . . and a good treat it was . . . for me at least. You are a good child . . . and I <u>do</u> feel loved.

Write or phone . . . or send a postcard . . . or throw a dead cat on the stage. . . . It's always nice to know you are around.

Love
Nonno

NOVEMBER 7, 1980
THURSDAY

Dear Mugs:

It gave me a very good feeling to know I helped get rid of Carter. I hope you voted for Reagan, too. It's incredible how I grew to despise Carter in the last week. It all started with his mealy-mouthed pandering during the debate.

How typically selfish of Carter to

concede the election at an early hour . . . (to show his "generosity") . . . and by so doing he destroyed any chance for the west-coast candidates to win anything. The people in California . . . Washington . . . etc. . . . just decided it didn't pay to even go to the polls because it was ALL OVER. . . . All this at 3:00 pm in their part of the country. Talk about going out in a blaze of dreck!

Well . . . hopefully this new regime will be better. It can't be worse. I was distressed to see that Richard Allen is back already.

L and K to all . . .
Nonno

Mother's prediction is exactly what did happen to Alfred Bloomingdale's nomination, or at least the trial balloon for it, as Ambassador to the Court of St. James during Reagan's second term.

NOVEMBER 13, 1980
THURSDAY . . .

Off to Tulsa . . . but gotta write my tochter before I leave . . .

Dear Mugsie Spanier. (Who's he?)

Yesterday Saginaw. Today Tulsa. Tomorrow the world. But I must say I still love the boonies. The small towns ARE different. I wonder if I was like the Saginaw dames when I lived in Eau Claire? Maybe I was and didn't know it. . . .

And now about the embarrassment of riches. . . . <u>Two</u> envelopes from you today . . . loaded with clippings. The Joan Rivers piece was funny. She has such a foul mouth, that lady . . . but she IS hilarious.

The [Bill] Safire piece was excellent. He is one helluva writer, that guy— altho' more conservative than my favorites. I have never met him, but mutual friends keep threatening to introduce me one day. As he pointed out . . . (and you caught it) Carter's big problem was his indecisiveness. The guy became paralyzed at make-a-decision time. . . . And as a result, he did nothing. But as far as I am concerned, he passed up too many good chances to show leadership and character. And he WAS <u>mean</u>. The way he treated Cy Vance was unspeakable . . . To Hamilton Jerrrden [*sic*] he was nice. It causes me no pain that all those jerks will be out of work. The latest poop from my pals in Washington is that they are all trying like crazy to get on as many good boards as possible and <u>MAKE MONEY</u>!

The tid-bit about the Bloomingdales was interesting—and logical. I can tell you the Annenbergs DON'T WANT IT. It's a lot of hard work and once you have had the "honor" . . . why take it again? I think Betsy and Al would be very good over there. Only . . . when it is announced . . . you can be sure someone will drag out that old smelly skeleton about how Betsy was fined for trying to slip some designer gowns through customs without paying. It was a real stink. Either she switched price-tags or some such thing. Anyway she was nailed and it was on every newspaper's front page.

Speaking of newspapers . . . I got a call from the <u>Modesto Bee</u> this morning . . . for a "comment . . ." It seems that they started to run my sister's column along with mine . . . (each three days a week) . . . and decided to take a poll . . . ask the readers which one they want six days. Well, it was Ann Landers about 15 to one. So-ooooo what did I think about it? I told the reporter that I had nothing to say. She said . . . "We are going to do a big story on it. . . ." and I told her she would have to do it without any help from me. Frankly, I think the whole thing is pretty tacky. Newspapers sure know how to make trouble between people. I hope Popo doesn't hear about this.

Incidentally, I loved your drawing of the cat. Have you considered art as a profession?

I gotta run. Take care of the clan and start cooking already. It's only 15 days till Thanksgiving. Kisses all around.

Your ever-lovin' Nonno

X GG
X Abra
X Tony
X Ali (my great-grandchild)

———————————— ⌒∞⌒ ————————————

Abbie Hoffman was three years ahead of me at Brandeis. He was not yet a political activist, and in fact, was then quite bourgeois. He drove a Corvette, often wore tennis whites, sold submarine sandwiches in the girls' dorms, and was an avid card player. We used to play gin rummy, I'd lose, and he'd make me pay up. After Brandeis, I saw him next in Chicago when he was a defendant in the Conspiracy Seven trial.

NOVEMBER 14, 1980
STILL THURSDAY . . .
BUT—I WILL HAVE IT HELD TILL FRIDAY. I
DON'T WANT TO SPOIL YOU.

Thigs, Dear Girl:
I already wrote to you once today but this came in the second delivery . . . and

I <u>MUST</u> respond. Besides . . . I just ran into an old schoolmate of yours in the hall. HE recognized me and said . . . "You haven't changed a day."

I didn't know who he was . . . and his six foot wife gave me no helpful clue. So—he says . . . "If you don't remember me, it's O.K. I am Abbie Hoffman."

Well . . . he's in town being interviewed by Mike Royko [legendary Chicago columnist] . . . and I must say the guy looks very spacey to me. His eyes don't focus or something. He asked me . . . "How is Margo?" and I told him . . . happily married in California . . . He said . . . "Meet my . . . . . . friend . . . We are happily living together."

If ever there was a good ad for staying away from drugs, he's it. From what I understand he has gone way to the right now . . . says Judge Hoffman was right all along. Isn't that beautiful?

Gotta run . . . Get busy and steal a turkey. You have several guests coming to dinner, you know.

Love to one and all . . . like always,
Nonno

---

*The following letter refers to the Thanksgiving
dinner at my house, during which Mother announced
she had voted for Reagan. Popo challenged her about
that being the truth, and frost descended upon the
evening. For whatever reason, she did not believe that
Mother had really voted Republican, having been so
publicly in Carter's camp the first time he ran.*

DECEMBER 3, 1980
WEDNESDAY

Margo, Dear Girl:
Here's proof . . . but I'll be darned if I
will send it to her. I am through
defending myself.
The more I think about it, the more I
am sure Ken is right. Everything was
rather nice until I said I was moving out
there.
Have a ball in Washington. I'm sure
you'll see lots of people you know.

L and K,
Nonno

[Enclosed were the following letters:]

NOVEMBER 1, 1980

Ronald Reagan
1669 San Oforo Drive
[The Reagans' actual street address
was "San Onofre," a few blocks from
where we lived.]
Pacific Palisades, CA 90272

Dear Ron:

I just spoke with Walter Annenberg
and he gave me your home address.

This is to let you know that for the first
time in 40 years, I am voting for a
Republican for President. When Jimmy
Carter announced during the debate
that he was discussing nuclear
proliferation with his daughter, Amy,
well—that did it for me.

Walter is predicting a Reagan
landslide. I am not so optimistic, but I
do believe that the level of the Carter
campaign has sunk pretty low and

many people are going to desert the party of their choice because their candidate has been a real disappointment.

My best to Nancy, and to you.

Sincerely,
Eppie {signed}
Eppie Lederer

NOVEMBER 24, 1980

Ann Landers
Field Newspaper Syndicate
Chicago Sun-Times
Daily News Building
Chicago, IL 60611

Dear Eppie:

Nancy and I were delighted to receive your letter and both of us are greatly honored that you made your first departure from the ranks of the other party in our behalf. Having been a Democrat most of my life, I have to tell you I understand completely your feelings when you crossed over for the first time.

We remember with great pleasure

that weekend at Walter's and hope we
will be seeing you soon. Nancy sends
her best, as do I.

Sincerely,
Ron {signed}
Ronald Reagan

---

*Mort Phillips's "buddy" was my father. They did
a lot of traveling together.*

*The "Jennifer party" refers to Jennifer Jones, then
married to Norton Simon. She would entertain for
Mother on visits to Los Angeles, and I went to a few
of those parties at the Simons' Malibu house. For
someone my age, they were amazing; I thought of them
as "dead movie star parties," because the guests were
old-line, top-tier screen stars. One night I remember
meeting Greg Peck, Walter Pidgeon, Henry Fonda,
Jack Lemmon, and Michael Caine. (Jennifer very
kindly asked me to pick my dinner partner that night
and I chose Caine.)*

*There is a reference in this letter to what I always
thought of as "the Hollywood Wars." Both sisters had
different show business friends. Though Mother didn't*

live there, her pals seemed to be the more established denizens of the movie business . . . Edie Goetz, the Kirk Douglases, Jennifer Jones, Cary Grant . . . while Popo's group tended to be more along the lines of Charles Nelson Reilly and Sally Struthers. By this time, Mother had decided that her idea of moving to L.A. was not a good one.

[DECEMBER 19, 1980]
THURSDAY . . .

Dear Thigs:

Think I'll move the carriage over a little so you can read this.

Gotcher your priceless letter yesterday and . . . gee, kid, you sure can lay it on the line. I love the way you express yourself. And . . . you were right on the money.

That, "I've been luckier than you, Puss" was the crowning crack to be sure . . . and it didn't go down easily with me. But why respond to anything so patently phony? This is not the first time she has said that to me. How that girl can talk and not <u>hear herself</u> is a deep, dark mystery. She has no idea how she comes off.

. . .

The way to deal with Popo is distance . . . and I plan to do just that. Of course we will correspond but she will not be seeing much of me. Actually I am rather happy this thing happened because it provides me with a very legitimate reason to see her infrequently—and Morton even less. When she said . . . "Mort finds it harder and harder to be in your company . . . because of all the name-dropping . . . and I I . . . me—me" well, I really didn't need to hear any more of that. You are right. He never did like me. I took up too much of his buddy's time. And now . . . they aren't even speaking. Irony, isn't it?

Yes, I am sure she will send over chicken soup . . . and lots of other things, but I am not for sale . . . "and all the perfume in Arabia cannot sweeten those little hands . . ." (McBeth??? [*sic*])

So . . . onward and upward. . . . I will be out there on January 13th for a few days and maybe we will get together. I'll give you a call when I return from New York . . . that's where I am going when I get back from Nashville. (I wrote

Louisville . . . I must be more tired than I think. It's past midnite!)

Love to one and all . . . kiss everybody, including Ali. I really like that hound. Sort of a 4th grandchild . . . looks like me, too.

Please don't be distressed by the Popo thing. I was truly wondering how I was going to deal with her trying to horn in and maneuver me to include her in my activities (remember the Jennifer party? Like a damn fool I let her trap me). Well . . . I don't have to worry about that any more. And it's a load off. Which reminds me . . . please . . . explain to me why she can't get in touch with anybody she wants to???? She has lived out there for ten years and they have a nice home and plenty of money and she is a celebrity. What in the world is the problem?

Sign me . . .
Baffled in Chicago

Love you—
Nonno

[APRIL 24, 1981]
TUESDAY . . .

Dear Thigs:

It seems as if we have been out of touch for a long time . . . but then both of us have been traveling a lot. I have been all over the country . . . making with the mouth circuit and attending annual meetings. Tomorrow I go to Topeka—Menninger's, natch . . . and next week there is New York . . . then Nashville . . . and Boston and Notre Dame . . . which gets me into May. . . . I also see Indianapolis on the schedule and Los Angeles. It seems horrendous when I see it on paper, but somehow I manage it just fine . . . and keep telling myself . . . "one day at a time, kiddo . . ." (Just like A.A.)

I LOVED the piece in the New Republic that you sent on homosexuality. It said a mouthfull. I do take the New Republic but confess I don't read it carefully. In fact, I rarely read ANYTHING carefully. The reader mail has wrecked my reading habits. In order to select column material, I must

read very rapidly ... scanning ...
skipping sentences and paragraphs ...
and if it doesn't suit the purposes, I'm
on to the next one. I appreciate having
another set of eyes (and a good, smart
head) out there looking for me.

Yesterday I had Cloris Leachman to
coffee. She is here at the Water Tower
doing Twigs ... (I was invited to the
opening and could not make it.) It
seems Cloris is going to be doing a TV
series about an advice columnist and
she wanted to talk to me about the
work ... how I do it ... what my office
looks like—etc. (I am sure she would
have loved to come to the office but I
don't allow anybody up there.)
Anyway ... she came promptly at
1:30 ... and at 3:45 I had to broom her
out. She is a non-stop talker ... having
been vaccinated at birth with the same
phonograph needle that they used on
dear Hubert Humphrey.

From the minute she sat down she
started to tell me the story of her life ...
and I must say ... she has had
everything happen to her. The dame has

five kids . . . four boys and a girl . . . and her husband, George English . . . or is it England?????? . . . a producer, whom she described as the world's handsomest man . . . well . . . after 25 years and many separations he left her to marry a young girl . . . and she is now pregnant (the girl—not Cloris). And Cloris is keeping her mother-in-law who is senile . . . and last month she started a fire in the CUPBOARD—she thought it was the fireplace. Also, the old lady has three dogs who have peed on every rug in the house. But Cloris loves her dearly and will keep her forever.

Why am I bothering you with all this? Do you care? I doubt it. ANYWAY . . . she is very expressive . . . very verbal . . . very warm . . . very tsu-drayt* . . . and interesting but a great time consumer. She would LOVE to see me again . . . is staying at the Ritz for six weeks . . . and well, what can I tell you?

. . .

It's stormy and cold here . . . a real

---

*"Tsu-dray," usually spelled "tsedreyt" means confused.

wind and rain storm . . . and I gotta go get a manicure.

Take care love . . . I am running . . .

Kiss the GG and the kinderloch* . . . including Ali . . .
Nonno

———————— ⚮ ————————

In the following letter, the address Mother speaks of was the commencement talk she gave for my son Adam's class at Eaglebrook. He was mortified. When it was announced that she would be the speaker, he asked his headmaster if they could please switch to Magic Johnson. Putting an R in every word referred to one boy's remark on Mother's Midwestern accent.

JUNE 12, 1981

Dear Margo:
Thanks for that great letter and Adam's perfectly wonderful term paper on Lin-Po. It was truly brilliant and I must say, I was surprised at the

—————
*"Kinderloch" means "children."

maturity and insight Adam displayed in his writing. It was most professional. He put in segments of Lin-Po's poetry—and his selections were truly superb.

I loved his little phrases, such as, "It is almost as if Po is uttering spontaneous messages from his soul, and not living up to a fixed style or method." Also, "It fascinates me, probably because I am part of a capitalist society based on competition, that these two men, rivals in what was then the Golden Age of poetry, were able to share friendship, trust, and, in some cases poetry."

It might interest Adam to know that when I was in the People's Republic, Lin-Po was very much discussed by the students and there were public readings of Lin-Po's poetry, "advertised" in Peking. This is the way the Chinese entertain themselves and, of course, everything is <u>free</u>.

Just between you and me—I was fascinated with the reference to "Tang"—and you and I know that Tang's first name was Poon, but of course, don't mention this to Adam.

I was delighted to hear about the "raves" in connection with my address. Any person who performs in public knows whether or not he is going over and I certainly felt the vibes from that audience.

I did work hard on that speech because I wanted it to be top-notch and I am glad Adam didn't have to faint from shame. The irony of it all knocks me out. Here I am getting 7 grand for a speech and very rarely do I make any special effort . . . I just talk, digressing from the text—and that's that.

I don't know the last time I wrote a special speech for a group and here I am speaking for nothing—not even expenses . . . and writing a brand new speech in the bargain which can never be used any place else. I loved the comment from one of the boys, "She puts an R in every word." It really knocked me out.

You always ask about "gossip." Well, here is some "newsy" gossip. Sara Lee Lubin [whose father named his baking company after her] married a guy

named Friedman several years ago. You
may have known him. Anyway, they had
4 kids, they parted, and he found
somebody he liked better than the
Cheesecake. So they were divorced
about two years ago. Nicki Harris fixed
her up with a blind date—a swell guy
from New York—also divorced with 4
kids. They were married last Saturday.
He has the kids, so now Sara Lee has 8.

I wonder if you remember meeting
Rosemary Breslin [late wife of Jimmy
Breslin] several years ago. Anyway—
she never failed to ask about you all
through the years—thought you were so
beautiful and very witty. A week before
Rosemary died, she called me from the
hospital. I knew it was to say goodbye.
She said, "I am just calling, Ep, to say I
love you." What a great girl she was.

Sister Helen spent the night with me
on her way to Paris. We went to see
Cloris Leachman in Twigs and I must
say, Cloris may be crazy, but she is one
hell of an actress. At least she was that
night. After the performance I took
Helen backstage and she was thrilled.

More gossip—I just came from the photo lab and saw Carmen Reporto [Sun-Times photographer]. He told me when he went to photograph Cloris to do a half page on her for the Sun-Times, she took off everything and I do mean the girl stripped to the buff. Carmen does not shock easily but he said that dame really unhinged him. [I knew from my days in California that she was often more comfortable without clothes.]

This is a magilla and a half, so I will sign off with love and kisses to the whole mob. Enjoy, enjoy, enjoy and we'll be in touch.

Your ever-lovin' Nonno—
who puts an "R" in every
<u>worrrrrrd</u>!

Larry Foster was a Johnson & Johnson vice president and very generous in sending products to me. I called him the "vice president for freebies," but I don't think that was his title.

For a few years Mother was one of the "nominators" for the MacArthur Foundation "genius grants." Jonas Salk was one, as well. Those people weren't supposed to tell anyone of their assignment, so of course Mother told me. She was always "nominating" research scientists, but didn't always succeed. In fact, I'm not sure if she ever succeeded. A close friend, and escort, of hers was Bill Kirby, who was the lead lawyer for the Foundation, having been John D. MacArthur's personal attorney.

CHI./CONN.
JUNE 22, 1981
MONDAY

Dear Thigs:

I LOVED the clipping on abortion from the <u>L.A. Herald Examiner</u> [a pro-choice piece, heavy on the science]. I am going to write to that doctor and send him love and kisses. I am also going to quote him . . . a lot. In fact I may even do a column on it.

You have a great eye for sending good things. Please keep it up. Which reminds me . . . what paper are you going to take NOW? Where are you near? I think it's Poughkeepsie. I am in the Poughkeepsie Journal (evening)— and it's not too bad. I would plotz if you took a paper that didn't carry me.

Larry Foster sent me a lovely "gift box." I called to thank him . . . and also to tell him I am coming to New York . . . he has been nagging me to have dinner with him for two years already . . . so . . . he told me he had sent YOU a gift box also. I said . . . "Oi. They just moved to Connecticut!" The dear man asked for your Connecticut address. So, I wouldn't be surprised if you ended up double-gifted. (Those boxes are neat!)

Blondie [Edna Brigham, a close friend from the Eau Claire days] and I had dinner last night at Jimmy's place [a restaurant]. I have not been there in a long time . . . and it is one of the few really good places that is open on

Sunday. She loved it . . . and so did I. Also, Jimmy adores you and is so thrilled that when you come to town you eat there. He asked me to send his love . . . which I am now doing.

Blondie was SO disappointed that you and Ken didn't get to Reno. She was really looking forward to it. Damned shame. You'd have had a spectacular time with the Brigs.

Actually, I hadn't planned on writing much of a letter, but it seems I always have something to say to you . . . more than I had planned . . . which is the story of my life. I wanted to send you this cartoon which I think is hilarious. I must say the election of grant recipients for the MacArthur Foundation's goody deal was a big disappointment. Some of those recipients need a grant like Johnstown needs more rain.

I had a ball at the Greenbrier . . . danced my feet off . . . (the Glenn Miller band yet . . . really my kind of music from the 40's) . . . and June Valee who was THEE hot band singer in those days along with Peggy Lee and Helen

O'Connell . . . sang with the band. She really knows how to belt out a song and I don't know when I enjoyed a vocalist so much. When I went up to compliment her she KISSED me . . . and said in a Brooklyn accent . . . "If my muthuh knew I was standin' heah . . . tawwwwkin' to Ann Landers . . . she would drop dead from hot failyuh!" It seems I am her mother's very most favorite and she has not missed me in 25 years. So—of course I have to send her "muthuh" a picture.

No air controllers strike. And you and Ken and kids on AMTRAK. Well—I am sure it will have been a terrific experience. One day I might do it myself. Trains can be nice. Besides, I do owe them something . . . that's where Ann Landers was discovered . . . thanks to her kid.

Much love to one and all . . . and let me know when you get a phone. Better yet . . . pick it up as soon as it's connected and call your ma.

Nonno—

The wedding in another country refers to my cousin, Bob Brodkey, marrying a Frenchwoman. He was one of two sons of Mother's eldest sister, Helen.

JULY 2, 1981
CHI./CONN.

Dear Fred Mugs:

This is a new typewriter and I am just learning how to use it so there will be two million mistakes. On the old one . . . to which I was accustomed, there were only <u>one</u> million. Anyway, please bear with me.

The enclosed I am sending because I was sort of put on the spot. I found it very interesting, strictly from a traditional point of view. I never have attended a Jewish (Orthodox yet) wedding in another country. Helen wrote this up for the rellies . . . and when we spoke on the phone today she asked me if I thought "Margo would like a copy." I could not say—NO . . . . . she then asked if she should send you a copy or would I send you <u>mine</u>. I told her I'd send mine. So . . . now you have it.

I am also sending a copy of my letter to Cary Grant since I cut you in on his original to me. A few days ago I received two marvelous color photographs from him . . . of the orchid tree. He put a white tea kettle beside the tree to show me the comparative size. It is a DARLING picture. He also says in his letter that if the tree should show signs of drooping or fading, he would send it over to Greg Peck's greenhouse for rejuvenation and added . . . "I am considering doing the same for myself." Believe me . . . he doesn't need ANYTHING . . . to help his looks along. As for the rest of it . . . well . . . I am not witness. I have heard a lot of stories about him being gay . . . etc. . . . but I just can't believe it. The guy has been married five times . . . not that that is proof of anything, but I have never heard his name linked with any male, but there sure have been a lot of women in his life.

I am going to Mary's for the usual birthday bash and will call you from there. This letter is a bore and a drag

but it's better than nothing—just barely.
I wonder if Grant Tinker being the new
head of NBC will mean anything to Ken.
I know they are good friends . . . etc. . . .
It sounds like a bigger challenge than
anybody needs. Their ratings are in the
cellar as you know.

Twigs is folding here this week. Cloris
had hoped it would run through the
summer . . . but it didn't make it, and I
am sure that series she was telling me
about (she made it sound like almost a
sure thing . . .) . . . will never come
about.

Gossip: The airline stewardess on my
way back from California told me she
just had Danny Thomas. He was
smashed and came aboard with his own
bottle of vodka. It is against the law to
carry your own booze on a plane so she
tactfully asked if she might pour it out
for him. He became very rude and
obnoxious and was mean as hell the
whole trip. I can't imagine him being so
nasty. . . . But she said he was one of the
worst passengers she had ever had.

I finally finished my Family Circle

piece and can enjoy my vacation without that hanging over my head. And now I am looking forward to Popo's book. I saw something in <u>Publishers Weekly</u> (courtesy Dan Herr) that didn't look very good. It seems she has put some of her "life's story" in the book and there is a squib they picked up that goes like this.

"My success was immediate and the column was in great demand but I walked around for seven years with a hole in my heart because my sister would not forgive me for cutting into her act. I even sent her an olive branch . . . which she ignored."

Now, mind you . . . I don't know what went <u>before</u> or came after . . . but THAT is what appeared in <u>Publishers Weekly</u>. The media . . . (especially book sellers) are always looking for controversy . . . and excerpting is a good way to get it. Anyway I am very sad that she chose to open these old wounds. Already I have had invitations from TV stations in Philadelphia and elsewhere to "discuss the sister's book" or "just come on the show WITH your sister who will be here on September 15th."

I do hope this doesn't end up creating real trouble between us. When I saw her a few days ago in L.A. (for coffee) she was sweet as can be. Not one word about her book, except that it would be out in the Fall.

This has turned into a real magilla. My love to one and all. . . . Your

Nonno

———————————— ⌇∞⌇ ————————————

The article referred to in the following letter was in Ladies' Home Journal. *It was an interview given by Popo in which she was gratuitously on the attack, and remarkably mean. It proved such an embarrassment that she tried denying having said what was quoted . . . until the writer, Cliff Jahr, whose professional reputation was being put at issue, threatened to release tapes of the interview if talk of "inaccuracies" and "misquotations" didn't stop. It stopped. I was to meet him, by chance, some months later, and he said Popo had been after me, as well, but he had left that part out. When my name came up, Jahr said, she replied, "Three husbands. I ask you . . ." That piece, I think, was one of the reasons I wrote my book. Mother would never respond to Popo publicly, but I felt that I could speak for her.*

"Lida" was Lida Sachnoff, one of the women who worked for Mother, and of whom she was especially fond.

AUGUST 17, 1981

Dear Margo:

What a wonderfully supportive girl you are! That phone call last night was really something. At least an hour and fifteen minutes. And Ken's remarks were a hoot. He really knows how to see the funny side of everything—and isn't that really the secret of getting through some of the lousier things that can sneak up on your blind side?

That magazine article was just incredible. I really feel sorry for Popo. I wonder what is happening in her life that is creating so much rage and anger and hostility. She must be miserable about something. And <u>again</u> I am the target. So help me I can't think of a single thing I have ever done to her that justifies this kind of bitterness. I read the magazine piece again and it is off the wall. That business of her ghost writing my early columns is so crazy I can't believe she said it—but of course she did.

I had the phone off the hook this morning so I could get through my exercises and breakfast. The minute I put it back on—it rang. Popo. She said . . . "I am JUST SICK. I read the morning paper. What can I say?" I told her if she was sick now she should wait until she sees the magazine piece. Apparently she had not seen the article. I don't know how I can possibly stay with her when I go out in September. She said . . . "Ep, you've GOT to forgive me. We can't let this come between us . . ." I told her I DID forgive her and that I honestly feel sorry for her because I know how much she must be suffering . . . but I just didn't think I could stay with her on my next trip out.

I am sure time will heal the wound. I

can't cut her out of my life completely, no matter how loony she gets. She is too much a part of me, but I must protect myself against her in some way. She is too unpredictable—and destructive. I can never be sure where she will be coming from next. This last unprovoked attack was very much like the Thanksgiving dinner at your house. WHAT A NIGHTMARE. And why? What reason did she have to humiliate me like that? Something that has nothing to do with me must be eating at her. [Your] Daddy's phone call this morning was typically Daddy. He started out . . . "THAT BITCH!" No hello . . . no how are you . . . nothing. I really had to laugh. He is just furious. I tried to calm him down but—no way. Finally he stopped for a minute and said . . . "How are you, Queen?" I told him I was fine and that I hoped he would forget about going to the newspapers with his anger. He said nothing could stop him—that it was time somebody let her have it and it was going to be his pleasure. I made him promise he wouldn't do anything today and asked him to call me in the morning. I hope to hell I can get him off the idea. His loyalty to me is beautiful but I don't want him to get any of this crap on himself. He is struggling to start a new business and please God . . . he should make it.

The dames in the office have been marvelous. Lida said . . . in her droll, marvelous way . . . "Of course her problem is jealousy. You have the figure and the dimples and the face and your column is so much better in every way she can't stand it. I'm not surprised she explodes every once in a while."

I received a lovely letter this morning (inter-office) from mine publisher, Jim Hoge. He wrote . . . "I feel a little sorry for anyone who has to give such an interview to a magazine. You, Eppie, to friends, and the public, in general, are the model of integrity and courage and grace under pressure. I know your indomitable spirit will continue to brighten our lives."

Well . . . enough of that. Tonight I am off with Bill Kirby to see Shelley Winters in Gingerbread Lady. It's opening night and Shelley's birthday. There's a birthday party after . . . and we shall be going . . . courtesy of Debbie Silverman who is the P.R. lady and never leaves me off a list. Bless her.

Gotta run, sweet girl. Keep in touch. Call from wherever . . .

I send much love to the mensch you are married to and you, my doll—well, what can I say? What a lucky Nonno I am. And to think—you might have been left at the Groruds' doorstep instead of our house!

All there is . . . in the whole world . . . and more
Love—Nonno

Mother's reference to the Cape was about Ken doing summer theater at a few New England playhouses.

"Eli's" was a very good deli on the Gold Coast, famous for its cheesecake.

The "Eau Claire Bears" was a minor league farm team, and the box we used was right next to the home dugout. I was therefore blessed with "tutors" who could not elude me . . . so I would lean over and ask all my questions of whichever players were standing around. Two of them did quite well later on: Bill Bruton and Hank Aaron.

AUGUST 27, 1981
SATURDAY . . . STILL AGLOW FROM THE TRIP
TO MY TAUCHTER'S BEAUTIFUL NEW HOME!
IT'S REALLY LOVELY.

Dear J. Fred:

Love your new stationery. Tres' classy. Also love talking to you from your various and sundry digs. The Cape sounds wunnnn—nderful. So glad it's a sell-out every night. Quality always makes it—except in prisons and insane asylums. (Don't ponder that last statement for too long. I'm not sure what it means either.)

. . .

I had a date with Abraham Lincoln Marovitz [legendary, long-serving federal judge] . . . and told him when we made the date three months ago, that I wanted to go to Eli's for liver.

Well . . . that's what we did and it was to die from. . . . The people literally lined up at our table. Between the two of us we knew everybody in the place and it took two hours to eat. Do you remember a guy named Chuck Tanner (I think it's Chuck . . .) a handsome baseball guy. . . . I believe he manages the Pittsburgh Pirates now. Well . . . anyway . . . he fell on my neck. . . . He used to play with the Eau Claire Bears when Andy Cohen was the manager. We recalled old times and it was fun . . . but I thought he would NEVER LEAVE. He pulled up a chair and it became a threesome. Esther and Eli always ask about Margo and they send their love. When I left, Eli gave me a cheesecake . . . chocolate chip yet. I guess they are famous for those cheesecakes which he makes in the kitchen . . . and they ship them all over. (He said, "For the freezer, Doll.")

The good judge is very interesting company. He really knows the local political scene . . . and, according to him, [—] is stealing this city blind. And, of course [—] is a real crook. . . . Abe calls them "a bunch of thieving bastards . . ."

Since the news went out that I am staying in Chicago . . . I can't tell you how many calls and notes . . . and bouquets of flowers I have received. I knew I had friends here but I didn't know how many people really cared. It's been a real love-in. And now I gotta go . . . so give the kids a hug for me and the hunk a special one . . . for taking you off my hands. . . . Call when you can. . . . I'll be home until Friday and then I'm off the Fisher's Island . . . and on to Dallas to speak. So it's L and K, Baby.

Nonno

The Critic was a Catholic literary magazine, for which I occasionally wrote. Mother was very fond of their two guiding lights, Dan Herr and Joel Wells. Herr ran the Catholic Press/Thomas More Association, and himself wrote books. A mention in Mother's column could move 30,000 to 40,000 books. And did.

SEPTEMBER 4, 1981
CHI./CONN.
FRIDAY . . . I THINK I'LL HAVE FISH
TONIGHT . . . JUST FOR THE HALIBUT.

J. Fred:

You are my best scout—so I decided to scout for you today. I assume you don't see the <u>New York Times</u> ALL the time.

All is well. I had a wonderful time Wednesday night. Ted Hesburgh came to dinner. Just the two of us. He is some guy.

He had read the <u>LHJ</u> [Ladies' Home Journal] twice and knew it by heart. In his opinion, Popo is sick. He said . . . "No well person talks as much as she did and says such things about ANYBODY, much less a sister." He also pointed out that even the reporter was shocked at the way she ran off at the mouth. I am sure Ted is right. She never did resolve the problem of sibling rivalry and when the envy gets too much she explodes.

Helen has been asking me to send Popo my phone number . . . which I am NOT doing. I have not responded to Popo's last letter and don't intend to.

Wednesday of next week I will be at the White House dinner for Menachem Begin. I shall let you know who was there, what was served . . . etc. From WASHINGTON I go to Atlanta to make a speech. . . . Happily I don't have to talk till 2:45 . . . if it had been a luncheon speech I would have had to pass up the Whitehouse [*sic*] dinner . . . no way I could have been sure of air transportation. This way, I have two sets of reservations . . . if one is cancelled, the other is sure to go.

I love hearing about the kids. Write or phone or send up smoke signals . . . or beat your Tom Tom . . . if you will excuse the expression.

The last issue of the <u>Critic</u> is a beauty. Maybe you will write and tell Joel and Dan? They are really grieving over its folding.

In haste . . . I send love to Ken and the kids and especially to you—

Nonno [with a lipstick print]

SEPTEMBER 25, 1981
CHI./SANTA FE
WEDNESDAY

Dear Mugsie:

I'm on my way to the airport—(the mouth circuit again).

. . .

I am <u>not</u> in touch with Popo. She does not have my new phone number—I have asked sister Helen (the self-appointed peace-maker) to <u>LAY OFF</u>. I've told her I am handling the matter with as much dignity as possible— making no public responses and to please leave me alone.

Popo will be on the <u>Phil Donahue Show</u> on Oct 5 and <u>Good Morning America</u> on the 6th. I'll be watching. It will be interesting to see if that magazine article comes up. Maybe she can make a deal with Phil not to mention it, but I don't see how she can control his audience—those women really come in out of left field with some doozies. Also—the phone-ins can be murder.

I had a lovely evening with Stanley Mosk (Supreme Court Justice of

California) and he told me he received a copy of Popo's book with a note—"If you saw the magazine article in the <u>Ladies' Home Journal</u>, I want you to know I did <u>not</u> say those things." Stanley has been in Brazil and had no idea what she was talking about. So—you can see, her defense is going to be denial.

I know Cliff Jahr has <u>everything</u> on tape and he said if she makes any public statements discrediting his reporting, he will open the tapes to one and all. He also told me that she had said some things that were so destructive he left them <u>out</u> of the piece to protect her. Can you believe it? I can.

<u>Honestly</u>, I think she had a quart of wine and blabbed her silly head off.

My anti-abortion mail is surprisingly light—and mostly lunatic stuff—like "Dear Murderer"—the mail in support of my position is amazingly heavy and of <u>good</u> calibre. What a surprise! I believe I asked the office to send you those two columns. If you don't get them, just holler. They are worth seeing.

. . .

I'll be on the speaking trail for a few days, but write or phone when the mood moves you. It's always a joy to hear from you.

Is Denver off or on? Keep me posted. And—how are you enjoying New Mexico? A different world, isn't it? I like the dry, clean air out there. Very little pollution compared to most of the U.S.

Kiss the roommate for me—and hug yourself.

Love you—

Nonno

P.S. How does Adam like Hotchkiss?
How's Abra doing?
And Cricket?

Never reticent to begin with, Mother felt it almost a duty to use her social friendships and professional clout to advance causes she thought important. Just as she put herself on the line for abortion rights and getting out of Vietnam (and gun control and cancer research), so she felt obliged to continue lobbying for or against new issues as they arose.

Not everyone would use the words "The MX Missile is a dog" when writing to the President of the United States. However, Mother was very direct and seldom bothered to gussy up what she was thinking. My favorite story illustrating this was, some years ago, her London friends—the Georgiadases—gave a small luncheon at Claridge's. There were no more than ten guests. Mother was seated next to King Constantine of Greece . . . certainly a king without portfolio (or a job). When they were introduced, Mother asked, "What shall I call you?" "Your Highness," he replied. Before she could get a grip, she instinctively said, "You've GOT to be kidding." He did not speak to her for the entire lunch.

SEPTEMBER 28, 1981

Dear Margo:
  Maybe I'm nuts—but I gotta try—

  L & K to you and the mensch—
  Nonno

[The following letter was enclosed:]

SEPTEMBER 28, 1981

The Honorable Ronald Reagan
The President
The White House
Washington, D.C.

Dear President Reagan:

To assume you will see this letter is a little crazy, but I must try.

Among my 70 million daily readers are truck drivers, housewives, shoe clerks, bus drivers, physicians, lawyers and corporate executives—from Joe Blow in Kokomo to Roger Smith of General Motors.

Cap Weinberger is a long-time friend. I will tell you what I told him at the White House dinner for Prime Minister Begin.

The sanest, most acceptable solution to the budget problem is to put the MX missile on the back burner. It's a dog.

The brightest scientific minds in the country say the MX will be obsolete by the time it's built. Also, the cost may be triple. The concept is loony, self-defeating and it is lousing up your chance to balance the budget in 1984.

Another thought: Put on "hold" the promised tax breaks for the affluent. They'll forgive you. The poor <u>won't</u> forgive you if they have to tighten their belts again.

Your recent TV address was superb! What a pleasure to have a President who can speak English for a change.

Bless you,
Ann Landers

EPL/km

cc: Caspar Weinberger
bcc: Michael Deaver, David Stockman, Donald T. Regan, Edwin Meese, Walter Annenberg

---

OCTOBER 7, 1981

Dear Margo:

You wondered about Popo's "last letter." Here it is.

I watched her on the <u>Phil Donahue</u>

<u>Show</u> today and he did, indeed, bring up the <u>Ladies' Home Journal</u> piece, and she did <u>not</u> say—"I didn't say it" or "I was misquoted." What she did say was, "I was quoted out of context, they took the worst parts and strung them together so it would sound awful."

I don't know when this will show in the East, but if I find out, I will tip you off so you can look at it yourself.

I'm on the run, as usual, but send love to you and Adam and all the workmen who are hammering night and day on the barn.

Nonno

The beginning part of the following letter is about information I asked for to use in my book.

As for the Salvador Dali bronze of JFK, neither of my parents knew a thing about art. For example, when I was in college we all met in New York for a weekend. I shepherded them to the Guggenheim Museum . . . not that I knew that much more about *art than they did. The museum was exhibiting Jasper Johns, and Father became fixated on a painting with the number "5" as its center. He was not so much taken with the painter's technique as he was with the number. Budget's motto, then, was "$5 a day, 5¢ a mile," and he wanted to buy it for the waiting room at his office! He actually made an inquiry a few days later. When told those paintings were not for sale, Father asked if Mr. Johns would consider painting another one. (He would not.)*

But back to the Dali.

The first drama with the Dali bust was, as Mother mentions, when Father discovered it was one of six, not knowing about editions. The next drama was years later when, during a visit to Chicago, Mother led me to her library where the bust resided on a marble pedestal. With a conspiratorial air she confided that she was sure one of the household help had knocked off an ear but was afraid to tell her. I took a look. The bronze was perfectly smooth and the patina, there, was the same as everywhere else. I think I calmed her down by telling her that, seeing as how it was a Dali, she was lucky that JFK had even one ear.

OCTOBER 8, 1981

Dear J. Fred:

That was some conversation we had tonight. I am jotting this note off . . . in the name of accuracy . . . bleary-eyed. It's 1 AM.

My biog sheet will be sent to you by Carmella . . . from the office . . . but this is from me . . . re: my medical afflictions [she meant affiliations].

First let me tell you how much I liked what you read to me on the phone. It is a remarkably good piece of writing. The interest never flags. It really has a marvelous rhythm.

Now . . . about that Kennedy head:

Daddy read about it in the <u>New York Times</u> . . . actually . . . It was a news story . . . (they weren't running an ad or anything like that . . .) and he was fascinated with the photograph. He didn't know anything about art but it looked classy—and he inquired about it . . . because he thought I would like it. He discovered he could get one through the Merrill Chase galleries in Chicago, and asked me if I would like it for my 50th birthday . . . and I said yes . . . it would be a lovely gift. It cost pretty close to 25 grand . . . which was the most expensive piece of art he ever bought . . . and when he learned there were <u>FIVE</u> others he thought maybe he had been ripped off . . . but I really loved it . . . and assured him that it was a bargain at that price . . . even though it was one of six . . .

Today it is worth many times that price because Dali did very few head sculptures . . . and this is a beauty.

Your call cheered <u>me</u> up a lot. I confess that Donahue show got to me a little. There she was . . . reinforcing the same old lies . . . that I was mad at her for seven years (again she mentioned the olive branch which I "ignored" and I swear to God I never got any olive branch from her) . . . and she even managed to cry a little on the show . . . to show how touched she was when I called and asked what they were doing on their 25th anniversary. I guess what bothered me was the fact that she was pulling the same old crap and the audience was buying it.

(page 2) . . . although I should get into

the bath-tub and shave my legs. I am going to New York tomorrow and I don't want them to think I am a baboon and put me in the baggage compartment.

The theme that ran thru Popo's interview was how IDENTICAL we are . . . how MUCH ALIKE . . . in every way . . . and how just yesterday someone in New York called her ANN . . . and how almost nobody can tell us apart . . . and we <u>think</u> alike . . . and even have ESP . . . I guess this galls the hell out of me because I really don't think we are alike at all . . . and neither do MY friends. In fact, the people whose opinions I respect and whose esteem I value keep telling me how different we are.

On the show she also said we were NEVER competitive when we were younger. This shows such a lack of self-knowledge that I am amazed. Or can it be that she really has deceived herself all these years and IS CRAZY?

Good night Irene.

Nonno

When Mother mentions "four years younger," she is in error; she meant "six years," which was the age difference between Father's second wife and me. Elizabeth was six years my junior.

Father's brief association with AA (Alcoholics Anonymous), though not successful for him, had a sweet footnote. He said he very much liked "the guys" and felt real kinship with them. He couldn't stop drinking, however.

Mother's remark, "Of course you knew before I did," refers to one of the worst and saddest things that ever happened to me. My father and I had the most wonderful, warm relationship for thirty-five years, but started to have serious trouble when he came to me—not my mother—and said he wanted to divorce her and marry a woman he'd been seeing, for three years, in Europe. He was asking my permission, really, and I said, in essence, "Everybody's gotta do what they've gotta do. You and I will still be fine." But he kept putting off telling my mother, all the while being seen more openly with Elizabeth . . . as though it might be an arrangement among the three people concerned. I was hearing from people—on two continents—that Father was seen in many places with, as the saying has it, a woman not his wife. I gave him a few deadlines to either change his mind or tell my mother . . . and when he didn't tell her, I did. He then blamed me for ruining his marriage.

He had put me right in the middle of this awful situation, and, as a result, we were estranged until shortly before his death, when there was a warm exchange of letters. He wanted both women, I think, and it was his extreme ambivalence that kept him from doing things in a direct way. One of my father's employees said that my parents' marriage never really ended, and this may be the emotional truth. Father told her years later that he had many regrets and had made a hash of his life. Mother, in turn, was a kind and generous friend to him until his death. Her gift for forgiveness and understanding far outstripped my own. Mother wound up being in touch with the second Mrs. Lederer for many years, and told me she found her to be a fine person—and someone for whom she had empathy.

OCTOBER 9, 1981

Dear J. Fred:

(JEEZ Louise . . . what a magilla . . . nobody should have to read anything this long!)

It's Yom Kippur . . . so of course I am not going to the office . . . but I am doing a little work at home.

. . .

A couple of fixes for your book: You asked me to remind you.

That "four years younger" needs fixing. It sounds like she is four years younger than Daddy. I believe she was 29 and he was 58.

Also . . . When Daddy sold Budget to Transamerica . . . (I don't think you ever mention the name Budget, which you really should) he took stock instead of cash . . . mainly to avoid the taxes. When you take cash for a sale you must pay taxes on it . . . NOT SO when you take stock. This, of course, was his undoing and damned near knocked me out when I heard he did it that way. What actually happened was . . . the stock was 42 when he did the deal . . . and it went down to <u>9</u>!

. . .

He was always very generous as far as I was concerned. He never once asked me what I paid for anything. He <u>never</u> was that generous with himself. In all the years we were married he never bought a suit without me. We had two luncheon dates every year set aside for shopping for his clothes. . . . One in April . . . and one in October . . . and we'd go to Brooks Brothers or Saks and I'd get him outfitted. We always bought two hats for him on these shopping excursions. . . . I would say—"one to <u>wear</u> and one to <u>lose</u>" . . . because he was <u>wonderful</u> at losing things on trips. Not a week went by that I didn't get a package from a hotel in Cleveland, New York, Los Angeles, Toledo or Pittsburgh . . . you name it . . . two pairs of his shorts and some socks or a robe that he had left behind. It got to be a family joke.

He also never bought himself a shirt or a tie or socks in all the 36 years we

were married. I had him measured at
Custom Shirts and every year the
swatches would come to me . . . and I
would re-order three or four dozen
shirts for him. I also bought all his ties
and sox and shorts. The shoes we would
do on the suit-hunting day . . . Bally was
his favorite.

As you already know . . . because I
told it on the <u>David Susskind Show</u>,
although he had told me in January
about Elizabeth he asked me if he could
please stay in the apartment and would
I please not go public with the news of
our divorce because he had some
business deals pending and if the news
got out it would be damaging to him . . .
"because everybody knows you are
solid . . . they will think I am a little
nuts. . . ." I agreed to do it . . . and I
kept my word . . . only you and Ted
Hesburgh and Mary Lasker knew. . . . I
let him stay in the apartment and we
shared the same twin-beds with the
single headboard for four and a half
months . . . like brother and sister. We
kept social engagements and although

his alcoholism was becoming apparent to many of our friends, no one knew that there was a divorce in the offing. One night during dinner at home he said to me ... "I gotta be crazy ... do you think maybe I should see a psychiatrist?" I told him it was up to him. He then asked me to make an appointment with one because "you know the best in town." I told him I would <u>not</u> make an appointment for him because <u>I</u> did not want to <u>SEND</u> him to a psychiatrist ..... and reminded him that he knows the same ones I know ... and if he felt the need to go to one himself ..... So ... he made an appointment with George Pollock, head of the Institute ... and George saw him the following day. That night at dinner he announced that he had been to the psychiatrist and <u>once was enough</u>. He was sure there were no answers for him there.

A few weeks later he asked if I thought he needed A.A. I said ... "Yes ... I think you do ..." So ... on his own he did attend several meetings. He seemed to enjoy them but he never did stop drinking. Finally he gave up on A.A. because "I have to travel a lot . . . and if it's going to work, you have to attend meetings consistently . . ." I reminded him that A.A. had chapters all over the world, but it made no impression.

Finally . . . I decided it was time for him to get out of the apartment and on with his divorce because I was beginning to have a feeling he was stalling . . . and if I didn't throw him out he just might <u>never</u> leave. So I told him I had a speaking engagement in Athens, Greece on May 15 . . . (It was the International Convention of YPO . . .) . . . and that I was leaving on May 13th . . . and when I returned one week later I would appreciate it if he was out of the apartment. He agreed that I had been "just wonderful" . . . and said with a smile . . . (he had SOME smile, that guy . . .) "I don't know of another woman in the world who would have put up with this arrangement for five months . . ." and I replied . . . "Neither do I."

Before I left for Greece I had Willie and Jerry stock his new apartment with canned goods, frozen foods ... everything I could think that he might need ... all the staples ... and I wrote the phone numbers of the druggist, the doctor, the cleaners, etc. and even arranged to have Willie's sister Sara come three days a week and clean for him. I then went out and bought two dozen pairs of black sox, two dozen navy and two dozen brown ... three dozen pairs of shirts ... a whole assortment of new ties and shirts and had them put in his apart [*sic*] with a note ... "Have a good life, Led. I wish you all the best." ... and you know I meant it.

I have really gone on and on ... but I think accuracy is very important and you have done such a terrific job I want the book to be really excellent in every way. If you want to ask me any more questions ... don't hesitate.

Something that really galled me on the <u>Phil Donahue Show</u> ... Popo said AGAIN ... that she was the first one I told about my divorce ... and she took the next plane and found me red-eyed and in pieces. Well ... that is a lot of garbage. Actually . . . she was one of the <u>last</u> ones I told.

Of course you knew before I did . . . but the first one was Ted Hesburgh and that was in January of 75 . . . I phoned him the morning after Daddy told me the news . . . (his timing was wonderful . . . just as we were leaving to go to the Palmer House where I was being honored by the Weizmann Institute). We were dressed in formal and he was already plenty stiff . . . and had made quite a stink about not wanting to be seated at the speaker's table. . . . That was the only fund-raising dinner I had ever allowed in my honor . . . because it really meant a great deal to me. . . . They established a chair at the Weizmann Institute in Chemical Immunology . . . in my name in perpetuity. I phoned Ted the next morning and as you know he cleared his whole day for me. . . . I went to South Bend and spent five hours with him and came back stronger, confident and "healed." He said . . . "Eppie . . . you'll make it—but I'm not so sure about Jules . . ."

The first "the World" knew about the divorce was when it appeared on July 1 . . . 1975 . . . ironically enough . . . the day before our 36th wedding anniversary . . .

WE WERE DIVORCED ON October 17th . . . 1975 . . . and during our many talks between January and May I urged him to get married as soon after the divorce as possible because I knew he was not a guy who could ever live alone. He promised me he would . . . which was a great relief because I was worried about him. He did indeed keep his promise and was married the week after the divorce . . . in London.

Love, Mother

———————— ⌘ ————————

Mother's immersion in telling me things about her life for my book had to do with the fact that I didn't tell her there was even going to be a book until its later stages . . . so she was trying both to be helpful and to get in her licks. My reason for not disclosing the project until nearly the end was that I did not want her spinning events or chirping at me to please leave out this incident or that person. The book was meant to be my memory of things, not an official biography.

The part of the letter where she writes, "NOW—I am going to try to be YOU" was hard for me to follow then and hard for me now, because I was accustomed to her voice in the letters. The content, though, is as close as she ever came to putting pen to paper articulating her overview of the Popo situation.

OCTOBER 27, 1981
FAIRMONT HOTEL
DENVER/P.PAL.

Dear Mugsie:

ME . . . WITH TIME ON MY HANDS? I can't believe it! I am in Denver for the Marvin Davis do. The brunch at their home is scheduled for 12:30 p.m. . . . and it's ten in the morning and I DON'T want to go look at the stuff that will be auctioned for the benefit . . . all Gucci!!! . . . so here I am. . . . My work that I brought for the trip is all done . . . read the mail on the plane. So—ooo I called down and asked if they had an electric typewriter and the manager sent his own . . . which is exactly like mine at home. It weighs a ton. I tipped the guy who lugged it up five bucks. I hope he didn't get a hernia.

This is the first time in 20 years that I don't know what to do with two hours— so, I am giving them to YOU. It won't take two hours, but it will take maybe 45 minutes. I am going to try and reconstruct the quill story and put it in proper context.

NOW—I am going to try to be YOU. . . . Here goes!

Jeez—this machine is giving me fits. . . .

Thanksgiving dinner at my home in 1980 was a nightmare. I phoned my mother the following morning to tell her I never again wanted to be in a small group with her and Popo. It was just too painful to watch Popo's attacks—her really cruel attempts to belittle my mother and put her down. Ken was horrified.

When we spoke I knew she was more embarrassed than hurt. She then described the relationship in a way that made me see all the ambivalence, all the pain of that multi-faceted twin-ship.

"We are like the porcupines in Schopenhauer's parable," she said. "We need each other for warmth but when we get too close, her quills prick me like needles and I have to move away to protect myself. So I do. Then the cold sets in and I long for her warmth so I move toward her again. She can be so dear and loving and so funny—hilarious—I laugh with her like with nobody else in this world. So we are close again. Then suddenly I feel a sharp quill, a remark about how Mort finds it hard to be in my company, because I'm such a name-dropper. So I move away again, knowing I'll get over the jab—because I must. I could never cut her out of my life—never. So I keep trying to figure out the safe distance. How close can I get without being jabbed by those quills?"

. . .

Well . . . now the phone is ringing . . .
So . . . bye for now.

Love to you . . .
Nonno

*Mother's admonition to "quit stealing flowers"
was referring to my going into public municipal
gardens—on very rare occasions, mind you—to help
myself to a few blooms.*

[UNDATED]
FRIDAY . . . LIGHT THE CANDLES—
AND <u>QUIT STEALING FLOWERS</u>!

Dear Margo:

All is well. I am busy as a one-armed paper-hanger with the crabs. Everything seems to pile in on me at once. I am BEHIND in my copy . . . a catastrophe, to be sure, and it doesn't happen very often. When I say "behind" it means I am not nine weeks ahead . . . only three . . . and that's not enough for me. It is practically deadline. And Bob Stolar is coming in town tonight. Ah klog. I can't NOT see him but I really could use this evening to work.

I still have not found time to flesh out the Viet Nam visit with General Westmoreland but I'll do it as soon as I find a minute. That magilla I pounded out in Denver should hold you for a while. Talk about having more information than you care about, that was the all-time prize.

Last night Don Regan spoke at the Economic Club. They had a record crowd—2,217 pieces of humanity (mostly corporate types) . . . hanging on every word. The speech was right out of the Oval office, and he came to life only during the Q and A. Art Nielson was my date . . . and he assures me that their stock is going places. The company is doing extremely well. I'm glad you have it.

Haven't heard from you in a while. We'll probably talk over the weekend. I am off to Nashville Sunday night. . . . You'll receive this Monday, I'll bet.

Tomorrow night is the PRITZKER costume bash and I am going as a hooker. Bill Kirby, my date, is going as a pimp. I hope we don't get arrested.

Love to the mensch and kisses to you, baby,

Nonno

NOVEMBER 1, 1981

Dear Mugs:

The enclosed is probably the most important column (cloutwise) that I ever published.

When it appeared in print the senators were literally swamped with mail from people who were "following my instructions." I really hit a lot of hot buttons . . . in fact nearly one million pieces of mail fell on Washington. There had never been anything like it . . . not even the war in Viet Nam. [The column began, "Dear Readers: If you are looking for a laugh today, you'd better skip Ann Landers. If you want to be part of an effort that might save millions of lives—maybe your own—please stay with me." Then she talked about the number of people cancer had touched and would continue to; the need for research; and finally she asked her loyal readers to write their elected representatives. She ended by saying, "No one can do everything, but each of us can do something."]

Stuart Symington called to say . . . "The mail in this office is stacked all over the place. Please Eppie. . . . tell people to stop writing, I got the message."

Alan Cranston called to say he had to put on three extra people to handle the mail that was coming in as a result of that column. Hubert phoned to tell me he had never seen anything like it. Chuck Percy sent a picture he had taken by the senate photographer. It was a shot of the mail room . . . sacks loaded on sacks of mail . . . it looked like Christmas in the N.Y. post office. Somebody had hung a big sign over the door . . . "IMPEACH ANN LANDERS . . ." Chuck said it was the most phenomenal reaction he had ever seen. Ted Kennedy was euphoric. Javitts [*sic*] was thrilled!

What happened? The response to that one column let all the Senators know exactly how their constituents felt about the National Cancer Act. So they took the message to President Nixon and he signed the bill which resulted in <u>100 million dollars for Cancer</u> research.

Night night . . .

L and K,
Nonno

Mother's history with her eldest sister, Helen—like all family relationships—went back to childhood. Mother and Popo were "the babies," then there was Dub, then Helen. My grandmother, though she ruled the roost with a firm hand, took to her bed more than occasionally with sick headaches. Helen's seniority made her the matriarchal sister in charge . . . the "bossy" one. Seven years older than the twins, she just got in the habit of telling the younger ones what to do . . . and never got out of it. Once, on a visit to Chicago, she actually started moving the furniture around in Mother's living room . . . with no conversational prelude. There were instances, over the years, when Mother felt it was necessary to restate the obvious: she was too old to be told what to do.

[NOVEMBER 4, 1981]

Dear Mugsie:

I am still a lousy mother. No time for a letter . . . so I am sending a copy of a letter I wrote to sister Helen. I decided it was time to let her have it. Again.

Every now and then I have to remind her that I am an adult and I don't need her to tell me when to make up with my twin.

Sunday Babe Nogg called just to talk. I haven't seen her in about two years and she is probably my favorite cousin. We grew up together as kids. She is exactly our age . . . and her mother was widowed young. (aunt Ruth . . . Daddy's sister) . . . MY Daddy . . . not yours. Babe's father owned a little grocery store and he was shot to death during a hold-up. It really was a family tragedy. Anyway she had it rough . . . no college . . . nothing. Just work.

Babe told me she was reeling from the <u>L.H.J.</u> piece . . . and that everyone in Omaha was talking about it. The consensus was that the twin sister who is giving advice to everybody needs some professional help herself. And Babe asked me THEE question . . . "what in HER life is so terrible that she has to try to make your life seem so pathetic?" Of course I had no answer . . . but it is interesting that she asked.

I asked her if sister Helen ever mentioned it to her (they are quite close). She answered . . . "ARE YOU KIDDING?" I still find it interesting that Helen never acknowledged to me . . . or to anyone that maybe Popo shouldn't have blabbed so much. You could be right . . . about her choosing sides long ago.

I will call as soon as I catch my breath. The work is piled to the ceiling and the end is not in sight.

Love to you.

Nonno

[NOVEMBER 6, 1981]
FRIDAY—AGAIN . . . BENSCH LICHT. . . .
(WOULD YOU BELIEVE I STILL DO IT EVEN
WHEN I AM ALONE—FRYING AN EGG?)
ANOTHER MAGILLA. BATTEN DOWN THE
HATCHES . . .

Dear Mugsie:

I loved talking (and listening) to you last night. Some of the material you read was spectacular . . . really first-rate writing [I was running by her parts of my book, Eppie].

I'm glad you have a sounding board like Ken. He is right about so many things. Taking the LHJ apart and challenging Popo point by point would not have been a good idea. Tempting as it must be, it would have dragged you down to her level. It also would have put you too much in your mother's camp. The way you handled it was, in my opinion, just right. You demonstrated restraint, even dignity . . . and a genuine sense of fairness and objectivity. The writing was excellent in many of those paragraphs. I like sharp, crisp sentences with strong words—and you really did some of your best writing there.

I know I have a tendency to "over-direct" (so what's new?) and I am trying hard to cool it, but I want so very much for this book to be a huge success. It's not easy to keep my trap shut . . . especially when I am the mother AND the subject of the book. Jeez . . . I am trying not to be a pain in the ass. I hope you realize how tough it is.

One thing that bothers me is that you have so much rich, untapped information—things that nobody else could know . . . because you are my daughter . . . and you are also a very fine writer. The possibilities are endless. . . . Yet you seem to be skimming over some facets of my career and my personal life in a way that barely touches my life as I live it. For example . . . the clout business. I have a file that we've kept in the office for years. It is actually called "CLOUT". . . . It's a record of the things I have managed to achieve in the area of reader response. The most spectacular was the National Cancer Act—100 million dollars of government funding (I wrote you about this two weeks ago—). It was that column in which I urged readers to write to their senators that produced an unprecedented response.

Dorothy Dix, who was the reigning advice columnist for 30 years, could not have done it. And Popo couldn't have done it either because her readers don't take her all that seriously. To this day I am using clout to get legislation through Congress . . . and it works. Of course Mary Lasker has been doing this for 35 years. She built the National Institutes of Health . . . from zero to billions of dollars of governmental assistance for research and public health services. But Mary is a philanthropist. For years she has given a hell of a lot of money to the members of the sub-committee on health whenever they run for election. (The Congressmen run every two years . . . so you can imagine what it costs her.) She also has had hundreds of fund-raising dinners for candidates in her home. In other words, they OWE her. I don't do this number. I never have. My clout is the fact that my readers believe in me. If I recommend something they DO it. And I have kept my skirts 100 percent clean by NOT doing commercials or testimonials or endorsements or game shows on TV. A mention in my column about a book, for example, is worth anywhere from ten to fifty-thousand copies. The publishers know this . . . and I am inundated with books and requests to "<u>read please</u>" and "a comment for the dust jacket <u>please</u>" . . . 99 out of a 100 go into the wastebasket. (The books AND the requests.)

If you want to see the CLOUT file ask me and I'll send it. Which reminds me of something I wanted to say last night and forgot. I think it might be nice (and USEFUL) if you acknowledged my principal assistant, Kathy Mitchell, for furnishing you with columns and information about my work. This would take the heat off me if I am asked . . . "Where did Margo get this and that and the other?" I will be able to say I gave my assistant permission to send you requested columns and facts and figures so that the book would be accurate and factual.

An example of what I call "skimming" when you could have tapped a very rich vein and hit the mother lode: That bit about me and President Carter. What an opportunity! . . . That jerk was president of the United States. People would eat up every word about what went on with him and me.

Actually this is what happened . . . Marge Benton [political activist and close friend] gave a luncheon early in 1975 (I can get the exact date for you if you want it) for Jimmy Carter. . . . It was at Maxim's and 36 people were invited. (I'm sure it was very early in Carter's campaign and nobody thought he had much of a chance.) Only 16 people bothered to show up . . . among the missing was <u>the hostess</u> who had more pressing business in California. I DID show up because I wanted to get a look at the one-term governor of Georgia and measure him personally. When I arrived, there were only about five people there . . . including Jimmy Carter, who came over to greet me the minute I got inside the room. He said, "I've been anxious to meet you and was so pleased when I heard you would be here." He asked if we might sit at one of the little cocktail tables and talk for a few minutes. . . . "There are so many things you could help me with. . . ." Before I could acknowledge his greeting almost he asked me for an autograph for his mother—Miss Lillian . . . he said she was a big fan of mine. I wrote a little message on a cocktail napkin that made me feel guilty and ashamed because I really didn't believe it. "Dear Miss Lillian . . . I'll see you at the White House. . . ." He was very pleased and I tried to assuage the guilt by telling myself . . . it was an act of kindness that would make a hopeful mother happy. Jimmy Carter and I talked at length. He wanted to know WHO he should know— who would be useful . . . "Because," he announced emphatically . . . "I am going to be president of the United States."

I said to myself, "This man is crazy. . . ." . . . but I admire his determination . . . his positive approach . . . and the faith he has in himself. I was also impressed with his gentleness and kindness . . . his warmth . . . his energy and what I perceived to be genuine sweetness. (So much for my ability to evaluate. Actually, after three years the only thing I had straight was his energy. . . . I discovered he was neither gentle nor kind . . . nor warm . . . and he was <u>not</u> so sweet to Cy Vance whom I liked very much, as well as several others.)

One of the people I suggested he get in touch with was Father Ted Hesburgh, President of Notre Dame. "Oh yes . . . of course," he said. . . . I was surprised when he wrote the name down that he didn't know how to spell it. He asked if he should just call Notre Dame . . . and I told him . . . "No, Father Hesburgh has a private number . . . and I will give it to you—but first I have to check and get permission."

I then gave Jimmy MY private number and told him to phone me at 11 P.M. the next night to find out if I had obtained permission from Ted—<u>and</u> would Ted be willing to help him. (This was also a testing mechanism. . . . I wanted to see how much on the stick the guy was. . . . Would he follow through?) Well, I called Ted. . . . He said he would help Carter ("God knows the Democrats need a new face!") and yes it was o.k. to give him the pvt. number. The following night promptly at 11 . . . the phone rang. A voice with a very southern accent said . . . "Hello, Beautiful . . . this is Jimmy." I must admit . . . I melted. He really knew how to get to a girl. . . . I told him I had spoken with Ted . . . that he WOULD help . . . and here's the number . . . call him RIGHT NOW. He's in his office. "At 11 o'clock at night?" Carter asked . . . I said, "Yes . . . that's when his energy level peaks."

Five days before the election Jimmy called me and said . . . "Eppie it's going to be very close. I need your help. I will be in Chicago tomorrow morning. I'm holding a press conference at the O'Hare Inn . . . national TV will be on hand. Will you meet me at 8 o'clock in the morning?" I told him I had just that minute walked into the apartment. . . . I had been in Cleveland . . . and if I had known about this I would have slept at the airport . . . it would have been a lot easier. A blizzard was predicted and the roads were terrible . . . but yes . . . I would be there . . . . AND I WAS. . . .

The roads WERE hazardous . . . slippery and miserable . . . and it was one hell of a ride. When I arrived, Jimmy Carter was walking out of the Inn with his entourage. It must have been a very short press conference. The cameras caught me immediately as I got out of the car and walked straight into Jimmy Carter's outstretched arms. I gave him The Big Hello and he beamed his appreciation. The first question I was asked by the TV reporters (this is on national TV don't forget) was . . . "What did you think about Jimmy Carter's lusting in his heart remark that appeared in <u>Playboy</u> magazine?" I replied, "He has already said he is sorry he said it . . . and I see no point in beating that horse to death. Now do you have a SENSIBLE question?" The reporter asked . . . "Why are you endorsing Jimmy Carter for the Presidency?" I answered . . . "I do not endorse candidates . . . but when good friends come into town I sometimes meet them at the airport." After that transparent remark I added a wink . . . as if to say . . . "Look Buster, I am for this guy . . . and I want everybody to know it . . . otherwise why would I come out in a blizzard at eight o'clock in the morning?"

The rest is history . . . but I must say, Carter did not forget the people who helped him. I was invited to the Whitehouse [*sic*] several times and he was very nice to me. After 3 years in the office, however, I felt he lacked the leadership this country needed . . . he simply would not unload his political liabilities (mostly from Georgia) and I was very much turned off by the way he treated people. It seems he didn't really need a cabinet . . . he wanted to do everything himself. . . . When his mother said "Jimmy is a beautiful cat with very sharp claws" I'm sure she knew what she was talking about.

Actually the turning point for me was when First Brother Billy urinated at the airport (he was meeting the gang from Libya . . .) and made the statement . . . "There's more Arabs than Jews . . . and the Jews in America can kiss my ass" . . . and Jimmy's only response when questioned about these statements was . . . "I love my brother . . ." . . . well . . . I knew I could not support him again—no matter who he ran against.

Kiddo . . . my hands are falling off . . . if you want more on my first meeting with Reagan at the Annenbergs . . . my impressions . . . and so on . . . let me know . . . I also have some shticklock about my meetings with Nixon . . . and of course there's Lyndon Johnson . . .
. . . . . .

In conclusion . . . said she, as her index finger fell off her right hand—maybe you aren't counting words but

sooner or later, the publisher MUST . . .
so you had better think about producing
a book that is big enough and juicy
enough . . . and detailed enough to sell
for a GOOD price. As long as you are
working your can off, you might as well
make it pay.

Goodnight, Irene.

Love you,
Nonno

———————— ⌘ ————————

*"Hubert," of course, was Humphrey. And because
Mother is, here, recalling details of her Vietnam trip
for my book—with a fourteen-year span between the
event and this letter—there is no way of knowing to
what degree, if any, her memory was revisionist,
colored by hindsight or historical perspective. I do
recall hearing essentially the same report upon her
return. She is mistaken, however, about the trip taking
place in August; it was May. I know this because my
youngest child, Cricket, was born May 17, 1967,
and I had a number to call at the State Department to
get word to her in Vietnam. When the war was over,*

there was a reunion, of sorts, for Mother and General Westmoreland . . . when they were guests at Stuart Symington's second wedding. The general—in a business suit—came to Mother's table and asked her to dance. He very modestly said, "I don't know if you remember me, but I'll never forget you." They danced and talked . . . in their way, two old war-horses.

Dr. John Merrill, whom she met on that trip, was to remain her close friend until his death.

Of all the things she did during her lifetime, certainly one of which she could be most proud was her hospital visiting while in Vietnam. Unlike most celebrities who popped into a ward or two for a photo op, she wanted to see as many of the injured as she could . . . which she did, from early morning 'til late at night. And she had with her a small, spiral notebook. All the military men she saw in hospital beds—and there were hundreds—were invited to give her names and telephone numbers for wives or girlfriends, or parents. When she got home, she took 3½ days and called every number she'd been given so she could relay greetings from the boys in the beds. Mother told me that if an injured man was in really bad shape, she soft-pedaled that when talking to his loved ones. And she received letters, for years afterward, from both the families of the boys who came home and those who didn't.

NOVEMBER 10, 1981

Dear Mugs. (J. Fred, of course.)

Before I head for the East . . . I had better get this unfinished business done. You asked me to "flesh out" Viet Nam. I never did it. Now I shall . . . even though it's late at night and I should be in the sack.

I went to Viet Nam because I was strongly opposed to the war and all my attempts to get Hubert to see the situation for what it was, were futile.

He kept insisting that he had "classified information" he couldn't share with me . . . and that the morale of our men was great and that we could easily beat back the Viet Cong if we sent over another 200,000 troops. Our arguments were becoming more angry and I could see that this issue was damaging our 20 year friendship. I also knew that it was not true as many people insisted—that Hubert didn't believe in the war, that he was just being a faithful vice-president and supporting the Chief.

Finally Hubert said he was sure I would support the war if I could understand it better and the one person who could explain it to me was General Westmoreland. I said, "Terrific . . . so how do we arrange THAT?" Hubert said . . . "I will see that you have a private visit with the General if you agree to go to Viet Nam." I had not counted on this but the thought came to me that I might be able to perform a valuable service if Hubert could somehow set things up so I could visit the soldiers in the hospital. I remembered the satisfaction I had as an A.W.V.S. volunteer when I visited the men at La Garde hospital in New Orleans . . . and I wasn't even Ann Landers then. . . . This trip could really be something. So I told Hubert I would go in August and that I would be happy to talk with General Westmoreland but in exchange I wanted to visit as many soldiers as I could . . . starting at 8 in the morning . . . until I fell down from exhaustion at night. He agreed and I must say the travel arrangements were marvelous, thanks to the Vice-President.

I went over on a U.S. Army plane, loaded with fresh-faced G.I.'s . . . from Chicago to San Francisco to Manila (where we picked up Dr. John Merrill from Harvard . . . he was going to inspect the kidney installations) . . . from Manila to Guam . . . from Guam to Tokyo . . . then to Saigon. This was a straight shot with no sleep-over. When we arrived I was met by lots of brass and Dr. Merrill (who had a Major General's credentials) was non-plussed.

On my first day in Viet Nam I met with General Westmoreland. He was extremely cordial, very attractive . . . almost as if he had been sent there from Central Casting . . . every inch the Man in Charge. I started out by telling the General that I was not there as a newspaper person . . . that our first visit would be strictly off the record and I had come because the Vice President felt it was important that I get a better concept of the war. After all, I was a molder of public opinion . . . one of the major voices in the U.S. in that area, and he felt if I REALLY understood the war I would stop talking against it.

I then decided that as long as I had made the long journey I should speak my piece to the General or I would hate myself forever for having passed up the opportunity . . . so I said . . . "This war is immoral, indecent and unwinnable. It is a disgrace that the United States has become involved in a war 10,000 miles from home . . . against a small, poor country . . . a civil war at that and we are going to lose." I told him, "We are supporting the wrong side—again . . . a corrupt clique of crooks and thieves . . . the Madame Nhu's and the Diems against the ragged, poor, starving under-dogs . . . and worse yet, they are going to kick us out." I also told Westmoreland that the war was tearing our country apart . . . that it did not have the support of the American people, that our campuses were aflame with protesters . . . students marching with banners and clenched fists yelling . . . "HELL NO . . . WE WON'T GO." I also told him that he was trying to solve a political problem with a military approach and it wasn't even our problem to begin with—and it all started when President Eisenhower was visited by Cardinal Spellman and agreed to send 3,000 "advisors" over to Viet Nam because the Catholics in the North were having problems. (Maybe you'd better leave this out . . . but this was the way it began, kiddo.)

Westmoreland asked me where I got my "intelligence" and I told him the real question was . . . where was he getting HIS intelligence. That his generals were bamboozling him . . . the notion that all they needed was 200,000 more troops was absurd . . . that we had already poured billions of dollars into that swamp and were getting our brains beat out. I also told him that we had no allies in this war (this is important). . . . We had a few troops from Australia . . . and some from Korea, but all our former friends backed off and told us they could not support our efforts . . . and they didn't.

What was scheduled to be a 20 minute visit turned out to be over an hour and 20 minutes and I must say he was a perfect gentleman the whole time. When I left he appeared shaken . . . thanked me and . . . asked me would I like a photograph with him. I said yes . . . and he had a photographer in two minutes. I told him I had no intention of reporting on our visit and he thanked me. Interestingly . . . when I arrived at the hotel a lt. handed me the picture of the General and me . . . on which he had written, by force of habit no doubt . . . "To Ann Landers, with warm regards and <u>THANKS FOR YOUR SUPPORT</u>." I couldn't believe it!

Good night . . . and no more of this sort of thing this year. I can't spare the time. Happy? I thought so!

Incidentally, I did go by and see Ellsworth Bunker but I knew he was <u>not</u> very crazy about the war either and decided not to talk to him about the merits of the mess . . . but simply to say I was there—to pay my respects . . . and also I congratulated him on his recent marriage to the Ambassador to Nepal . . . I felt sorry for him . . . being tapped to be Ambassador in that miserable unpopular place . . . so soon after his marriage when he really wanted to get out of there in the worst way. But he was a statesman . . . and a good one who saw his duty and he did it.

Nonno

My letter to the editor of the Book Review *had to do with* The Sunday New York Times' *review of my book. I had a hunch the reviewer may not have read it, but perhaps was more annoyed that she had called it "a polite little biography," when, in fact, I had two threatened lawsuits. (And Mother was right: The* Times *didn't print my letter.)*

Regarding Ellen Goodman, she was always gracious to me when I moved to Boston.

[SEPTEMBER 23, 1982]

THURSDAY

Dear Margo:

That was quite a letter you wrote to the <u>N.Y. Times</u> letters to the editor. I doubt very much that they will print it. But one thing is sure. They will SEE it . . . and so will Fran Schumer [the reviewer].

I didn't think the review was that bad, except for the inaccuracies which were a dead giveaway that the information didn't come from your book, but from a piece about me. I didn't see any hostility in it. Actually it was a valentine to me (better it should have been one to <u>you</u>) and I dropped Fran a short note and thanked her. I have learned over the years to always say thank you. You never know where the writer or editor or publisher or reporter may turn up next, and it's better to have a friend than an enemy. Fanning taught me years ago never to complain about a lousy story, even if it is filled with downright insults and inaccuracies. He also taught me never to write to "the boss" and complain. Bosses have a tendency to stick up for their own. In other words, his theory was ignore the bastards. Act like you didn't see it. This certainly proved true in the case of Ellen Goodman. She was the only important columnist in the business who rejoiced in print about my divorce. It was an ugly and mean thing she did. Ellen was new in the business and maybe she was miserable from her own tsores.* Anyway, I saw her a few months later . . . in 21 of all places and she had a hard time looking me in the eye. I was very nice to her and I'm sure she regretted what she had done to me 1,000 times over. Several years later we were on a panel together in Washington for the National Editors' convention. I am sure she was remembering (while I was obviously forgetting) what she had done to me. Another victory. For me.

It's not easy to overlook such stuff but it really pays off. Maybe I am, as Daddy always said, a Pollyanna, but I would rather be generous than mean and I would rather forgive than hold a

---

*"Tsores" means trouble.

grudge. Actually I wish you could soften up a little toward Popo, for example. She did a lousy thing to me, true. That <u>Ladies Home Journal</u> was a real knife in the back, but she has paid for it dearly in many ways. I hold no animosity toward her. Not a shred. It has always been, and will always be, a love-hate relationship. But I love her a lot more than I hate her and I am not being magnanimous when I say there are lots of things about her to love. She was very nice to you, if you will recall, and you even told me once that she is better company than I am—which I can understand. Almost <u>anybody</u> is better company than a mother for crissake. I understood what you meant and didn't take offense. The girl is really hilarious and GREAT fun. Enough of this already. . . . Who put a nickel in ME? Actually what I am trying to say is I feel a little guilty maybe because a big part of your feeling about Popo is tied in with your loyalty to me. I hope all this makes sense and that you will find it in your heart to be a little easier on the kid. One thing in her favor, she never said one word to me about your book. I appreciated that. This is some magilla, Mugsie. I'm off and running. Love to the G.G. . . . Have a happy, healthy, productive New Year . . .

Nonno

———————— ⌒∞⌒ ————————

"Jessica" was Jessica Savitch, the late NBC newscaster. I felt bad when she died a year later (in a car/water accident) because she had spent her last Thanksgiving and Christmas with us! ("Us" being my starter husband—John Coleman—whose date she was, my three children, Ken, and me.) We were giving the blended-extended family approach a try. (It didn't work.)

[DECEMBER 30, 1982]
THURSDAY

Dear Mugsie:
  I LOVED your letter today . . . the one telling me about the stationery . . . and other things. I have no time to respond properly . . . but I did want to get this off to you in the mail.

The piece about Jessica is O.K. I thought. If she is into coke she is not going to last long, believe me. I had lunch with Barbara Walters and she also mentioned the drugs in connection with Jessica so there must be plenty to it.

Also . . . Carl Bernstein ran into me in an elevator at the Ritz-Carlton and said . . . "You are Margo's mother!" We had a brief but lovely talk and he said . . . "Margo and my ex-wife were best friends at Wellesley." I told him you went to Brandeis . . . but that you were indeed very fond of Nora . . .

Jeez . . . this machine is eating the paper but I am NOT going to do it over.

I am putting it in an envelope and letting it go as is.

I LOVED THE HESBURGH PIECE. Thanks for sending it. Yes . . . he IS quite a guy. I have known him for almost 30 years . . . real first class mensch in every way.

We'll talk,

Nonno

"Mr. Brown at Pebble Beach" owned the store where I had a particular type of stationery made. Mother admired it, so I got some for her, and she was inquiring about how to re-order. (Having not experienced the Depression, myself, I had no trouble spending money.)

Edie Goetz was one of the doyennes of Hollywood—the daughter of L.B. Mayer and the widow of Billy Goetz, an A-list director.

[JANUARY 4, 1983]

Dear Margo:

The be—yootiful stationery arrived half an hour ago and it is only fitting and proper that the very first letter on it be written to you. The only trouble with this stuff is—it's so damned knock-out that I will be awfully stingy about using it. I simply GOTTA get over this feeling of poverty that was instilled in me during the Depression. I must keep saying to myself . . . "SPEND YOUR MONEY, HONEY. . . . YOU GOT IT . . . AND PLENTY—AND YOU AIN'T POOR NO MORE!"

I have already written to Mr. Brown at

Pebble Beach and asked about the price. I am sure when I get his response I will need a cold rag for my head. But I am determined to class up my act and continue with this stuff . . . no matter how much it costs! It is also a wonderful gift for someone who has been generous . . . like Jennifer [Jones] . . . and Edie Goetz . . . people who have everything—so I do thank you from the bottom of my motherly heart.

I envy Abra's ability to buy the right gifts. This is a talent I definitely lack. It was extremely thoughtful of her to go to all that time and trouble . . . even though I am pretty sure she used her father's plastic.

[What is excised here is Mother talking about a problem one of my children was having.] I'll keep praying. I may be nuts—and foolish, and childish and even ignorant, but I do believe that there's something out there. It has been a great help to me to pray—and I haven't missed a night in 60 years. And, I must tell you, I've gotten an awful lot of the things I've asked for.

I'd better sign off before I sound like Orville [*sic*] Roberts or that nut on the 700 Club. Love to you and the Mensch . . . and thanks for this gorgeous gift.

Nonno

I had (apparently) mailed Mother something about Ted Hesburgh, Andy Warhol, and sex. She had a kind of shockability and puritanical propriety about some things that appeared either in print or in movies . . . and of course was also protective of friends.

The judge business had to do with a publishing situation I was involved in where I was considering going to trial. I do not remember, now, the details of why I thought the judge might know Mother and therefore recuse himself.

"R. J. Walker" and "Jill whatzername" are Robert Wagner and Jill St. John. Mother often didn't know the names of movie people unless she actually knew the people. Once, getting off a plane, the special services agent said there were some people who would

like to meet her—Peter, Paul, and Mary. She had no
*idea that they were a famous singing trio, and proved
this by telling me she had met three people "who did
something together, and they all had biblical names!"*

*The reference to cows reflected her amazement at my
having a house in a rural setting. Though the cows
were not ours—they were Farmer Twing's—they
grazed in one of our meadows, and I told her I loved
to look at them. I also told Mother that Farmer
Twing, in gratitude, "repaid" us with liquid
fertilizer in one of the meadows and that we definitely
knew when it had been delivered. She said it served me
right for allowing cows "on the lawn."*

JANUARY 13, 1983
TUESDAY NIGHT

Dear Margo—My One and Only Chick:
I returned from the west coast last
night to find a <u>second</u> long newsy
magilla from you . . . the first I got just
as I was leaving for the airport . . . one
week ago. But before I delve . . . let me
tell you—you've been a very good kid
about writing lately. Donkey-shine.
(That is farm talk for donkka-shayne.)
. . .

That bit about Ted Hesburgh wasn't funny. It was tacky and crude. To mention him in the same breath with Andy Warhol is the mischief of the infidel and he (or she) will burn in hell. As for Ted DROPPING OUT of sex. . . . I can tell you with complete certainty that he never DROPPED <u>IN</u>. I have told him more than once if I ever found out that he was <u>not</u> celibate, and I wasn't the one, I would kill him. (And probably her.)

Please keep me posted as to when Ken's stuff will air. I do not consider it bragging. Just tip me off, please. And . . . that reminds me . . . let me know when your piece on John Warner appears in the <u>New Republic</u>. If it has already appeared, I missed it. I do not see every piece in every magazine, so be patient with your gray-haired Nonno.

. . .

On to the next page. Mother is not through yet. Hang on, Rosalie.

And now. . . . Here come da judge!

Sorry I didn't understand what in hell you were talking about. It did not make sense to me. None of it. If I knew the judge I would KNOW I knew him . . . and if he knew me well enough to recuse himself from the case, we would know THAT by this time, wouldn't we? Enough of that already. Now—let us pray. . . . Oh excuse me . . . you have decided there is no God. Do you mind if I pray?

Your evidence is only circumstantial and would not hold up anywhere. Please tell Ken God is not a virus. Meanwhile herpes has dealt a death blow to the one-night stand. People are being a lot more careful than they used to be. Need I tell you Phyllis Schlafly is very pleased? (I hope her husband gives her a dose.)

I had a ball in California . . . lunch with Claudia and Morey Mirkin . . . who send their love. Visited Norton Simon in the hospital twice . . . with Jennifer . . . and had lunch at Edie Goetz's house. They all send love. Edie was expecting to hear from you when you were last out there. I told her I didn't think you made the trip. Did you? Anyway, she wanted to give a party for you . . . and have "kids" your own age ... like R. J. Walker and Jill whatzername? Incidentally, "their" therapist says R.J. will never marry Jill. She moved in too fast—or something.

I did see <u>Tootsie</u> and enjoyed it. I also saw Sydney Pollack at the Hereditary Disease Fdn. dinner. He is a doll ... and his wife Claire is terrific. I loved Sydney in that role as the agent. We had a lovely long conversation and I was surprised to learn that he grew up in South Bend. What a sweet guy! She told me that just before they were leaving the house to come to the dinner, they got into an argument and Sydney began to get real mad ... and SHE said ..., "Cut it out ... I've already seen you do this number in the movie!!!!!!" It broke him up.

Well ... tomorrow is <u>20-20</u>—Barbara Wawa will be here and I gotta decide what I am going to say when she asks me about Popo ... and Margo's book ... and what it's like to have a daughter married three times when I am advising the whole world ... and if she asks me if I have had a face-lift, I'll tell her if she will confess, so will I. So . . . this is it . . . doll. I am looking forward to seeing you here, like you wouldn't believe.

Kick the cows . . . kiss Ken . . . and have one yourself.

Nonno

Dear J. Fred:

. . .

I introduced Walter Cronkite at a media luncheon today . . . and was, if you will pardon the immodesty . . . a smash. It was a rather brief intro . . . but apparently I did it just right.

Please . . . give me some guidance with the grandchildren. I DO need help. I don't want to lose touch with them altogether, but it seems odd that the only connection I have is thru gifts. HELP! Talk it over with Ken and tell me what to do. Maybe the "gift connection" is better than none at all.

Gotta run . . . I'm having a quiet dinner with Walter at the apartment tonight. We decided if we ate out everyone in the place would come and sit with us. Also it would be a nice item for the newspapers, which we don't need.

L and K to you and the mensch,
Nonno

———————— ⚭ ————————

The New Republic piece Mother refers to is a humorous essay I wrote about Nora Ephron's book Heartburn. That piece was the end of our friendship, which I greatly regretted. When Nora and I were friends, I found her to be a generous, great girlfriend.

A "reefer" is newspaper/magazine jargon for "refer to," like a line on a cover or front page essentially saying, "See this article."

Chris Ogden, then Time bureau chief in Chicago, was the son of a newspaperman friend of Mother's.

The end of the letter shows, once again, how

Mother was a devoted stage mother, literary division, where I was concerned. She absolutely thought that I should be on the magazine cover for a single-page essay at the back of the book!

JUNE 17, 1983
CHI./CONN.
THURSDAY

Dear Mugsie:

I'm on the plane from Wash. D.C. to Chicago. Last night was the General Motors dinner. They gave 3 awards, $100 grand <u>each</u>, for the researchers who have done the best cancer research. It was a very classy affair (an annual event—and my third) held in the State Dept. dining room. Probably the most elegant and distinguished room in the country. It is furnished with magnificent antiques.

Invited [W.] to be my escort. He was divorced (last month) and called to say he'd love to see me. So—he turned out to be the <u>ideal</u> date. Very handsome, very elegant, and people kept coming up to him (men 15 and 20 years his junior) saying "You were my professor at MIT!"

[Mr. X] was there with a nice (average looking) lady and I felt his eyes on me all evening. It is over between us—finito—THE END—and I am relieved. I didn't feel the slightest twinge of <u>anything</u>. When it's over, it's over. And now I am thanking my lucky stars I chopped it before it landed in the <u>National Enquirer</u>. It could have ruined me for sure.

I re-read your piece in the <u>New Republic</u> and it is absolutely the classiest writing you've ever done. Truly professional. You not only caught the essence of the book, but your x-ray of Nora's head was terrific. If she is mad at you for this—tough luck, Lady. She got better than she deserved from you. A dame who writes a book like that lets herself open to everything and anything.

I was really proud of you when I ran into a few references I couldn't understand. What's a roman a clef?

. . .

At first I was mad that you didn't get a

cover reefer—or even an identification in the table of contents, but Chris Ogden cooled me down by explaining "Washington Diarist" is always a "semi-secret." My question is, <u>why</u> should it be? Your piece is by far the best thing in the magazine.

This is it for now, my tochter. Do keep in touch.

I send love to you.

Nonno

———————— ⌀ ————————

Jim Hoge was a great favorite of Mother's. He worked his way up to editor-in-chief of the Chicago Sun-Times. *From there he went to the* New York Daily News, *and now is number one at* Foreign Affairs, *the magazine of the Council on Foreign Relations.*

The restaurant "Cricket's," named for my younger daughter, was in one of the Chicago hotels owned by her father.

Dear Mugsie:

All is well. We will be talking soon . . . meanwhile I am really looking forward to my next trip . . . because it means I will be seeing you and Ken and the kids. WHAT A TREAT! I can't tell you!

Thursday was the Marriott stockholders' meeting and Daddy came in for it. We had dinner together at the International Club the night before and that was some experience. He is still very much overweight—but his hair is no longer white. It is blond again. I mentioned it and he said . . . "My barber puts some stuff on to BRING out the gray." I told him the last time I saw him he was snow white (without the seven dwarfs . . .) and that his barber was making him a blond. No comment.

Meanwhile . . . his once handsome face is lined with age (the booze and years of heavy smoking haven't helped), and he looks old old old. His deal is still pending and I don't know if he is hallucinating or what. If it comes off it will be a shocker to the financial world . . . and he will certainly be on top again. I am keeping my fingers crossed, but so many of his stories don't match, it is very hard to know how much is fact and how much is fiction. I told you he has moved to Westport, Conn . . . and loves it there.

At the Marriott stockholders' meeting (that's what Daddy came in town for) all the Grays showed up . . . Shell, Avram and their father [Sheldon Gray, a close friend since high school]. So many people asked about you . . . including the brothers Gray . . . and there was Peter Bennzinger . . . Gabe and Janet Joseph . . . Nicky Pritzker. Everybody wants to be remembered.

Last night was the party for Jim Hoge's 25th anniversary with the <u>Sun-Times</u>. Marshall Field gave it . . . at Cricket's . . . and it was lovely. I sat at Jim's right . . . and Jamee Field was at his left. . . . Next to Jamee was Mike Royko . . . who got very drunk, for a change. . . . His language when he is sober isn't very clean. WELL . . . what

can I tell you? A good time was had by
all . . . I will give you the details in
person . . . if you are interested, which
you may not be.

Gotta run . . . so much work to do I
can't see straight. Also, it is 95 degrees
out and I am walking home.

Love to you and the G.G. Bless him . . .
and you, too, tochter.

Nonno

---

*My dear chum, and Mother's, Ilana Rovner, now
sits (and was the first woman) on the Seventh Circuit
Appellate bench. Marjorie Benton was a major
political player who, with my mother, urged Senator
Percy to make the Rovner appointment to the federal
trial bench, from which she was later elevated.*

AUGUST 2, 1983
SUNDAY NIGHT

Dear Mugsie:
You have been good about writing . . .
and I enjoyed YOUR comments on the

Christmas cards. Pure Margo. A knock for everybody. I guess I shouldn't complain. You seem to like me—and that's what counts.

I walked with Eunice Johnson today (93 degrees by the lake!) and she always asks about you. Her daughter Linda has a swell fella . . . and it looks serious. The guy is with Goldman and Sachs (Chicago branch) and Johnny met him first . . . the guy called and conned his way into a business meeting by being both smart and charming. When Johnny laid eyes on him HE immediately called a staff meeting (Linda is Vice-President). . . . The smart pa saw the kid's possibilities as a son-in-law immediately. Can you believe it? Well—it's true. Anyway, Eunice is already talking wedding dresses.

. . .

Ilana is once again fired up over the possibility of getting a Federal Judgeship. If Chuck Percy doesn't appoint her <u>this</u> time he is crazy for sure . . . also he will lose two good friends . . . me and Marge Benton. We have put him on notice.

This is it for now, pet—so write when you can . . . keep those hilarious clippings coming . . . and I'll hold up my end . . . if you will excuse the expression.

Love to you and the Hunk.
Nonno

―――――――― ⌒∞⌒ ――――――――

[OCTOBER 1983]

Bella Molto—which means "Very Pretty" in Italian (I think):

I'm in another one of those deadly meetings. They are now discussing fragments of the monocule and its laminer domains and its oncological receptors that relate to carcinoma of the neo-plagia. Of course I already know all this, in fact I wrote the definitive paper on it when I studied in Zurich last year, so I am bored to death.

Everyone is making notes, so I am writing, too—only I'm writing a letter to you. If you haven't guessed, I'm in Washington, at a meeting of the

National Cancer Institute. Boring—don't ask! Others seem riveted, so maybe I am just ignorant.

I am having a room-service dinner tonight with Muffie Brandon. Just US. What fun! She knows all the gossip so I'm sure to get an earful. It's so nice not to have to go to a restaurant. We'll take our shoes off—order up and yak. I really do enjoy that girl. She knows everything—and is very hip politically. Having been the White House Social Secretary for nearly two years, she knows lots about what went on at the top.

Now they are showing slides. Oi—when they bring out the pictures of diseases I want to plotz.

My seat-mate on the plane to Washington last night was Tom Cochron (Corchoran? . . . wrong name?). Anyway, he's the Congressman running against Percy. The guy is a Notre Dame graduate—Very good-looking Irishman and he just might take Percy in the primary. If not—there's Paul Simon in the general election. I do think Percy is going to get beat.

<u>I fell asleep</u>—So help me—
More later. For now this is it . . .
Hello again—
this is the next day—
I'm back in Chicago and <u>swamped</u> with mail to answer—
Much love to you and the G.G.

Nonno

———————————⌘———————————

DECEMBER 12, 1983

Dear Margo:

First—the swing albums are simply fabulous. You could not have bought me a better gift, no matter what.

As I told you on the phone, I've been dancing every night and it's such great fun. I hope no neighbors within telescopic distance range have their equipment trained on my library window. They would surely call the mental health authorities, and drop a net over me.

Here I am—at 11:00 at night—middle-aged (?) lady, dancing all by myself for 15 and 20 minutes at a stretch!!!!

It was great fun seeing you and Ken here. You must come more often.

. . .

Tonight is Cindy Pritzker's 60th birthday and it's going to be an all-out, no holds barred bash at the Hyatt Regency. Where else? Of course, Mr. Kirby is my date (he's also been A. N. Pritzker's lawyer for years). I know the music will be terrific and Kirby is one hell of a good dancer.

Cindy called me this morning to ask if I would take the overflow of the flowers she is receiving. I said, "Sure, send them down." Well, the first was from Marvin and Barbara Davis, Denver, natch, and that arrangement must have cost $350.00. Haven't seen such flowers since the [Mr. X] days.

Last night, would you believe, I went to the opera? <u>La Boheme</u>. I do not care for opera, even good opera. The gentleman that asked me is a real pussycat. Bill Graham is Chairman of Baxter Travenol. Bill's wife, Edna, died last year and every widow and divorcee in town is chasing him. He is nothing to look at, but probably the smartest businessman in these parts and very sweet.

First, we went to the Governor's cocktail party, then to the Casino for dinner, then to the opera. He is great company. I am sure he is not looking for romance, just looking for someone to go with.

This is quite a magilla so I will sign off with L and K, to you and the G.G.

Nonno

At this time, Mother did not know Kitty Kelley. When they met, they became friends.

The remark she repeats from a conversation with my father, "Shut your mouth, Esther," was a set piece between them, always said with affection. It was his way of saying he didn't want to hear about it, because he'd already thought of it. As for misspelling her own name, this was either a typo or the best example, yet, of her indifference to spelling.

[DECEMBER 26, 1983]

MONDAY

Mugsie, Dear Girl:

This is a legal holiday—another example of the way the unions have ripped off our country. There is no good reason people should not be expected to work the day after Christmas—unless, of course, they are too hungover. But that should be considered a "sick" day—or just plain absent due to drunkenness. Anyway, my office is closed and I am working at home.

This was, I decided, an ideal time to clean out the shelves and get rid of a lot of the stuff that has been gathering dust and cluttering my apartment. Also I have been thinking for a long time that I should get rid of the hundreds of love letters [Mr. X] has written me over the years—starting in February . . . 1976. They are all in his own hand and he is a <u>magnificent</u> writer. But the handwriting!!! (He should have been a doctor.) I learned how to decipher his script and could make out every word.

I was up until two o'clock in the

morning with [Mr. X's] epistles and I must confess it was a traumatic experience. His writing is pure poetry and in those letters I relived some of the most exciting and loveliest days of my life. It made me wish it could have lasted forever, but I know that was not possible, for many reasons, and it's foolish to look back. So—I shredded his gorgeous letters by hand . . . and the pile was two feet high! In it I found one you had written to him . . . and am enclosing same. (He had sent it to me.)

Oi; the typewriter is eating this letter. My eraser tape is out and the ribbon is also going. . . . But to continue. . . . I am glad I was able to find the good sense to destroy those letters. It would not be good if someone found them in 30 years, after I am gone. I shall do a lot more ripping up one of these days when I go through my VIP files in my office. An ambitious secretary could make quite a bundle selling my files to Miss Kitty Kelley or her successor. Maybe in 30 years no one will be interested, but some people might. I only had one secretary in all the years I've been writing that I suspected was "making notes" for later . . . and I canned her.

It is still bitter cold and I am sitting here with Daddy's maroon wool sox on . . . and a heating pad under my feet! By the way, he phoned to say he was going to London for the holidays. Sounded fine. Sober . . . hopeful. I hope the New Year is a good one for him financially. I think he is living quite well on his consulting fees from Avis AND Hertz (!). When I suggested to him that this might be a conflict of interests . . . and somewhat unethical he told me . . . "Shut your mouth, Ester [*sic*]."

This is it for now, doll girl. . . . My love to you and the GG and those great kids. Let me know how the holidays went with the Aspen end of the family. I hope the eldest has found employment and a decent guy to keep her company.

Much love . . . and may the new year be a humdinger for all of us.

Nonno

P.S. You were dear to phone on X-

Mas . . . and I loved talking to Adam and Cricket.

———————— ⌗ ————————

[APRIL 4, 1984]
TUESDAY EVENING

Dearest Tochter:
Moved that you used the last half a cartridge to write to your old chestnut-haired mammy with the white roots. I'm answering, post haste.

. . .

LOVED the monkey picture and the comment about too-much ice cream. Actually my weight is pretty good (for an old bat). Age has a tendency to pile on a few unwanted pounds. Which reminds me . . . I saw Popo at the Gridiron and she was wearing a sequin outfit with a matching COAT. This is a bad sign. When they start wearing "matching coats" it means something has to be covered and usually it's the behind. I know that Jennifer [Jones] uses matching coats and to a great advantage . . . for both afternoon and evening. The last time we were in New York together we went to Halston . . . her designer, not mine . . . and when she took off her "matching coat" to try something on, I was amazed at how beefy she was. Which reminds me, Halston has very clear memories of you and Chicago and sends his love.

Did you get a call from Bert Convy's manager . . . or agent? He called me at the office and wanted to know if I was going to be in California "around April 28th. . . ." It seems they wanted you and me to do Tattletales. Mother and daughter team. (I guess Florence Henderson and her daughter did it and they thought it was very good.) I told him . . . sorry, on April 28th I will be in Tampa . . . getting an honorary degree. I then added, rather gratuitously, that we don't do mother-daughter gigs. I could have talked all day without saying THAT. It was, I realized later, rather graceless and totally unnecessary. (When will I learn?)

. . .

Did I tell you Marty Peretz was here for cocktails and we had a marvelous visit. He is ca-razy about you and Ken . . . and says you two are a real upper. He and Anne love it when you visit them. They are on a high for four days, he said. Also . . . he hopes you will come to them for Passover. (That's the holiday where they have the hemstitched crackers, honey.)

I thoroughly enjoyed seeing Marty. He really is a fascinating guy—and he has the most beautiful hands. Have you ever noticed? We know a lot of the same people . . . on both coasts . . . and the time just whipped by. He came for cocktails only . . . that night he was the speaker for Hebrew University.

Well, kiddo . . . my fingers just fell off . . . and I got a night's work to do yet . . . so nobody can say I was not a good mother today.

Write when you can and so will I.

Nonno

I was parked in Dallas for some weeks during the filming of a television movie, and reading, as always, the local papers.

[MAY 7, 1984]
MONDAY . . .

Dear Margo:

That Andy Rooney column on the Kennedy boy was very good . . . until he got into the stuff about . . . "would the boy have been on drugs if he were one of two children?" What garbage! That Hinkley kid was one of two and he had been spaced out for years . . . as well as a schizophrenic. Also, there are loads of only children who are on drugs.

True, nobody needs 11 kids . . . but some large families are great . . . (not 11 . . . but 6 and 7 . . .) because their parents paid attention to them. As for me . . . I liked having just one. And YOU had three. . . . How are THEY???? Do tell.

Sorry you prefer the Times Herald. I was in that paper for years but they did me a lot of dirt . . . took Popo on and played her column on the EDITORIAL page and I was back with the truss ads and pimple creams. Felix was the one I held responsible for this. My dear, sweet pal, Felix McKnight. I still have a soft spot for him but he really did double cross me.

I stayed in the Herald for many many years . . . and then they interviewed me when I was at the Greenhouse [a spa] with Mary Lasker and Lady Bird. I have in all my life never seen a more bitchy interview on anybody. They made me look like a pampered, rich, spoiled, society dame who had come down there to loaf and spend a ton of money. I was furious when I saw that . . . complete with a stinkin' picture . . . (the worst they could find . . . they took dozens . . .) and I SHOULD have gotten out of the paper then.

Well, two years ago Ralph Langer called . . . the new Editor . . . and he said, "We must have you in The Dallas Morning News . . . price no object. We'll pay you right up front . . . print every word you write . . . and treat you the way you deserve to be treated. . . ." So I called the syndicate and said . . . I want <u>out</u> of the <u>Times Herald</u> and I mean IMMEDIATELY . . . (we have to give them 30 days . . .) . . . Notify them <u>NOW</u>.

When Steve Jahorek knew I meant business he said, "O.K. but the <u>Times Herald</u> is going to hang very tough." I told Steve . . . "Sorry this is it . . . I should have done it years ago." So— when I called Ralph Langer and told him I was coming over . . . they threw a party in the city room . . . put up BILLBOARDS all over town. . . . I was on the trucks . . . on the rack-cards on every corner . . . and my first column was in color on the front page! They wanted to fly a balloon over Dallas with a banner saying "We've got Ann Landers" but I wouldn't let them go <u>that</u> far. Anyway . . . I love the people. I love the paper. . . . They pay me TRIPLE what the <u>Times Herald</u> was paying . . . and I feel loved, which is more important. By the way . . . the News has the bigger circulation and it's getting bigger.

I am off and running . . . trying to get a hold of Abra and make a date . . . Keep in touch . . . I love your letters . . . and I'll write when I can.

Love to you.

Your . . .
Nonno

───────────── ❦ ─────────────

[MAY 15, 1984]
MONDAY. <u>8:45 AM</u>!

Dear Fred:

I'm in another one of those deadly National Cancer Institute Advisory Board meetings and Armand Hammer just completed a 20 minute dissertation (prepared by his Washington "ghost," no doubt). He maintains this dumpy but savvy little broad, at considerable expense, so that he won't look like a moron at these meetings. I guarantee you, he doesn't know from my linka foos (left foot) about what is going on here. (He's the <u>Chairman</u>!—a Reagan appointee.)

I must say, the old gaffer is in pretty good shape for 86!! And his wife, Florence, is <u>82</u> and she looks fabulous. No beauty, but in awfully good shape.

Armand signed off and some Doctor from Detroit is now putting everybody to sleep.

I just took the floor. In my half-open ear I heard the speaker complain about the objection to the use of heroin for the terminally ill hospitalized cancer patient. I made the observation that perhaps it is because all the "legal" substances used in hospitals—valium, dalmane, demerol, amphetamines, etc. wind up in the hands of physicians, nurses and other hospital personnel and many become addicted or <u>dealers</u> and we certainly don't need to add heroin to the list of drugs that get into the pipeline via legitimate channels. Applause.

We adjourned for lunch and returned at 1:45. It is now 2:15 and my eyelids feel as if they have 10 lb. weights on them. I had to get up at 6:00 <u>AM</u> to make this friggin' meeting. La Salle

Lefall [Washington oncologist] picks me up at 7:45. I need 45 minutes for my exercise and 30 minutes to get my face on, my clothes on—and run up to the 10th floor to grab a couple of delicious coffee-cakes for La Salle and me to eat in the car (the N.I.H. is 30 minutes from the Washington Hilton).

. . .

Just heard the National Cancer Institute budget for 1984 is <u>One Billion - 77 Million</u>. Not bad, eh? Mary Lasker is largely responsible for this. (My assistance was minimal—although she says I helped a lot. Mary has a way of giving credit to others whenever possible.)

. . .

Well, kiddo, this goes in an envelope and off to you, my pet. So—L + K to you,

Nonno

JUNE 4, [1984]
MONDAY

Dear Mugsie:

Gotcher letters today. Two of 'em. . . . What treats! Who is Aaron Spelling? And why does he send gifts with engravings like "Glitter" and "Hotel." He MUST be a producer. I get Spielberg mixed up with him. . . .

I am giving an ADVICE "Shower" for Linda Johnson. I'm sick of people who invite you to parties and expect a gift. I HATE showers of any kind. Most of those poor suckers have to go to three or four and buy a wedding gift, too. So— to my party they can just bring some advice. It's going to be fun. . . .

The market is going to pick up. Hang in with Avacare. It may take a long time but it's going to be GOOD. Also . . . stick with Dunn and Bradstreet . . . if it isn't too late. I'm hanging on to mine. If you want to trade or buy . . . Bell South is very good. They just split 3 for 1 . . . so it's cheap. Also . . . Have faith in Baxter Travenol. Actually, the best bet for US is tax-free bonds that pay 9 or 10%. A good, sharp guy can find them for you.

Bob Burnham (suggested by Will Munnecke) found mine. Bond shopping is an art. I hope your man is good at it.

Gotta run, my little one . . . More later. I love your letters . . . also your husband. Such a doll . . .

XX's . . . your ever-lovin'
Nonno

⌒◯⌒

"W." was one of Mother's "gentleman friends." He was, by then, divorced and someone she had known while married to my father. "W." had been a college president, morphed into an author, and always reminded me of a pint-sized George Hamilton.

I was at the Bret Harte School, in Chicago, for just one year (first grade), before we moved to Eau Claire.

JULY 10, 1984
CHI./CONN.

Dear J. Fred:
The beautiful silver flask (for perfume, not gin) arrived today and it is THEE perfect gift for me. I always have

trouble with purse atomizers. They leak . . . or don't work . . . or the glass chips. This beauty will solve all the problems. Also, what a classy thing to take from one's bag—and nonchalantly dab a little behind each ear. A real conversation piece. Added joy . . . Margo gave this to me for my birthday!!

So thank you, dear tochter, for this ever so thoughtful and elegant birthday gift. I love it!

[W.] and I had a wunnn-nnderful time on our little trip. I hope to be talking to you on the phone soon. We have never been so out of touch!! I really don't know where you are. The last I heard (on the 4th) was Port Angeles . . . and that is really where Christ lost his shoes. I also received BACK some stuff I sent to you at the Beverly Hilton. Don't those guys have a forwarding address? So—I have sent everything to Connecticut . . . where I will be sending this—for want of a better address.

If you call me between now and when you go to Connecticut all the news in this letter will be stale. For example:

You are going to have a half brother or

sister in November. Your father may make the <u>Guinness Book of Records</u> . . . two kids—44 years apart. Yes . . . Elizabeth is pregnant. He seemed thrilled when he told me on the phone several weeks ago, and asked me not to tell anyone until the tests came back . . . amneocentisis [*sic*]. Elizabeth is 38 or 39 and they were concerned about Down's syndrome no doubt. Anyway . . . that's it. I wonder what the grandchildren will think of it. If they were upset about their father—they will wig out when they hear their GRANDFATHER is expecting.

As you know, your father and I are in touch by phone . . . he calls at least every three weeks . . . "just to check in" . . . and when I told him [W.] and I were going to rent a car and drive around the Berkshires he insisted on providing a Cadillac for us . . . no charge . . . at LaGuardia . . . for as long as we wanted it. The car was a beauty. AND . . . the Berkshires are gorgeous. You guys sure know where to live. I had a feeling we were close . . . very close to your place.

We went to Tanglewood and heard Isaac Stern . . . Ozawa of the Boston Symphony was conducting and HE is more of a treat than Isaac. It was marvelous. In spite of a terrific rainstorm, the place was packed. (At $34 a ticket, nobody stays home.)

We stayed at Wheatleigh's . . . a lovely Inn in Lenox. It is the place in the Berkshires that everyone wants to get into . . . but there are only 18 accommodations . . . (very expensive, by the way) . . . so reservations have to be made a long time in advance . . . like months. [W.] had been there before so he had some clout. And now . . . guess who owns it???? Linfield and Sue Simon. Sue is Sue Rittenberg who went to Bret Harte with YOU. I'm sure you remember her well. She certainly remembers you. You told her the first dirty joke she ever heard—and she didn't get it! Anyway I hope you will call her and maybe you and Ken can drive over there for dinner one evening. The food is DIVINE. The best in that part of the country. Their chef is Swiss . . . and he is fabulous. Trust me.

Mary's party was gorgeous and we all had such a good time. I am signing off for now because I am almost sure I will be hearing from you before you receive this. Also . . . the painting by Cricket arrived. It is very good . . . I think . . . but what do I know? I would think so, just because she did it.

L and K to the G.G. and we shall keep in touch. . . . Again thanks for the be-yoootiful gift.

P.S. the card was SMASHING! Looked just like you.

Your ever-lovin'
Nonno

⸻ ❧ ⸻

Cricket continued with her painting, first at prep school, then Vassar, and after she graduated. Now a physician, she still paints.

[JULY 1984]

Dear Mugsie:

You do send me the best stuff. Today's mail brought that George Will piece on Jesse Jackson. A masterpiece. And so true. But—Jesse played that convention hall like a harp. I heard this ayem that the head of B'Nai Brith is looking to get together with him to "work something out."

Meanwhile the Republican convention will be a real sleeping pill. They will have to bring in the clowns . . . or a talking dog . . . something to relieve the boredom.

By now you are at home in your little nest and loving it. You are also inundated with mail . . . at least six pieces from ME. And before you know it, you'll be heading for the Cape. A rough life you have kiddo. . . .

You mentioned that Cricket really wanted to go to the Rhode Island School of Design. I'm guessing at the name. I hope you and Ken will change her mind. She can always do the art number but never again will she have an opportunity to get four years of Liberal Arts. Just think of what you would have missed if you had not gone to Brandeis. And what Ken would have missed if he had not gone to Amherst. You would have been different people. Cricket really needs to be in that kind of learning environment . . . in fact . . . it was one of the very good things that came out of her visit with Ted Hesburgh. He advised very strongly in favor of four years for a B.A. . . . and THEN art school. Please please talk this over with Ken . . . and TELL her this is what she is going to do. You will never do her a bigger favor.

There are times when kids should not be allowed to make decisions that affect their lives in a serious way, and this is one of those times. I remember when Adam thought maybe he would like to live with his father . . . in New York . . . or go to school there . . . some damned thing . . . rather than return to Hotchkiss. You and Ken very wisely let the matter sit for a few days . . . and then when it looked like he just might make a definite move in that direction, you TOLD him . . . nothing doing. In retrospect you can see it was the only direction to go. Kids don't always know what is best for them. That's why God gave them parents.

. . .

This is it for now. . . . Keep in touch with your old gray-haired Mother who is sitting in her rocking chair crocheting doilies.

Love and kisses,
Nonno

―――――――――― ⟨≫⟩ ――――――――――

The reference at the end of the letter is to Ilana Rovner's being appointed to the U.S. District Court for the Northern District of Illinois; "Chucky" was Senator Charles Percy.

[SUMMER 1984]

Mugsie . . . my darling tochter:
Just back from the coast (as the racetrack crowd says) and found your

warm and loving letter. I ate every word
with a parfait spoon . . . and it could not
have come at a better time.

For openers, a letter from a Harvard
kidney specialist telling me that my
dear friend John Merrill died suddenly
in the Bahamas. I am sick at heart. He
was a lovely guy—a real contributor—
and never received the accolades due to
him. I was in the process of getting him
Harvard's highest honor . . . The Medal
for Distinguished Service . . . and the
prospects were extremely promising for
the Spring. It would have been the
highlight of his life. He was a graduate
of Harvard Medical School and never
left . . . just stayed on to teach . . . his
whole life. He trained the world's
finest—which he was himself—and
never got the acclaim or the thanks he
had coming. That man did all the basic
work on transplantation. . . . All the
heart and liver transplanting would
have been impossible without John
Merrill's research. Actually, he should
have received the Nobel prize. It was
John who opened up the entire field.

John could have made a fortune in

private practice, but he never cared about money (He inherited a bundle, I should tell you, from his father who was one of the first big-time insurance people out of Hartford . . .) but unlike a lot of rich folks who always want more . . . John dedicated himself to serving humanity. He was a rare guy— a class act. The likes of him will not soon pass this way again.

I have been trying to reach Sue [Merrill]—her line is busy. And I leave for Florida tomorrow (the mouth circuit again) . . . and the phone is ringing like crazy. (I just took it off the hook.) I gotta finish this letter and get to work.

. . .

Meanwhile I am back with my rags hanging from one trip and am leaving tomorrow to talk at Novo University in Fort Lauderdale. Why? For $10,000.

Glad you liked the sweater. Barbara picked it out. She has a very good eye. As you know I think my gift-buying ability stinks. I never know what to get and always feel that I bought the wrong thing.

. . .

This is a real magilla . . . for which I apologize. I gotta get to work. It is piled to the ceiling and I'm off again tomorrow! Jeez, Louise! The weekend with [W.] was wonderful . . . and HIS family is something you must see to believe. He warned me but I still was not prepared. But that is another letter—his mother's 90th birthday party. And the brothers . . . 9 years his senior . . . are out of this world. On the way back to the hotel I told him I was sure they found him in the bullrushes along the Nile . . . or his mother must have fooled around. There is not one shred of resemblance between him and his brothers <u>or</u> his mother. He looks as if he came from a different town . . . forget about family.

I'm signing off with joy in my heart for Ilana . . . who called me when I was in L.A. to share the good news! Chucky DID come through . . . and ain't it wunnnnnn-derful!

Love to you . . .

Nonno

SEPTEMBER 4, 1984
CHI./CONN.
SUNDAY NIGHT—ON MY WAY TO CHICAGO VIA
ST. LOUIS—OZARK. OY!

Dear Mugsie:

I'm on the plane returning from the Sioux City reunion. It was fabulous. I swore I wouldn't go—and at the last minute, when Morey Mirkin said <u>he</u> was going, I decided to make the trip. So did Popo.

Well—Morey took a very sudden turn for the worse, didn't make it, but Popo and I did go—and we had a terrific time. God it was fun! We saw people we haven't seen in 40 years, and it was a <u>blast</u>!

Many people asked about you—especially Trudy Shulkin. She was Miss Iowa in 1960, and what a gorgeous girl she is!!!! She raved about how beautiful and smart you were and wanted to know what you have written lately. I didn't realize you were friends.

I'm so glad I didn't pass up that event. Another life lesson! Always bet on the come. Be a do'er—a go'er. Be a can-do lady. Don't miss out on the goodies. Sure, you'll run into a turkey now and then, but it's worth the chance. I can't tell you how much fun I had in Sioux City—and to think I almost didn't go.

. . .

I'll be home in a few minutes where the work will be piled to the ceiling, but it was worth it.

Love to you and the Mensch.

Nonno

[SEPTEMBER 13, 1984]

Dear Mugsie:

I'm back from the Hubert Humphrey honors in Washington . . . had a terrific time, which frankly I wasn't expecting. I thought it would be a pro forma thing— that I was obliged to attend for old time's sake but lo and behold it was a fabulous affair, from beginning to end.

The dinner was given by Dwayne Andreas, at the Capitol. This was only the sixth time in our nation's history that a dinner was given at that site. The first was for Lafayette—a thank-you for helping us win the Revolutionary war. George Washington was the host. The most recent was the State dinner for Queen Elizabeth. I don't know how Dwayne pulled this off—but he must have twisted a lot of arms. Naturally it was a black tie. The Marine band played some terrific music and there was dancing. The food was fabulous, too. I was seated between David Brinkley and Charlie Wick ... (you remember HIM [he was a member of Ronald Reagan's "kitchen cabinet"]) ... and it was indeed Dwayne and Inez's table. Across the table was Bob Dole and his wife, Elizabeth ... Senator [David] Durenberger and Chief Justice Warren Berger [*sic*] and his wife, Vera ...

Loads of people from Minnesota, of course, Orville Freeman, Walter Heller, Jerri Joseph and naturally John and Gee Blatnik. Gee told me, "I had 10 minutes to get ready. The first I knew about it was when John came downstairs in his tuxedo." (Same song second verse) "I said, 'John, where are you going so dressed up?' He said, 'Oh, I forgot to tell you . . . there's a dinner honoring Hubert Humphrey's memory . . . or something like that . . .' " . . . ". . . so I said, 'Wait a minute. I'm going with you!' " (Incidentally they ARE being divorced, but still living under the same roof . . . for the time being.)

Fritz and Joan [Mondale] were there . . . and he spoke. Everyone died! If ever there was an opportunity for him to shine, it was there. After all, Hubert was Fritz's mentor . . . Mondale laid such an egg, he should save it for Easter. David Brinkley leaned over and said, "Right here is the best example of why this jerk is going to get creamed. He is a horse's ass." I then looked at Bob Strauss who was at the next table with Muriel [Humphrey]. He had his head in his hands. Muriel looks very old . . . but pretty . . . and smiling. Her husband looks like a nice small town dentist, or maybe the president of the Chamber of Commerce from Lincoln, Nebr. All the kids were there.

The next day at the Whitehouse [*sic*], Reagan was fabulous. He gave a beautiful and moving tribute to Hubert, "The Happy Warrior." Many people wept. And that is one of the reasons Reagan will win very big again. He knows how to connect with people's feelings. Maybe Ken would like to run for President? Actors are in. Lawyers are out.

The best stuff is on the next page. I went to see Sally Quinn . . . and she is Nora Ephron's best friend. Can you stand it?

PAGE II OF THE DEAD SEA SCROLLS . . .

Ben and Sally's house is spectacular. It's a 250-year-old sprawling mansion and has 11 working fireplaces. Sally is decorating it herself . . . and doing a very good job. Their little boy was born with a defective heart . . . has had surgery and is doing fairly well. He is darling looking and very lovable. . . . Now THAT is a heartache. On to pleasanter things . . . like our friend Ilana . . . the judge . . . and the big G about Nora [Ephron].

Sally is Nora's best friend . . . in fact, Nora is the baby's godmother. It seems Nora (all this according to Sally, of course) . . . has been trying to get a divorce from Crazy Carl for three years. Carl is being a real bastard.

    . . .

Nora has a swell guy . . . a Nate Pledgy [this is Nick Pileggi, a well-known writer] or something like that, and they want to get married, but Nora can't get loose. Meanwhile Nora will make a load of dough on her book which she has sold to the movies . . . but until then she is totally self-supporting and not exactly rolling in moola. I thought she had rich parents but I was wrong. Her mother is dead and her father has emotional troubles. Sally says Nora's children are wonderful and she has never been happier or in better shape. If only she could get rid of Carl . . . But the end is not in sight. She will have to spend a bundle to defend herself in court. . . . End of saga.

    . . .

And now I have to go to work or lose my job. I am so far behind it is an

international disgrace. Don't say I
haven't written any letters lately . . . not
to mention all the clips and stuff I have
sent in the last two weeks. Ain't I a nice
Nonno?

Love you,
Nonno

———————— ⌘ ————————

*I would send Mother her column from different
papers when I traveled. She liked to see what editors
were doing with it.*

Ken was opening a Bernard Slade play, Fatal
Attraction *(nothing to do with the movie of the same
name), in Toronto.*

NOVEMBER 5, 1984
CHI./TORONTO
SATURDAY

Mugs:
   You have been a very good kid about
writing . . . or sending things in the
mail. Please keep sending the columns
to me. This is a great help. And, you

should know, Toronto is my flagship paper in the entire country. Highest quality and highest circulation.

I must give you a phone description of the Johnson wedding [John Johnson's daughter, Linda]. . . . IT WAS SENSATIONAL. In my life I never saw anything like it—and never will again. They left no stone unturned and no dollar unspent. Forbes says they are worth 100 million . . . Well . . . no more.

I took Jay and Cindy Pritzker and Jo and Newt Minow in my car . . . (two blocks to the 4th Pres.) but it was bitter cold . . . and who wants to walk in pink satin 5 inch heels anyway? There was a mob of gawkers outside the church . . . probably started to gather at 4:30 and when I arrived there was huge APPLAUSE. Cindy and Jo almost died laughing. . . . "My God" . . . they said . . . "we forgot you were a celebrity!" WELL . . . if they applauded like that for ME, I can imagine what they did when Sammy Davis, Jr. arrived.

Anyway . . . when we seated ourselves in the church the usher came up and announced that the Johnsons requested that Mrs. Lederer be seated with "the family." I was torn about leaving my friends, but they insisted . . . so I went forward, and do you know who "the family" was . . . Sammy Davis, Jr. and Altovise, Jessie [*sic*] Jackson and his wife, Mayor Harold Washington and his fiance . . . etc. . . . So . . . there I was, right up in front . . . in a far better seat . . . Jessie asked me if I had seen him on <u>Saturday Night Live</u> and I said . . . Yes. . . . He asked what I <u>liked</u> <u>best</u> about it. I said, "The end." He looked surprised, so I told him that if he is trying to be a statesman he shouldn't also try to be a TV comedian . . . that it diminished his status . . . especially after his uplifting and spectacular speech at the Democratic convention . . . one of the best political speeches I have ever heard. He thanked me for my opinion and said "I value what you think because you have an awful lot of common sense and know the score in lots of areas." His wife is very nice . . . and we had a good visit.

The wedding was SPECCC TACULAR . . . and the dinner and

music . . . and flowers . . . and food . . . and well . . . Linda's gown was gorgeous . . . (Robert Sherrer of Paris) . . . and Eunice almost outdid her daughter. She wore a shocking pink and purple beaded gown that was heavenly! The whole ceremony . . . 12 beautiful bridesmaids . . . and 12 handsome ushers was something to see. Andre [Rice] kissed her with such passion at the altar that she had to pound his shoulder to get loose! More on the phone . . . I gotta go to work or I will lose my job. I am determined to belt out a brilliant week . . . and I had better start NOW. Love to the hunk . . . and so let me know how the opening goes. I am making a brawche* that this one is a smash.

Love you—
Nonno

---

*"Brawche," more commonly spelled "brocheh," was Mother's very individualized spelling of the Hebrew word for blessing.

The survey Mother refers to received an extraordinary amount of publicity. Based on a letter she got, she asked her women readers if they would rather "cuddle," or engage in "the act." More than 90,000 responded, and something like 70 percent of the women said they would prefer to cuddle.

[FEBRUARY 1985]
SUNDAY NIGHT

Dearest Mugsie:

Gotcher "Dear Nonno" letter in the batch yesterday when I returned from California. I love your letters. They always bring me joy. Even the short ones. The magillas make me euphoric.

California was wunnnnnnnnnnnnnderful. The social highlight of the trip was Mary's black tie dinner at Bistro Gardens. She had about 60 people, my least favorite of which was Danny Kaye. Je—sus, he's a terrible person. [W.] said, "That is the most obnoxious man I have ever met." For openers he greeted me the minute we walked in with . . . (IN A LOUD VOICE so everyone could hear . . . including Mary who was standing beside him) . . . "HERE COMES ANN LANDERS . . . FRESH FROM HER SURVEY! WOULD YOU RATHER FU— or HUG?" I thought I would go through the floor.

The guest list was somewhat second string . . . about 20 people had the flu or were out of town. Among the <u>missing</u> were Cary Grant and Barbara, Mary Martin, Betsy Bloomingdale, the Artie Deutches, Edie Goetz, Otis Chandler, Dianne Feinstein, Sydney Potier [*sic*] and others. Among those <u>present</u> were Kirk and Anne Douglass [*sic*], Deeda and Bill Blair, Jennifer [Jones] Simon (no Norton . . . he has Guillen's Beré [Guillain-Barré syndrome] . . . and cannot walk) Francie Brody, Edward Lasker and his three sons and Dennis and Carrie Stanfill . . . etc. . . . etc. . . .

The music was fabulous and you know how this kid loves to dance. Well—Kirk and I put on a floor show. Lord he's a good dancer! [W.] is pretty good, too . . . tho' quite self-conscious about his dancing. I had to damn near drag him onto the floor. Incidentally, he was wearing John Coleman's black patent leather shoes. I fall down every time I think of that story. [W.] said he never had shoes that fit as well as John's.

For Valentine's Day, [W.] sent me some gorgeous roses . . . and brought along a lovely sterling silver pill box . . . unique . . . for aspirin only . . . with a sliding top which secures aspirin totally. I asked him for a pill box because the one I have keeps opening up and spilling the premarin and ornade all over my purse. I also asked him to get me some chocolate chip cookies . . . from Ivy's . . . which are the best thing in the world. So . . . the dear fella schlepped himself to Melrose and Robertson and got me three dozen. They are to DIE!

Abra called a few minutes ago. She is all excited about the prospect of going to The Culinary Institute of America in Hyde Park. I think it's a swell idea . . . in fact I suggested it several months ago. I know she is not college material and she hates regular school, but this would be ideal for her. The course is 22 months and when a person gets a diploma from <u>that</u> place, the job offers are terrific. Abra was thrilled with the pearl earrings I sent for her birthday. (Ron Brodkey took care of it.) I do love that child. There's a lot of very good stuff there. I was hoping maybe she and Tony Gray might get back together but she said . . . "No romance. Just good friends."

It's cold as the dickens here . . . but then I'm spoiled. California was 84! I'll be going back there in March to visit Mary . . . and then, within a week after THAT I meet [W.] in Washington for Gridiron.

Nonno

P.S. Popo tried to be sweet but it was hard . . . what with all the publicity I've been getting on the sex survey. She did not say <u>one word</u> about it . . . and neither did I.

I am so sorry I won't be able to see your friend Yo Yo Ma but I have another party that night. Darn it.

Nonno

The issue being discussed here was that Mother's friend, Dan Herr (editor of The Critic, *a Catholic literary magazine), had sent her galleys of a piece I had written for him. I thought it odd that an editor would send a piece, before publication, to the writer's mother. As a result, she then got after me to remove a phrase.*

AUGUST 17, 1985
FRIDAY

Dear Margo:

If you felt awful after our last conversation, I can assure you I felt worse.

I don't believe I deserved to get landed on that way—and I'll tell you why.

First, I am not a meddlesome, interfering mother. I think I have stayed out of your business pretty good. But— when I see something that might cause you real trouble, and there is time to get out of the way of the Mack truck, I would be a pretty peculiar friend, let alone a mother, not to say something.

That phrase "sexual-industrial complex" suggests without a shadow of a doubt, that the three people you named WERE named because of something about their sexuality. That, in itself, is not a decent thing to do. Also it's uncharacteristic of you.

. . .

When I read that reference I was uncomfortable. The piece in its entirety is excellent. It is warm and human. When I finished it I went back (after my first phone call) and read it again—and that one part bothered me even more. The more I thought about it the more I felt you would get yourself into trouble with those few words . . . and why do it???? They didn't add that much. I decided to call you back.

I was stunned when you fell on me— outraged and insulted. Surely you know I am not picky nor am I nuts. As for other magazines not sending me your pieces before publication, of course they don't. But you have sent me several yourself, which made me wonder why you were so angry that I had seen it.

Whether or not Thomas More edits, I have no way of knowing. I imagine that all publishers edit in the interest of grammar, punctuation, length and taste. I would, of course, not say one word to them, but maybe you might want to, after you read this letter. Believe me, tochterel, the mess you could make for yourself because of that single reference would not be worth it. I assure you that line will not go unnoticed.

I would hate to think that I could not offer a suggestion that might save you a lot of grief because you don't want to hear anything I have to say. If that is the case, we don't have a very solid relationship.

I won't mention this to you again, but if you want to—I will listen to anything you have to say. Meanwhile I hope you will share this with Ken. I send my love to you both.

Nonno

*A great old-Hollywood comedy writer and wit,
Jerry Davis, mentioned that a best-selling novelist was
a recent widower. I asked how he was taking it . . .
occasioning the "honest grief" remark. Davis's
conversation was maybe the fastest I had ever heard;
most things he said sounded like dialogue straight
from a Noël Coward play.*

SEPTEMBER 3, 1985
TUESDAY

Dear Margo:
Just back from the Vineyard and am
drowning in paper work. Even though
the office sent me a 10 pound package
on Friday I still came home to a pile of
it. So—no time for a letter now, but I did
see Rose and Bill Styron—had dinner
with them and Buchwalds and Bill is off
the booze (liver and kidney trouble) and
what a different person he is! I had
never seen him sober before. He's less
jolly, but terribly sweet. Rose is a doll.
Loved the comment on [—] . . .
"somewhere between honest grief and
Claus Von Bulow." He [the
novelist/widower] folded out of an
appearance on Oprah Winfrey

tomorrow and <u>A.M. Chicago</u> called frantic. Could I come on? I could not.

This is it for now, Kiddo . . . more when I get my head off the deck.

Nonno

Dear Mugsie:

Before I forget . . . I want to tell you how much my mouth watered when you mentioned that you were cooking fresh tongue! I had almost forgotten about it. And now I must ask you how you do it so I can tell Regina. I remember bay leaf and a pressure cooker, but that's about all.

Yes . . . the letter with all the gossip went to the Beverly Hills Hotel and they either sent it back via dog-sled or threw it out. I cannot remember a single thing I said so I'll just have to start fresh.

I had a swell time on the Vin [Martha's Vineyard]. The Cronks [Walter and Betsy Cronkite] are always great fun. Helen, Walter's 93-year-old mother was there . . . as usual. She comes when the first robin chirps in June and stays until the last leaf falls in September (or is it October?). Anyway, God forbid she should give Walter and Betsy a day alone together. Betsy could absolutely plotz. Helen, as I said, is 93 and looks 70 . . . and has plenty of energy to go everyplace they go . . . if invited . . . and if NOT . . . she often invites herself. The old girl complains endlessly about arthritis, but the minute the music starts, she's the first one on the floor . . . and the last to go home from any party. Walter's father was a dentist in St. Jo, Mo . . . Helen divorced him when Walter was 3 . . . and she has been a millstone ever since. This is 65 years worth!

I had a swell time with Buchwalds. Art had a lousy case of shingles but is O.K. now. Anne was sick almost a year with her open-heart surgery. They couldn't have been nicer . . . offered full room and board for the duration if I was uncomfortable at Coleman's. I told them I have NO trouble with HIM . . . but sometimes she can be quite "icy." I really don't blame her. What fourth wife wants an ex-mother-in-law as a house guest? Actually, John told me if she didn't behave, SHE would have to leave . . . not me.

You are right about Marty. I was supposed to get HIM an honorary degree. I think we agreed to "help" each other. So . . . now that he has spoken on my behalf, I must get busy and drum up something for HIM. So far I have been VERY lucky. I have not had to give but one commencement speech, and that was in Athens, Greece. All expenses paid round trip, first class. Not exactly a hardship.

Politics in Chicago and Illinois are heating up. Adlai and Hartigan will chew each other up in the primary and Thompson stands a good chance of winning again. Ilana said the Democrats stole at least 100,000 votes last time. (That's why the election was so close—Adlai damn near beat him.)

. . .

Popo and Mort are in Minneapolis. Jay [Morton's father] was hit by a golf cart and has a broken hip and leg. For a man in his 80's this is very serious. Poor Rosie [Morton's mother] . . . she is still grieving for Helen [Morton's wonderful sister, ill for many years]. Too bad they have such problems so late in life. It's tough enough when a person is young.

Tomorrow night we celebrate Dan Herr's recovery at Jackie's, his favorite restaurant. Todd Brennan and his wife and Candy (sister Candida Lund) and Nonno. Did I tell you she was suing the greeting card company for using her picture on a card that said . . . "You may kiss me but don't get into the habit!" It was a photo of her . . . many years ago . . . in full regalia . . . nun-type. The card company said they thought it was a model "in costume." Well . . . she's got some case, kiddo. And if they get in front of a Catholic judge, Candy can retire on the French Riviera.

This is it for now. . . . Write when you can and so will I.

Love you,
Nonno

I had picked up the phrase "Every move a picture" from Mother. The situation of the moment, calling for "get well" flowers, was that she had been running (!) up an escalator at the paper, tripped, and required several stitches. She had tried to be sketchy with me about the nature of the accident, but her office gave me the precise version. Mother was famously always in a hurry, but her racing around seldom landed her in the emergency room.

SEPTEMBER 13, 1985

Dear Margo:

Your flowers were simply beautiful—several orchids in there and a few other unidentifiable blooms in a magnificent blue-gray ceramic vase.

Best of all was your trademark—the world's best sense of humor, and I am not kidding. Your card really knocked me out—"Every move a picture."

Gee, I love you and I'm so glad you were not left at the Groruds'.

Much love,
Nonno

MAY 11, 1986

Dear Tochter:

The flowers—on <u>MY</u> day—Kiddo were simply magnificent.

Solly Hammer really out-did himself. He always does well by me, but this was truly <u>extraordinary</u>!!

The signature—"Your child" was dear. Yes, you are my child—in so many ways and I couldn't ask for a better one.

I have never regretted having only one. You were always enough (sometimes maybe too much!) but such a source of joy—unending—and you continue to be.

Thanks for avoiding the Groruds' and being mine.

Love,
Nonno

Ken and I were in Paris for three weeks with the American Repertory Theatre production of Robert Wilson's Alcestis. *Ken was clearing his head from* Dynasty *and* The Colbys *by spending a year at Harvard with his old dean from Yale Drama School, Bob Brustein. This was during a time of terrorist violence, and I thought we were very clever and cautious not to stay with the company on the Left Bank, but rather at the Plaza Athenee, where the security was quite tight. I felt less clever when someone told me that that's where a lot of Middle Easterners stayed . . . and it was against rich Arabs that some of the attacks were directed.*

The lack of hostility Mother refers to was Ken's being the first established performer to spend an entire season with the A.R.T., a traditional repertory company having no stars.

SEPTEMBER 12, 1986
FRIDAY

Dear Mugsie:

This letter is going to Paris . . . oo la la! It should take no more than four days to reach you. In the old days it took a week at least, maybe ten days. I'll be happy if it gets there at all. The address was such a magilla.

. . .

Did you know that Oprah Winfrey beat the socks off of Phil Donahue on the west coast last week? They had a highly touted "ratings contest" in L.A. [W.] told me about it . . . and Oprah took Phil to the cleaners. If this happens others places it could wreck Donahue. One thing I like about Oprah's programs— they aren't heavy into kinky sex the way Phil is—(or maybe was).

. . .

Yesterday I went to the Thompson-Stevenson debate . . . and Adlai [the younger] took Jim—no question about it. His wry wit knocked Thompson out. Also Adlai came well prepared with facts and figures, quotes proving that Jim has been wrong a lot . . . about many things. It was pretty devastating. If Adlai wasn't running on a split ticket set-up he would surely win. He may win yet. They had a big crowd, in spite of the rain. It came in buckets.

Paris should be gorgeous now. I kept

wondering what you will do there during the day. No doubt you will hang out with "the folks" from the troupe. You said in your letter yesterday that there was no hostility toward Zoon* and that they treated him "like a Prince." I am not surprised. They are probably thrilled to have him there. He is SO good . . . and so professional. Also, he is nice to people, without being condescending. He will do just fine, wherever he is.

I had a wonderful time with [W.]. He is great to be with. And about his daughter—well—you sure did hit it. The girl doesn't care to deal with it—as you said. So if she wants me to be "a friend of the family" that's all right with me. Actually, I haven't seen [W.'s ex-wife] in ages. [She] is a very nice person although [W.] wasn't too thrilled that she had a guy living in the house when the boys were in Junior High . . . (after he left).

. . .

---

*"Zoon" was one of Mother's names for Ken. Traditionally spelled "Zun," it means son.

Hello again . . . TOP SECRET . . . don't breathe a word . . . guess who Pamela Harriman's guy is . . . and she would like to marry him! [—]! Oy . . . married to [—] for 38 years at least . . . maybe more. Marge said they've been seeing each other for a LONG time. I cannot imagine a more unlikely couple. With names to her credit like Churchill and Leland Hayward and Averell Harriman she's after a Jew from [the name of a state]! Can you believe it?

Nonno

P.S. You knew Hank Greenberg died last week. It was in the <u>N.Y. Times</u>, page one . . . I assumed you saw it.

———————————— ⌇∞⌇ ————————————

Elita Georgiadas subsequently divorced to marry her longtime friend F. W. De Klerk, president of South Africa before Nelson Mandela.

After reading that a woman was killed when lightning traveled through the phone line while she was talking, I passed this on to Mother. Aberration or not, neither of us ever again would talk on the phone when there was thunder and lightning outside.

SEPTEMBER 26, 1986
FRIDAY
CHI./LONDON

Dear Tochter:

Yes—they all came on the same day! What a windfall! THREE wonderful letters from you this morning and I lapped them up like a thirsty hound in the middle of the Sahara.

First—before I forget. My friends Tony and Elita called from London to say they were coming to the states. (They are the Greek ship-builders . . . the Georgiadases. . . . Elita is beautiful and Tony is RICH. . . .) I told them you and Ken would be at Claridge's for "a few days" . . . unfortunately they will be in Africa. But he said, "I would love to send them flowers." So . . . remember the name and don't return the flowers to the desk saying . . . "wrong . . ."

I laughed out loud about charging $30 a day for the dog. Jeez Louise! But I can see where it would be a source of great revenue. Actually they should charge more when one considers the damage they do in hotels. The little darlings chew the rugs, scratch the furniture, knock over lamps and pee on the Oriental rugs. They also bark at night when left alone and annoy the other guests.

. . .

I am NOT worrying about you. You are right. It IS all luck. And now you are reading this in London . . . so you made it.

. . .

I sent Abra a tin of homemade goodies and you would have thought they were rubies or emeralds. She was THRILLED. Ruth Edelman's cook makes the best stuff and all I have to do is "put in my order." Next week I will send another tin.

Has it been 12 years since you saw Marcel [Marceau] and his brother? I can't believe it! I thought the mime was the best I have ever seen—he does have an international reputation.

As for Sam Pisar [an international lawyer] . . . he did not fake his "history" . . . believe me. The tattoo is on his hand there is plenty of documentation. The guy is a pain in the ass socially . . . but he did go thru plenty and is an authentic survivor of the Holocaust.

Well, Kiddo, my hands are falling off . . . and I am calling it a day . . . altho' it is pitch black outside and looks like midnight. Actually it is NOON. We are having a lulu of a storm here. I want to call the office but I will NOT use the phone until the storm abates. Thanks for wising me up. You were absolutely right.

Write when you can . . . and I'll do the same. It will be great to know you are back in the States. Let me know the minute you land on US soil.

Sunday I go to Texas . . . the LBJ ranch . . . or did I tell you this in the last letter???? Anyway . . . 68 means a few rocks in the head . . . so you'll just have to forgive me if I get repetitious. . . . Lady Bird is having a small dinner party for me and I am speaking for the LBJ Library.

This is it for now ... Kiss Zoon for me ... and enjoy, Ketzeleh* ...

I send love,
Nonno

⌒✕⌒

OCTOBER 4, 1986
CHI./LONDON

Dear Margo:
You and Ken are now in London ... my favorite city in the whole world. Enjoy!

I have been sending you all kinds of reading material and hope you are liking it. You have been very good about writing—and soon I will be getting things from LONDON! The last week in Paris you outdid yourself.

Thank God you are out of France already. I see by the <u>N.Y. Times</u> that they have cancelled all leave for police officers ... in anticipation of more bombings. Jeez. I know the tourist trade has suffered a lot. Nobody wants to go there.

---

*"Ketzeleh" means little kitten.

Tonight is the Ireland Fund dinner . . . a black tie dinner-dance. I'd give $1,000 if I could stay home. It's been raining for a week . . . cold and miserable. Lake County has been declared a disaster area. Those poor people didn't have a lot to begin with and now their furniture is floating and they have had to abandon their homes and go to sleep in churches and schools.

. . .

John Coleman has gotten more rotten publicity. It seems the people who own the Ritz Carlton name are SUING him because his hotels do not meet their high standards and they want the name back. The story in the Wash. Post said the hotels do NOT have decent service. . . . The switchboard doesn't answer, the room service is very slow and the hotel rooms are filthy. This is serious stuff. It could ruin him. I heard this from him on Monday . . . and again from Bonnie Swearingen yesterday at a cocktail party.

. . .

ENOUGH for now . . . write when you

can. Love to you and Zoon. . . . WRITE
SOON . . . OR CALL.

Nonno

---

*The enclosure mentioned below was that of a letter
from a reader complaining about a Dr. Ruth column.
The underlined quote said, "A man was having
trouble breathing while having oral sex with his
girlfriend. Her answer was to keep trying, because
practice makes perfect." Mother never cared for Dr.
Ruth, regarding her as an embarrassment. In addition
to sensationalizing her sexual advice, Mother felt her
doing commercials and bit parts demeaned the business
of giving advice. She held the same opinion of Joyce
Brothers.*

OCTOBER 11, 1986
CHI./CONN.

Dearest Mugsie:
  We just had the BEST visit. It's
Saturday night and I am at home—
trying to make an honest living. Your
phone call was <u>GREAT</u>!

Going through the mail I ran across this. Can you believe it???? How a family newspaper can print this is beyond me. And when you think that when I started to write, 31 years ago, the words "damn" and "hell" were considered "unfit" for print. Even sex was not discussed in a paper. I mean everyday, ordinary, marital sex. The word SEX was not even allowed . . . unless you used it in the context of whether the sex of a child was female or male.

Happy New Year to you and the G.G. In fact, you are a pair of G.G.'s. Please know that Monday is Yom Kippur . . . the holiest of all days. It is the only holiday I honor. I do not go to the paper. (I may eat a hot dog but I don't go to work.)

L and K,
Nonno

The Ann Landers "replacements" were necessary when Mother left the Sun-Times *for the* Chicago Tribune. *The* Sun-Times *held a much publicized contest for a new advice columnist who would write under a new name . . . the name Ann Landers now belonging to Mother. They ultimately chose two people to write it together, though that column is no longer running.*

[JULY 24, 1987]

Dear Margo:

Hardly worth the postage but I know how you love to get mail from the colonies . . . so here is something to enjoy with your coffee. The new Ann Landers replacements have bombed out. I wouldn't be surprised if they pulled 'em. Zazzlo [Jeff Zaslow] thinks he is Samuel Johnson with his essays and I don't know who that Crowley dame [Diane Crowley] thinks she is. Jane Austen she is not.

This is it, doll . . . Oh . . . Helen Cronkite age 95 broke her hip yesterday. The birthday party is on the 19th. . . . I'll bet she makes it.

Love to you and the Zoon, Nonno

———————————— ⁘ ————————————

The drama of the moment, causing Mother to praise my strong mettle, was the exploratory surgery I was about to undergo in London. Actually, I was in better shape than everyone close to me. I have come to think that being the center of a health scare is easier than being an onlooker. Always worried about me to begin with, Mother of course was frantic . . . though trying to seem very upbeat and sure of a good outcome. I later learned she spoke with two oncologists, by phone, several times a day. She did not come to London until after the surgery, convinced that if she came before, I would think I was dying for sure. When Mother did come, it was with cut orchids and caviar in her garment bag. Cricket's presence in London was because Ken had sent for her to see me—and him— through the surgery.

AUGUST 10, 1987
MONDAY

Dear Margo:

Today is Monday. We talked a couple
of times and I shall try to call you
tomorrow. You are made of wonderfully
strong stuff. I am proud of you.

What is this in the envelope you ask?
Well—you won't believe it but it's true.
Your last letters came to me a few days
ago and the stamp was not cancelled. It
looked so inviting . . . and temptingly
usable. So—I peeled it off with great
care, affixed it to an envelope with
library paste and am sending it back to
you. I have a thing about uncancelled
stamps. I simply cannot throw them
away. It's like throwing away MONEY.
Of course, reusing a postage stamp is a
federal offense and if I get caught I will
be ruined. Over the years I have re-used
several hundred dollars worth of
stamps. It's a compulsion. I just can't
pass one up or throw one out. Everyone
has an area of petty cheapness and this
is mine.

Today the girls (and Joe) [her
chauffeur] are moving from our

temporary offices in the <u>Tribune</u> to our permanent ones in the Tower. It's a helluva job and Kathy and Barb and Laurie and Marcy have been saints. Those dames have been working out of boxes for five and a half months. Also, their chairs are awful and they all have back problems . . . so they sit with pillows. It will be wunnnderful to see them in a classy, elegant office with good chairs . . . beautiful desks and orthopedic chairs . . . ordered specially for the walking wounded. The <u>Tribune</u> has spared nothing to make me and mine comfortable. It was a great move.

I went to a cocktail party this evening . . . a rare occurrence for me. But Jewel La Fontant [a prominent lawyer] gave it . . . and I had never seen her place (Water Tower) and knew it would be lovely. The party was for a fellow Board Member from Washington. Jewel is a lawyer . . . very attractive and being both black and a woman, she is a good one to appoint to a board. The dame she gave the party for . . . Nancy Clark Reynolds was a V.P. at Bendix when all the shmutz was going on with

Mary Cunningham and Bill Agee . . . so she must know plenty. [The Cunningham-Agee romance, then marriage, was the corporate version of a May/December love affair: He was top management; she was very junior.]

. . .

This is it for now. I will write again tomorrow . . . and try to find some good stuff to put in the envelope.

Love to you and Zoon . . . and Cricket.

Nonno

———————— ⌒∞⌐ ————————

The surgery that so worried Mother revealed no malignancy.

Her reference to the starter husband's flowers, and oxygen, was that the arrangement was so large and lavish that one of the nurses asked if it had come from Texas!

"Dawson" and "Sheppard" were the two Harley Street docs taking care of me. Sir Anthony Dawson was known as "the Queen's bowel doctor," which amused me because I didn't think they would go public with the fact that the Queen had bowels. Mr. Sheppard

was the oncologic surgeon. (Surgeons in the UK have the title "Mr.," not "Dr.") And it had been Mother's connections in London that led me to Dawson.

AUGUST 13, 1987]
CLARIDGE'S LONDON [STATIONERY. SHE WAS
IN CHICAGO.]
THURSDAY

Dearest Margo:

I just spoke with you and you sounded tired but wonderful. Yesterday—getting the good news was one of the happiest days of my life. It was the best present I have ever received.

I guess there is something of value in even the shreckiest of troubles. It makes us realize how lucky we are just to get up in the morning and have no major worries hanging over our heads. It reminds us to be thankful for every day—and how blessed we are to have one another. I am sure that is what Ken was trying to say yesterday when he gave me the call I have been waiting for, for a week. He was SO relieved . . . and just sort of numb. He said it hadn't hit him yet. I know what he meant.

I'm glad you liked my flowers. I called Michael Bently, manager of Claridge's, and asked him to take care of it for me. I knew they would be nice because he ordered the flowers I sent Deedy and Chris [Ogden]—and I SAW them with my own eyes.

I am sure Coleman's flowers are using up all the oxygen on the entire floor. He really made me crazy for a whole week . . . calling twice a day. And yesterday—(that was the day of the surgery) he drove me nuts. I finally said . . . "PLEASE don't call again. I will call you when I know something."

. . .

So now . . . all you have to do is get your strength back and feel well again. All I can say is you were shot full of luck to be in London . . . and gotten tied up with the likes of Dawson and Sheppard.

I gotta run now . . . but I will be calling again in a couple of days. (I will let you rest tomorrow.) Meanwhile I am glad Crick is there!

I will write again very soon. As of now you have plenty to read. I've been clipping like mad . . . and the August <u>Vanity Fair</u> went out Fed. Express yesterday . . .

Much love to you and Zoon and Cricket,

Nonno

———————— ⌒∞⌒ ————————

The flat we stayed in in London belonged to Doug Fairbanks Jr., who was called "Dougie" by all the help—certainly not a name he had in the States. This five-story apartment building was attached to the Basil Street Hotel, and their executive housekeeper looked in on me during the day. Mother came for only a couple of days, Cricket returned to school, and Ken was filming Strange Interlude *with Glenda Jackson, David Dukes, Edward Petherbridge, and Kenneth Branagh, who played a small role. (Though Branagh was already a leading man, British actors, by tradition, play any role that interests them without regard to its size.)*

"*Horrids*" (*her intentional spelling*) *was Harrods, a mere half block away.*

"*The Dukes and Bern*" *Mother mentions meeting were the late actor David Dukes, his novelist-poet wife, Carol Muske-Dukes, and the playwright Bernard Slade.*

And I get the idea, from this letter, and others . . . though I have no particular memory about it . . . that I must have been a bit of a prima donna in my behavior. Though she is clearly being lighthearted and hyperbolic about it, her remarks are of a piece with my recollection of her saying, over the years, that I was more high-strung than she.

[AUGUST 1987]
SUNDAY

Dear Margo:

I'm one hour from Chicago—30,000 feet in the air and have just put in 6 solid hours of work—with time out to visit with Roger Ebert who is seated across the aisle. (He, too, is hip to the Bubble—Business Class.) He's a swell fella and thinks your pieces in the New Republic are <u>delicious</u>. He loved the

Vanna White demolition job—says you are a terrific writer and the <u>New Republic</u> could use more from you. (And he's not your mother.)

If you still have the <u>TRB</u> piece about the 10,000 year old mummy, <u>please</u> send it to me. I want to pass it on to a few pals.

Oops, I just noticed that this page has a chewed off bottom. Sorry about that. I am not starting over. Let's just say the dog ate my homework.

I must say, this was the best trip ever. How wonderful to be flying home after a good news visit. I feel so wonderfully happy and grateful. I'm sure it has given you a new and deeper sense of appreciation for things you once took for granted.

I love your flat—and marvel at the way you change money and shop in the grocery store—and go to "Horrids" and make friends everywhere.

London is <u>so</u> special but for Christ sake—don't buy anything except maybe another bag at Tobias! When I think of $60 American for that nothing bra!!!! And $700 for a "cheap" sweater. (The better ones for $1,000!!!) You gotta be crazy to go for such prices.

If you haven't made reservations for the Bubble in business class—do so soonest. The bulkhead would be the best for Long John Silver [Ken was 6'6"]—which I'm sure he already knows. I really love British Overseas. They do everything just right.

Thank you for the truly warm hospitality. Yes, this was the <u>nicest</u> you have ever been. Just "out of hospital" and you steamed my clothes!!!! I had a terrific time. More later—for now this is it. Write me a longie when you can.

Much love to you and Zoon—

Nonno

Blue Cross finally did pay, which surprised me. Also unexpected was that private medicine in the United Kingdom costs markedly less than in the United States.

AUGUST 16, 1987
SUNDAY

Dear Margo:

Well—it's all over . . . and the fat lady sang. I have never heard such beautiful music in all my life. I honestly believe it's a good thing to have a few rotten experiences in one's life so we can have something to compare the good stuff with. People don't know how good they have it until fate slings 'em a zinger. I've lived long enough so that I wake up in the morning and thank God for every day.

Like Barney Sordoni said on the phone . . . "It was providence . . . that she should be in London and get those fabulous doctors . . ." and I believe it. That girl is a real doll . . . a class act. I have loved her for 35 years . . . we were YPO wives that far back, and I've seen her through 2 widowhoods . . . both swell guys. She lives not far from Boston and one day we will meet there. She remembers you with great affection.

Coleman is an odd duck. As you said in your book . . . you carried rebellion a little too far. But there is some good there—and he does try. I must say I was surprised at the depth of his concern. He pestered the hell out of me. I am glad he had the good sense to leave Virginia and John Jr. off the card. I find the Ice Queen pretty rough to take. But I'm sure I stick in her throat like a halibut bone. Who the hell needs an ex-mother-in-law in the picture? Some women have to put up with an ex-wife when they have kids . . . but an ex-mother-in-law????????

Hang tough with Blue Cross. All those insurance outfits are momsaireem* . . . and thieves. Just yell a lot . . . be insistent . . . and don't let the bastards grind you down. They will try everything before they pay . . . but in the end they WILL pay. In London for Crissake how could you get a second opinion from Cornell?

. . .

I am pleased that you appreciate the wonderful things in your life and that you feel you have been very lucky. I

---

*"Momsaireem," usually spelled momzarim, is the plural of the word

agree that you have. After two klunkers to have landed the most generous, loving, handsome, intellectual, funny, warm-hearted guy . . . is quite remarkable. And he DOES appreciate you . . . and he cherishes you . . . and that makes me feel wonderful.

I am glad you think your father is "interesting." That is as good a word as any. If I had to describe him in a word I don't think it would be that one. Tragic is more like it. He had everything going for him and threw it away. But there was so much good there. In his glory days he was a wonderful husband and an adoring father. We did get his best years. Funny how booze was such a destructive factor in both your marriage and mine.

I am truly happy you don't harbor any resentment against Topsin . . . and that you just remember the good days. That's the best way to go.

I am frank to admit that I was ready for the worst. Not [W.], however, he was extremely optimistic and kept me afloat with positive thoughts. I told nobody else . . . but Stolar and Milton Wexler. Also Jordan Gutterman [an oncologist at M.D. Anderson]. He was <u>wonderfully</u> helpful. They were both very upbeat. But now, thank God it is OVER and I told Ken and Dub [her sisters] yesterday. Now that the news is good I have told my "girl friends . . ." Mary Lasker and Jennifer . . . etc. I feel so happy I could FLYYYYYYYY! Funny, when my new financial advisor was here I was thinking how little all my worldly goods meant to me. It's people that count . . . not things—and I know it now as I never knew it before.

Nonno

———————— ❧ ————————

"Call me Joe" (Cardinal Joseph Bernardin) was Mother's great friend. She loved his down-home quality.

The pope Mother refers to here is John Paul II.

Mother's mentioning how we both felt about "cards" was our perhaps snobbish feeling that greeting cards were not quite as correct as a note.

"The Minneapolis thing" was a party given by Popo's in-laws to which Mother was invited, then disinvited.

[AUGUST 19, 1987]
CHI./LONDON

Dear Mugsie:

It's Monday night. . . . I am looking at the telly as I type. (I always turn on Channel 7 at 10:30 at night and see what Ted Koppel has on.) Well—right now it's William F. Buckley debating a blind man who is attempting to sail the Atlantic . . . alone. Well . . . are they ever going at it!

Buckley is telling the man he has no right to attempt such a thing . . . that he is not helping the blind. The man is telling him . . . "Who are YOU to decide such a thing for me or anyone else?"

Buckley is now saying a blind person should not be going to the ballet—that it is just foolish to think he can really enjoy it. The man is furious and saying . . . "Maybe I might enjoy the music." Well—it's getting very rough and Buckley is getting in way over his head. He is going to get some murderous mail for this. I am surprised that he was so foolish as to get into this.

"Call me Joe" (His Eminence) came to lunch today and hit me up for $$$$$$ for the Parochial Schools of Chicago. I believe in the system and think they are an essential to the community. Children who attend Catholic schools in Chicago get a better education than the public school kids. I have seen the difference— many times, when I have gone to speak at both public and Parochial schools in any number of different cities. The discipline in Catholic schools produces much better students. While the kids at Hyde Park High are throwing books at the principal who is on the stage . . . trying to get the kids to be quiet so he can introduce the speaker (me). . . . I am ready to walk back to the car in the parking lot.

I am going to put my money where my mouth is. "Call me Joe" was delighted. He is the best Cardinal in the country and has pulled Fatso's fat face out of the fire more than once. (I'm talking about the pope, of course.)

. . .

I am climbing into the bathtub now with a few hundred letters and will write again tomorrow. I am trying to stagger the mail so you will get something every day. How'm I doin'? I also told Popo. (She called when she heard about it.) She said to give you her love . . . and she meant it. She truly was concerned. Helen Brodkey asked for your address in London so she could write. Both Helen and Dor were very much concerned when I told them you were in the hospital. I know you feel about "cards" the same way I do—but I think you are going to get a few from Omaha. (Sorry about that. I can't help it.)

Gotta go soak . . . so L and K to you and Zoon . . . and Crick if she's still there . . .

Nonno

P.S. I had not heard from Popo since the Minneapolis thing. I am sure she was too ashamed to write. Anyway . . . Dub told her about you and she called me to see how you were. When I told her she said, "Give Margo my love. It may not mean anything to <u>her</u> but it means an awful lot to me."

Actually she is not a bad sort . . . really. She has had a rotten year because I have beat her brains out. The publicity because of my moving to the <u>Tribune</u> and the contest . . . nothing has generated such interest in the newspaper business for years . . . and it goes on and on. First I move into the <u>Chicago Tribune</u> and they put her in the comic section. . . . And then I move into the <u>Los Angeles Times</u> which is her parent paper. Next—I get invited to speak to the Middle Management group of the <u>L.A. Times</u> . . . an audience she would LOVE to have. . . . Next I show up at Malcolm Forbes's party of the Century and appear in <u>People Magazine</u> with [W.]. It goes on and on. . . . I can understand her hostility and anger. The competitiveness will never end. She will never be comfortable with me. And now she <u>knows</u> I have her beat. I really do understand it and am not bothered by her "dirty tricks." She just couldn't face having me at the Phillips party and did what she had to do to keep me from being there. She must have been plenty tortured to have gone so far . . . it was irrational . . . and I feel sorry for her because I know that she is kicking herself for having been so foolish. The worst agony is not what people do TO us, but what we do to ourselves. Enough of this . . . already. Good night, Irene.

L + K to Zoon and you—again
Nonno

[SUMMER 1987]
WEDNESDAY

Dearest Mugsie:

It took me until now to get my act together and thank you and Ken for the warmest hospitality ever. I love sharing your little nest and was so glad to get your letter of joy about the Eppie Duck. Also, it's lovely to know I have a standing invitation to lay my blonde head (with the gray roots) on a pillow in "My" room at [my apartment in Cambridge].

Wanna hear a killer? My sis must be losing her grip. As you know, the <u>L.A. Times</u> is a great star in my crown. Recently, I was invited to speak for the <u>L.A. Times</u> middle-management group . . . a very good audience for me, need I say . . . several hundred people who are the real working stiffs at the <u>L.A. Times</u>. I'm scheduled there next week. Well . . . Kathy heard this morning from the guy in charge of the program that Popo called them up, her hair on fire . . . furious that they had invited me to speak when SHE has been in their paper for years and lives right in L.A. (Actually I was sure she had spoken for that group but apparently she has not.) The girl must be off her rocker to have made such a call. It is probably all over the paper and will do her no good. It also gives a new life to the rumors that we are feuding and bitterly competitive. Such crap does neither of us any good.

. . .

This is it for now. Write when you have something to say . . . and I will continue to write even if I have nothing to say . . . as always.

Love to you and Zoon . . . and the cows and Farmer Wing or Dingaling [Twing], whatever his name is. . . . This letter (?) is going to Connecticut.

Enclosed are the stickers you asked for. How about getting more made with your new address?

XXXXX's . . .
Nonno

———————— ⌘ ————————

[SEPTEMBER 17, 1987]
BOCA RATON HOTEL AND CLUB
BOCA RATON, FL.
WEDNESDAY

Dear Margo:

I'm in the back of one of those huge limos—in Boca Raton, heading for the airport after making a speech to the Illinois Savings Institute. About 1,000 loan sharks and their wives. Great audience.

It's hot as hell down here—and raining in Chicago. The sheep is in the meadow and the cow's in the corn. You are in Connecticut, but this letter is going to Cambridge.

Your last phone call was <u>the best</u> ever! To hear you say, "I feel terrific" is worth the world to me. I know you've been schlepping for several months and it has been a real effort, but you didn't complain. Thank the good Lord for the English doctors. So now Madame Bovary has gotten rid of that lousy ovary, life should be great again.

Be sure to let me know when <u>Strange Interlude</u> airs. I'm sure there will be some promotion but I want a little advance notice so I can set the tape.

Is Ken a "visiting professor"—"a visiting instructor"—a "professor"—an "instructor"—or what? [W.] asked and I didn't know. No matter what the title, I know he's going to make a great place for himself on that campus. What a lovely place to be! I've always loved

Boston—and it <u>is</u> the cradle of true intellectuality. Did you ever think when you went to Brandeis that you would be <u>living</u> there?

I plan to go to Notre Dame this weekend for a football game—actually I'm going to see Ted. I don't even know who Notre Dame is playing! They have a great new coach (Lou Holtz)—and he's going to do a terrific job. Notre Dame did poorly under Terry Brennan. There was a lot of pressure on Ted to can Terry but he refused to do it. (Actually, he was hoping Terry would quit—but he didn't.) So, the once great football school was looking pathetic for five years.

What do you think of the Bears?!!! I had to go to a dinner for Helmet [*sic*] Schmidt so I got home just in time to see only the last half of the game, but it was a thriller!!!! As you know, they beat the Giants 34 to 17 in one of the most exciting games <u>ever</u>! McKinnon ran <u>93 yards</u> for a touchdown and Mike Tomczak proved that the Bears <u>can</u> win without McMahon. I was never very

much interested in football but the
Bears made a real fan out of me. It all
started when Mike McCaskey came to
town. Mike and [W.] taught together at
Harvard many years ago and have been
good friends for a long time. Mike is
married to a nifty lady—Nancy—and
[W.] and I have "double-dated" with
them several times. Great company.

. . .

Nonno

———————— ∞ ————————

*The joke about "Kathy's call" was that she had
instructions from Mother to "call Margo" should
Mother ever start to seem wacky.*

[OCTOBER 12, 1987]

Dear Margo:
   You are in New York and I am going to
Orlando tomorrow . . . back Tuesday.
   [W.] was in Cincinnati yesterday, back
tonight. Tomorrow he goes to Monterey.
And Gorbachev is in Moscow and
Helmut Schmidt is in Berlin and Dong

Chou Ping is in Beijing and they are just about to take me to Cherokee.

I knew this work would get me sooner or later . . . and now it has happened. Don't wait for Kathy's call. I am telling you myself. I have wigged out.

Love to you and Zoon,
Cell 23

———————— ⌘ ————————

Don Michael was the managing editor when I was at the Chicago Daily-News. *We started out with a prickly relationship, largely due to my spelling. (It was he who memo'd the editor-in-chief, who was my editor: "Tell this girl to use a dictionary.") We ended up great friends.*

Mother was reporting on Adam and Cricket visiting her at a Los Angeles hotel. Kristin was Adam's ladyfriend at the time. He was then twenty-three. The film reference was that during one of his "time-outs" from Amherst he starred in a few movies.

My best guess regarding the welcome flowers from W. is that he and Mother had called it a day, so she didn't understand why he was sending flowers.

[MARCH 21, 1988]
TODAY IS FRIDAY—

Dear Margo:

I'm on the plane—from L.A. to Chicago. A most successful speaking engagement in Torrence—a suburb of Los Angeles. Don Michael and his wife came—and—as always, he sends his warm regards to his "star."

Seeing the "kinderlach" was <u>wonderful</u>. They look great—came on time and we had fun. They didn't want <u>anything</u> from room-service—instead, ate the fruit and macaroons and drank the bottled water and orange juice. Kristin is on a diet. (She looked great to me.) Adam biked in so he wore shorts and a T-shirt. He's very excited about the film. Also, I noticed that the kids are very respectful of me. Adam slipped and used the F word and quickly said, "Excuse me, Gram"—Cricket didn't smoke in front of me but the minute she got into the corridor, on the way out— she lit up. When she combs her hair (probably next October) God knows what she will find—maybe a couple of sparrows and a wren. But it was a great joy to see them and I'm so glad we got together.

When I checked into the Beverly Hilton I was greeted by a bouquet of beautiful roses. The card read—"Love—[W.]." I do think the guy has flipped. None of this makes any sense to me.

The food service starts in a few minutes so this is it for now. I'll sign off with L + K—

Nonno

————————————— ⁓❧⁓ —————————————

"The Washington bash" was the Gridiron dinner. The reference to Bill Farley reminds me that a few of us had named Mother "the private plane slut." As she got older, her preference was to fly in friends' planes as opposed to going commercial . . . and so she would often choose an escort to Gridiron whose accoutrements *were a tuxedo, a plane, and two pilots. I kidded her that she should update the old axiom to say, "A journey of a thousand miles begins with a private jet."*

The signature "Sister Mary Nonno" was a name Ken had given her to signify her optimism and positive outlook.

[MAY 27, 1988]

Mugsie:

I am between trips.

. . .

The Washington bash was a gas. We had a great time. Popo came up to me at the after-party (I had not seen her at the dinner at all. . . .) and she made a monkey face and hugged me. This was a signal that all was well. Meanwhile, Morton stiffened up when I went to greet him and he literally dragged Popo off. He really is hostile.

On the way to Washington I showed Bill Farley the Editor and Publisher ad and asked if he thought this was cause for her to stop talking to me. He said . . . "That is crazy . . . the two of you have the market locked up and she has no right to be mad because you out-polled her."

. . .

I received a lovely thank-you from Cricket for the birthday check. She is a darling girl and I know she's a great joy to you.

. . .

I am off to Houston tomorrow . . . then home a day and off to Nashville. Call when you feel like it . . . I'll be home after that.

Love,
Sister Mary Nonno

———————— ⟨∞⟩ ————————

"Playing Chicago" meant that, when we met, Ken was starring as "Dr. Dysart" in Equus.

"The Vassar event" was Cricket's graduation. She was the first—and only one—in our family to get a college degree. Mother didn't graduate, nor did I or my other two children . . . and Father never finished high school.

MAY 15, 1989
CHI./CONN.
MONDAY

Dear Margo:
I'm writing this on the plane—from Hartford to Chicago, to tell you I had a wonderful time in your country place. What a heavenly spot!

It was a real Mother's Day—being with my one and only chick and the big rooster that she fell into by sheer luck when he was "playing Chicago" twelve years ago.

I'll never forget one little thing he did. When you brought out that divine apple-pie and I had the chutzpah to ask if by chance you had anything so dangerous as vanilla ice-cream in the freezer, he slipped out the back door to go to the store and <u>buy</u> some! And, of course, taking me not only to the airport but to <u>the gate</u>—was wonderful! I'm sure he told you how I started to run off to the gate in exactly the wrong direction—& then, after he straightened me around, I tried to go to <u>Dallas</u>. Bless his heart. What a mensch.

. . .

I'm looking forward to the Vassar event—so this is it for now.

Lots of L&K—to one and all—

Sister Mary Nonno

This letter was on the occasion of the death of my aunt Dub, the second of the four girls. Aunt Helen was too ill to make the trip from Omaha.

JULY 4TH [1989]
AMERICAN FLIGHT 220
FROM L.A. TO CHICAGO
3:30 PM—

Dear Margo:

Your phone calls meant so much to me—and you'll never know what it meant to Aunt Helen.

. . .

I called Helen from the hotel, and she said, "Margo called and we had such a wonderful, warm conversation. So many warm memories. I loved talking to her."

Reaching out when people are in pain is a real "mitzvah"—and they never forget it. I know Helen must have been suffering terribly—not being able to go to her sister's funeral—they were very close—18 months apart, and even tho' they were very different, there was a lot of love there.

A death in the family makes you look at things in a different way. It makes you wish you had done more, and it also makes you want to do better by those who are living.

One thing this funeral did for me—I have never spent so much time with Roger and René [my aunt Dub's son and daughter-in-law]—and Bob and Ron—and I learned that they are wonderful, warm-hearted, first rate people. I have always had a tendency to be too critical of everybody. (I'm sure you got this trait from me, and it's not a good one.) We write people off in a hurry if we find things wrong—as if <u>we</u> are perfect.

Jeez, I didn't intend to go on like this—but I guess the dam burst. Enough already.

I'm signing off. This pen is running out. I've barely enough ink left to say—

I love you—
Nonno

The subject of this letter was Mother's response to my telling her I was seriously considering ending my then twelve-year marriage, finding it increasingly difficult to deal with an issue that seemed insoluble. Surprisingly few letters between us exist on this matter . . . the reason being that the subject was discussed mostly on the phone or during in-person visits. A large portion of this letter is excised because it spells out what she thought of the eligible men she knew (not much) and whom she identifies by name. Her purpose in so doing was to encourage me to try and stay in the marriage . . . her point being, I guess, that everybody had something wrong with them. Then there was her advice about what she thought I might do regarding the problem, which I have no wish to be specific about. She had great affection for Ken Howard for all of her life.

SEPTEMBER 27, 1989
CHI./CONN.
SATURDAY P.M.

Dearest J. Fred:
That was a loving and thoughtful call I received this morning—to let me know that "today is a better day. . . ." It lifted

my spirits about twenty stories and I actually began to chirp again. When things are tough for you, they are tough for me, too.

. . .

So, the message is—maybe it's best to hang in there with what you have . . . warts and all and give it every chance to shape up. You can always ship out, but doing so prematurely could be a mistake. A big one.

. . .

As I write this, I don't know if he is still there or what is going on. But I do hope you will make things comfortable. If you think maybe it's not fair that you should have to do so much bending, let me tell you this is the way it's been from the beginning of time. Women have always had to give more to get less. Personally I think it stinks but I can't change it.

I guess I am back to that old question . . . "Would your life be better with him or without him?" . . . and from these 71 year old eyes that don't miss much I have to say . . . <u>with</u> him . . . even though it might mean some separation from time to time. I really believe there is too much wonderful history to let it all go.

Call me when you can. I'll be home from Menningers on Wednesday . . . afternoon.

Love to you and Zoon,
Nonno

———————— ⟨✈⟩ ————————

To underscore my point about Mother rarely recognizing celebrities, I offer only the P.S. from this letter:

NOVEMBER 16, 1989

. . .

P.S. The affair in New York was great. Do you know who Karlie [*sic*] Simon is? I sat next to her and had never heard of her, but everyone in my office did. She's a darling girl . . . and very tall!

———————— ⟨✈⟩ ————————

Walter Annenberg and Mother were like girlfriends, in a way; they talked on the phone often, shared gossip, and had the same sense of humor. They also seemed to become increasingly deaf at the same rate, so the two of them on the phone was a high-decibel affair.

Her writing, "My hair FROZE," reminded me of an old Saturday Night Live *skit. Mother was famous, for some years, for a very lacquered hairdo with "wings." One night on SNL someone said the line, "Did you hear? Ann Landers fell down and broke her hair." I think it was this, along with my encouragement, that convinced her to finally change to an easier, more natural hairstyle.*

DECEMBER 26, 1989

Dear Mugsie:

I loved the clip about the couple who were fined several times for having a fist fight aboard a Continental Flight . . . and then they tangled with the crew.

As you wrote . . . "very dignified."

I sent it to Walter Annenberg. He has a weird sense of humor and loves this kind of stuff. You sent me another clip about some battling couples and he laughed his head off for days.

It's cold as hell here. My hair FROZE last night walking from Beth Janis's [daughter of an escort] house . . . I was some sight when I got home. . . . It was only 3 blocks and I was sure it would be no problem . . . of course there were no taxis . . . Xmas night . . . and Joe [her chauffeur] is in San Antonio for the holidays (my holiday gift). Next year I think I'll keep him here for Xmas and give him Ground Hog day off.

We'll talk soon, Shirl.

Nonno

⸺⁂⸺

JANUARY 22, 1990
CHI./CONN.
SATURDAY

Dear Margo:

Back from St. Louis where I had a great time.

I spoke at a Seminar for Working Women . . . really middle-America.

They call it "Survival for Working Women" and they surely are heroic ... many of them holding down two jobs and trying to raise kids without a husband ... and we think WE have it rough?

...

All is well ... I am too damned busy and don't know what to do about it. I just have to start saying no to a few things, but it's tough because I want to go every place and do everything ... don't want to miss anything. Am I crazy? Please don't answer that.

Now about the question ... should you invite [—] and [—] [to my 50th birthday party in Chicago]?

I say ... it's always best, when in doubt, to err on the side of generosity. In this case I don't think it would be a mistake. If they accept, they can't hurt the party—and if you <u>don't</u> invite them ... and they find out there was a party, they would be crushed ... and you would never be able to make it right. Ever. I am sure you'd feel guilty.

So there is my "professional"

opinion . . . and it is worth what you paid for it.

I send lots of love,

Nonno

Regarding the annual Berkshire-Hathaway stockholders' meeting (in Omaha), Mother always went if she was free—being very fond of both Warren and Susie Buffet—and being a stockholder. She once told me some words of wisdom from Chairman Warren that had me convulsed with laughter. It was something he had said with which she totally concurred: "If any problem can be solved with money, it is not a problem." I said, "Mother, WARREN BUFFET is saying this!" She didn't get the joke.

May 3 [1990]
Chi./Camb.
Thursday

Dear Shirl Your Own Self:

I just got a real load of great garbage from you and hasten to reply. I have been running around the country like a real bum ... Palm Springs ... home for ten minutes and then off to Omaha. Meanwhile, the desk is groaning under the weight of the work (undone, of course) and I am up to my hocks in notes that say "urgent" and "must do immediately." Ah klog.

Thanks for the "mother pile." I loved it. I don't know where to send this letter ... Cambridge or Connecticut but I'll either figure it out or give you a call to make sure. Meanwhile that 1986 letter from Barnett Singer was fascinating. I think this is the first time I have seen it ... altho' it does seem vaguely familiar ... that part about the imitator and the original rings a bell. He sounds like a very insightful and interesting guy as well as a real Margo fan. I wonder what kind of a guy he is. But ... one must not get involved with the fans ... a cardinal rule of survival.

. . .

I haven't even told you about the Omaha trip ... Berkshire-Hathaway stockholders meeting and dinner in

Lincoln . . . via mini-bus . . . guest of Warren Buffet and Kay Orr, a Republican dolly who has a good figure and no brains.

Well . . . this is it for now. I'll have Kathy call you tomorrow and find out where to send this. Until then . . . love you, baby . . . write when you can and so will I.

Nonno

———————— ⌘ ————————

I have no recollection of the vacation or who the other "boy" would have been, in addition to Adam, who was then twenty-five.

[JULY 11, 1990]
TUESDAY NIGHT

Dearest Mugsie:

You are now back from your vacation on the French Riviera . . . or at least . . . it cost as much. You were nice to give the kids such a treat but I still think you should have said something to the boys who had two appetizers and everything on the menu they thought might be tasty. Actually, that is nothing but pigishness and you shouldn't have stood for it. You can be certain they would not have ordered like that if THEY were paying for it.

No time for a letter. I am drowning in work. . . . Your mother has turned into quite a party animal and she is paying the price. So—this is it for now, tochter miner . . . (no relation to Asia Minor) . . . and as you can see I am getting punchy . . . no relation to Sulzberger. Call the wagon . . . your mother has gone around the bend.

L and K,
Nonn

Part Four: Cambridge

INTRODUCTION

In 1991, after fourteen years, Ken Howard and I separated, with great sadness. Wanting to see deciduous trees, I left California and moved to Cambridge, Massachusetts. There, after six years, I met and eventually married a man my mother adored, as I did—and still do. A Boston couple, friends of my parents, made the introductions. And it was, coincidentally, about the time I moved to Massachusetts—thirty-three years into our correspondence—that the frequency of Mother's letters diminished, and most of the letters were faxes. Though she was a miracle of energy and good looks even into her seventies, the machinery was starting to wind down. As she casually writes to me, in a noncomplaining but portentous way, the column is taking more out of her and requiring more time.

The aging process was as much a surprise to her as it was to me. We were both so used to the vitality and energy with which she lived her life, we unrealistically imagined things would continue that way until the end. My dear mother was not interested in getting old. *Being* old, perhaps . . . but not getting old. This was the willful, power-player part of her. She assumed—because she exercised faithfully, did not drink or smoke, and kept her mind active—that she could protect the machinery from the depredation that happened to other people her age. She did not want to go gentle into that good night. If truth be told, her wish would have been for there to *be* no night.

By the time Mother reached her mid-seventies things were decelerating. Most of her close friends had died. The prospect of a rewarding second marriage was no longer viable. No new challenges remained. Having built the most widely syndicated text column in newspaper history, the professional part of her life was complete but static. Newspaper economics, in fact, were such that many two-paper towns were down to one.

Though I never heard a word about it from her, Mother was dealing with health issues. And so we played a game: that things were as they had always been. We pretended she was operating with her same old vigor and acuity; we pretended that her health was perfect. On visits, I would notice a frailer version than the time before, but of course this was never a subject for discussion. We were both aware, nevertheless, that things were winding down; we just didn't talk about it. Mother would have regarded such an admission as complaining and burdening me. She also would have seen it as ceding her position as the one with the authority. The elephant in the room was Mother's advancing age. Moreover, as she edged toward eighty, her judgment was not as shrewd, across the board, as it had been. And when she did become eighty, she finally seemed old. But her letters, as you can see, were meant to be gay and upbeat—and so they were. Her wish, as it had been from the beginning, was to protect me, and her mantra was "No complaints."

We had journeyed a long way together and it

was hard for her to think about the end—and it was hard for me—so the best we could do was continue our mother-daughter dance of normalcy . . . and we did it with the written word.

———————— ⟨∽⟩ ————————

Derek Bok was then-president of Harvard. The dinner referred to was an event that he and I planned together to recognize Mother's gift to Harvard Medical School. The scholarship program she endowed was in honor of Bok's distinguished service to the university; and the medical school was dear to her heart because she had served on its Overseers Committee for twenty-one years, a record length of time. She wanted no note taken of her gift, but I persuaded her that the connection with the medical school had been a special one and therefore merited a celebration. She acquiesced, and so at lunch one day, in Harvard Square, President Bok and I planned a dinner . . . small, as such affairs go. Over a lifetime of Mother doing so many meaningful things for me, this turned out to have been one of the few things I was able to do for her. Many out-of-town friends flew in, and an undergraduate singing group—the Krokodiloes—

serenaded her with special material. Mother said afterward that she'd found it to be one of the truly special honors she had received. And this from a woman who'd been awarded thirty-six honorary degrees.

[FEBRUARY 25, 1991]

Dear Margo:

I think I had better be a bit more clear about what I want in regard to the Derek Bok dinner.

While I don't want Harvard to make any announcement that I am giving this gift, I think it would be perfectly appropriate for Derek Bok to tell the people at the dinner WHY he is honoring me . . . and to mention the amount would be fine.

. . .

No doubt a few lines about the dinner will appear in the <u>Harvard Gazette</u> or the <u>Crimson</u>, which would be fine with me . . . but I am NOT giving this to the <u>Boston</u> <u>Globe</u> or any other paper. This gift is not about publicity . . . it's really to honor Derek.

L and K, baby,
Nonno

—————————— ⁓⁕⁓ ——————————

*This particular wedding of Miss Taylor's was to
Larry Fortensky, a friend from rehab.*

*The beau of mine mentioned as getting "the deep 6"
was known to all my friends as "The Bad Boyfriend."
Mother found him so unsuitable that, when we got
back together, I did not have the heart to tell her.*

[OCTOBER 2, 1991]
SUNDAY NIGHT—

Hello, there, Shirl:

I'm on American #127, heading for
Seattle—to run my mouth for a Ladies
Club. I'll be home tomorrow night! I
can't think of an easier way to make 10
grand in less than 24 hours.

I took along your last two batches of
newspaper clippings—to read on the
plane. Please know how much I
appreciate them. You <u>do</u> pick the best
stuff—and even tho' I don't comment on
each and every one, I <u>do</u> enjoy them.

. . .

Liz Taylor's wedding is going to be a zoo. I was sure Popo would be invited. They serve on the AIDS board together, and Liz <u>never</u> misses a meeting. But—I was wrong. Popo has <u>not</u> been invited. Via fax, she informed me that the wedding is going to be a "media event" and that's the way Liz wants it.

I spoke with Jennifer [Jones] Simon yesterday and I know she and Liz are pretty good friends. Well—she wasn't invited either. Jennifer said, when I asked her why Liz was marrying this guy, "She hasn't made a film in ages and she needs to keep her name before the public, so she sells that perfume for the 'exposure,' and the wedding is sure to be a colossal media event." I guess Jennifer is right.

I've written two solid pages of nothing but drivel. For shame.

The plane is getting a bit bumpy so I may sign off in a bit if things don't calm down.

. . .

Need I tell you, I'm mighty pleased

that you gave [—] the deep 6. He's really into <u>control</u>, <u>power</u> and game-playing. One thing, I can't help but factor in— you met him thru Coleman. That's a bit of a minus for starters.

Abra will be visiting me next weekend. We're having dinner at The Palm—her idea. It's good for her to get away from Maxwell and Chris [her elder son and her husband] for a night. She really is a devoted Mother.

I'm signing off, Shirl—and will probably talk to you before you get this—but, maybe not. I head for Dallas almost immediately.

Am I nuts? Don't answer that!

Love you, Doll—
Nonno

Rosie Phillips (Mrs. Jay Phillips) is Popo's mother-in-law, a remarkable woman whom Mother loved. She was very direct, often unintentionally funny, and coined phrases without thinking they were anything special.

[SEPTEMBER 4, 1992]
WEDNESDAY NITE

Dear Lolly Baby:

This is hardly worth the postage but I am sending it anyway.

My desk is a mess and I trying to straighten it out before animal life forms. Jeee-zus . . . I don't know where all this stuff comes from. I gotta get unwound from some of the organizations and social stuff that seems to take over my life.

I got to Washington for the Kennedy Center affair where Michael Feinstein is playing . . . and then to the White House. It was lovely of him to invite me to be his date. I hope Bush doesn't throw up in the receiving line.

I will call soon . . . meanwhile, I had a nice chat with Cricket who seems very up and happy.

L and K . . .
Nonno

P.S. IF YOU GET THE <u>N.Y. TIMES</u> I AM SURE YOU SAW THIS STORY. THE SIGHT OF IT BROUGHT HOME TO ME

HOW I HAVE INFLUENCED AMERICAN CULTURE . . . AND IMPACTED ON THE LANGUAGE.

"WAKE UP AND SMELL THE COFFEE" FIRST APPEARED IN MY COLUMN MANY YEARS AGO . . . AND MANY TIMES SINCE.

I GOT IT FROM ROSIE PHILLIPS. SHE USED TO SAY . . . "JAY . . . WAKE UP AND SMELL THE COFFEE. . . ." AND I THOUGHT IT WAS VERY FUNNY.

I'LL BET THE HEADLINE WRITER AT THE <u>N.Y. TIMES</u> HAS NO IDEA WHERE THE LINE CAME FROM.

HO HO . . . TEE HEE . . . WHAT FUN . . .

L AND K . . .
NONNO

Mother and Joseph Cardinal Bernardin forged an unusual and warm friendship when he came to Chicago. She thought him a gentle, wise, and spiritual man. They would visit over late afternoon tea. She was deeply aggrieved by the false molestation accusation made against him—later recanted—and was prepared to put her reputation on the line as a character reference, should it become necessary, in a court of law. It was not necessary.

NOVEMBER 12, 1993

Dear Margo:
Popo has faxed me three times already this morning about Cardinal Bernardin. She seems convinced that he is guilty. This is a copy of the fax I just sent to her:

Bella, Bella:
You asked why a kid would make up such a damned tale. Ten million dollars—that's why. This Diocese, unfortunately, has had several priests who were found guilty of child molestation and the Church has paid off millions in litigation and damages.

Some smart lawyer decided this was an easy way to make a name for himself, plus a few million dollars.

This False Memory Syndrome has been beaten to death and in my opinion there are a great many therapists in this country who have encouraged patients to make these charges because it's certainly an easy out. Who could prove anything?

I have got a ton of work to do this weekend and am not stirring from the old plantation. The weather forecast is rain, rain, rain and flooding, and I am thrilled that I don't have to go anyplace. I hope you are in for the weekend, too.

Let me hear from you soonest.

L & K,
The Ep

P.S. I just spoke with the Cardinal two minutes ago and told him that I would be happy to be a character witness. If this means a trip to Cincinnati—I will go.

JUNE 24, 1995

[ON WHITE HOUSE STATIONERY, POSTMARKED CHICAGO]

Dear Margo:

Well—here is your very own Nonno—in the Lincoln bedroom of the Whitehouse.

When I phoned and told you where I was, you said, "Steal a towel." I wouldn't dare—but I <u>did</u> load up on the stationery.

And—I did have a <u>marvelous</u> time. The Clintons are very easy to be with—and this place is spectacular. The original manuscript of the Gettysburg Address is framed and hanging on the wall.

We'll talk soon and I'll fill you in on the details.

Lots of L & K—
Y. M.

P.S. I was seated next to Colin Powell at the Women in the Military function. He <u>is</u> a honey—and would be a formidable opponent if he should decide to run.

[The noticeable absence of letters and faxes from this period—more than a year—is because the correspondence from this time is either not of general interest or it is too personal.]

———————————— ❦ ————————————

A few days after Bernardin's death, Father Velo brought Mother a keepsake of the Cardinal's: a red porcelain bird—a cardinal—perched on a branch. It was one of her treasures and she placed it in her living room. Because she loved it, it is one of her things that is now with me.

NOVEMBER 14, 1996

Dear Margo:

It's a very sad day in Chicago and my heart is heavy. Our dear Cardinal Bernardin passed away.

I received a phone call at about 12:15 last night from Father Ken Velo, who is the Cardinal's right hand and a great friend of mine, and he said—The Cardinal is sinking fast. Would you like to come over? We'll send a car for you right away. I said I'll be down in the lobby in 5 minutes. Incidentally, the Cardinal's residence is about 5 minutes from me. I threw on some clothes, ran downstairs and was driven over to the Cardinal's home.

There was media all over the place, so they sneaked me in the back door. I went upstairs and there were 3 or 4 bishops around the bed—people I knew, long-time friends—and there was that darling Joe, eyes closed, looking as though he was sleeping very peacefully. I held his hand and kissed him on his forehead, and his face was quite warm. I stayed about 20 minutes, just holding his hand and reminiscing with a few of the bishops who knew him so well.

After I left, I tried to work, but of course, it was useless—so I turned on the T.V. just before crawling into bed, and the word was—Cardinal Bernardin passed away at 1:35. He was one of the sweetest people I have ever met—so beloved by everyone in this town—quite a departure from the last Cardinal, who got into a few scandals, you may remember. His name was John Cody.

I had a dinner date tonight which I

cancelled. I sure as hell don't feel like going out.

More later. So sorry this is such a downer.

L & K,
Nonno

———————— ⌘ ————————

The following fax came in response to one I had sent asking whether everything was all right, because Mother sounded so frazzled about her work. (In addition to writing back and forth, we spent a great deal of time on the phone.)

[JANUARY 5, 1997]

SHIRL:

EVERYTHING IS FINE BUT I DON'T THINK YOU REALIZE HOW DEMANDING IT IS AND HOW IMPERATIVE THAT I KEEP THE QUALITY UP. IF YOU READ POPO'S COLUMN YOU WILL SEE THAT SHE HAS AT LEAST FOUR VERY MEDIOCRE (OR POOR) COLUMNS OUT OF SEVEN.

THE ONLY THING THAT KEEPS HER
GOING IS THAT THE PAPERS NEED
SOMETHING TO COMPETE WITH ME.

I AM VERY HARD ON MYSELF AND
REFUSE TO RUN LETTERS THAT I
FEEL ARE MEDIOCRE. SOME NIGHTS I
WILL READ 500 LETTERS BEFORE I
FIND ONE THAT I THINK IS GOOD
ENOUGH TO PRINT. AND THEN I'LL
HIT A HOT BATCH AND FIND FOUR IN
A ROW.

I AM CONFIDENT THAT THERE IS
NOBODY AROUND WHO CAN TURN
OUT AS GOOD AN ADVICE COLUMN
AS MINE BUT IT TAKES ONE
HELLUVA LOT OF ENERGY. I JUST
THANK GOD THAT I HAVE IT.

LOVE YOU,
Y.M.

The mention of the "Jeanne participation" refers to Popo's daughter—my cousin Jeanne—who claimed she had been writing "Dear Abby" since the late '80s. She stated this on Larry King Live *in June of 2002. Until this public admission (which came after my mother's death) it had only been an educated guess on the part of some people that Jeannie had taken over from Popo. The reason was Popo's increasing mental impairment, which, of course, concerned Mother on many levels. For all the ambivalence they had lived with, rational discussion had kept them tethered to their shared history. It was frightening to Mother that Popo was fading off into what was clearly Alzheimer's because the "wiring" is often the same in identical twins. And Mother, by this time—at eighty—was experiencing problems with memory. In addition, Mother's judgment was not as keen as it had been. She functioned well much of the time, but there was some "slippage," as she called it, of which she was aware. Mother's increasing deafness did not help matters, because it often precluded her from hearing what was said . . . thereby making her responses sometimes seem a little off. Mother and Popo were not aging in the same way; Mother did not have*

Alzheimer's, as was confirmed after her death . . . but she was getting old, with the probable beginnings of senility. The fabulous days were behind her; the main thing linking the past to the present was her work.

"The Heart Doc" (a cardiac surgeon) is Ron Weintraub, who was my then beau, later my husband. Mother could not have been more pleased. That I would make a brilliant match in middle age astonished both of us . . . although my lucky number had always been 4.

JULY 18, 1998

Dear Lolly Baby:

Your note with the Popo interview says that Popo looks O.K. and sounds rational. The "Jeanne participation" is a very old story.

Popo and Jeanne read every interview I have ever given, and the answers SHE gives are identical to mine. They must keep a file and Popo reviews my responses before she gives an interview. That piece in <u>People</u> magazine was a fine example.

Her faxes to me indicate that she is quite fogged up. There is rarely anything original. It's almost always a few words written on the bottom of my faxes . . . or a picture of monkies. I cannot remember the last time she initiated a fax to me on her own.

. . .

I don't know if you read her column but I do every day and it is obvious to me that <u>she</u> reads <u>mine</u> very carefully . . . and many of her responses are patterned after mine. Of course it annoys me a lot but there is nothing I can do about any of this.

. . .

I gotta go to sleep. It's 1:35 . . . usually I cash in my chips at 2 A.M. but I'm going night-night early . . . Love you . . . and XX to the Heart Doc.

Nonno

MARCH 1, 1999

Dear Margo:

You labeled my response to "R.N. in Alberta" inadequate. Actually, the Boston Globe butchered it to the point that it almost made no sense. I am sending you the original so you can see what they did to it.

Meanwhile, there is nothing I can do when a paper performs this sort of mutilation, but I must say, I don't know of any other paper in the country that does the butchering job that takes place at the Boston Globe. Please—don't complain on my behalf—let it alone. Third party interference can be hazardous.

L & K,
Y.M.

———————————⌘———————————

"Prudy" or "Prudie" is the Dear Prudence column I write for the online magazine Slate. *Mike Kinsley, my editor at the* New Republic *some years earlier, had been asked by Bill Gates to create an "e-zine." That I would wind up doing their advice column was total harmonic convergence. I had not even been writing for*

a couple of years. If I'd needed to put down "occupation" on a form, the honest answer, at that time, would have been, "Entertaining myself." And right about then, the Heart Doc had encouraged me to go back to work. Factor in that Kinsley was the best in the business, everything happened on e-mail, Herb Stein (the creator of "Dear Prudence") had given it up—and it all seemed quite right. Kinsley knew I had said no to writing advice my whole professional life . . . thirty years . . . but the timing and the Internet were the right combination. Mother thought "Prudie" was terrific, which greatly pleased me. Though I had, years earlier, declined to carry on the Ann Landers name, my once-a-week column for Slate *felt just right. Surprisingly, I loved giving advice.*

[SEPTEMBER 6, 1999]

DEAREST LOLLY B:
WE JUST SPOKE A WHILE AGO, AND IT'S JOY TO THIS JEWISH MOTHER'S HEART TO HEAR YOU CHIRPING AWAY . . . SO HAPPY WITH YOUR HEART DOC, MAKING TRAVEL PLANS AND MEETING HIS FRIENDS. I

CONTINUE TO <u>LOVE</u> PRUDY WHO SEEMS TO BE TAILOR-MADE FOR YOU. SHE IS NOT TOO DEMANDING . . . AND GIVES YOU AN OPPORTUNITY TO EXERCISE YOUR CONSIDERABLE TALENT FOR EXPRESSING YOURSELF WHILE GIVING REALLY SOUND ADVICE.

I HAVE A TON OF WORK ON MY DESK . . . AND AM BEAVERING AWAY . . . IF YOU WILL PARDON THE EXPRESSION. IT IS AMAZING TO ME THAT AFTER ALL THESE YEARS . . . LIKE NEARLY 44 . . . I STILL LOVE THIS WORK AND AM STILL PRETTY DARNED GOOD AT IT . . . SAYS SHE, IMMODESTLY.

SO NOW I DIG IN . . . AND AWAIT THE NEXT PRUDIE WITH JOY.

LOVE TO YOU AND MR. WONDERFUL,
LOLLY SR.
AKA SHIRLEY ANN

"Dr. Pussycat" was the name by which the Heart Doc was known to Prudie's readers. It was actually my name for him before I went to work for Slate. Given that cardiac surgery is such a macho specialty (both for the intensity and length of the operations) that nickname was an anomaly, to say the least.

Appended to this letter was the following note from me: "Shirl—this is kind of funny. Your old pal, Ashley Montague, just died at 94. His name had been Israel Aronberg!!"

NOVEMBER 29, 1999]

Lolly:

He wasn't exactly my "pal." I pegged him as a phony early on. Wouldn't you say from "Israel Aronberg" to "Ashley Montague" is quite a stretch?

When I first met him he bragged about having scored with Eartha Kitt. That didn't sit well with me.

I've got a ton of work to do tonight— but had a <u>great</u> pizza for dinner so I'm a happy camper.

Kiss Dr. Pussycat for me and have an X for yourself.

Shirley Ann

Myles is Dr. Myles Sheehan, a Jesuit gerontologist. When Mother had rounded the bend of eighty, I wanted her to have this kind of specialist. Ron asked the head of gerontology at one of the Harvard hospitals if there was anyone she had trained and thought well of who was practicing in Chicago. The head of gerontology said Myles Sheehan. This turned out to be serendipitous because when my husband had been a young attending, Myles was a medical resident. He had not been on the surgical service, of course, but Ron remembered him for the kind and careful doctor he had been. The four of us together—Mother, Myles, the Heart Doc, and I— dealt with the last leg of the old girl's journey. I have no doubt that if Ron had not been a physician and selected the doctor himself, Mother would have told me to mind my own business and would have refused to see a specialist. As it was, she referred to Myles as "the nutritionist," food being more pleasant for her to contemplate than aging.

[FEBRUARY 11, 2000]

Dearest LB—

I like Myles a <u>lot</u>. I told him about all the junk I eat, thinking he would tell me to quit it. But, he did no such thing. He said I was in excellent shape, extraordinary for my age, and to just keep on doing whatever it is I'm doing. He was impressed that I exercise every morning and walk around the apt a lot. My vampire hours didn't faze him. He said, "If it works for you—fine." I like his style.

I <u>love</u> the way you have dinner parties—so effortless—way to go, girl!! (Ron's influence, again.)

<u>Love</u> your faxes—Keep 'em coming.

XXXXXXXX
XX for H.D.
Shirley Ann

The fact that Carly Fiorina is actually the head of Hewlett-Packard should not be construed as an example of Mother being fogged up. In point of fact, she had been making these confused identity mistakes for many years—and Ms. Fiorina, like Kurt Vonnegut, found it easier to play along rather than correct her.

[APRIL 17, 2000]

LB:

I just got back from the Econ. [Economic] Club dinner. The speaker was Carly Fiorina, head of Fed. Express. (A woman.) I saw her in the ladies room before she spoke and told her Fed Ex "misplaced" a <u>very</u> valuable book on its way to me. She asked from where was it sent. I told her Boston. The response was—"That's one of our worst trouble spots." And she added—"It would have to happen to <u>you</u>—<u>of all people</u>—our worst nightmare." I told her not to worry—that I wouldn't put it in the column.

And now I hit the desk which is oy vay.

XXXX

Shirley A.

———————————⟨✠⟩———————————

[MAY 8, 2000]

Dear LB:

I have a <u>ton</u> of mail to read and a column to put together. Thank God for the work. It still fascinates me—after 45 years. Amazing!

Give the H.D. a hug from me. As I told you, if anything happens to the relationship, I'm keeping <u>him</u> and throwing you out.

XX Shirl

In the following letter Mother speaks of "this trauma," and traumatic it was. She and I were having a go-round the likes of which we had never had before. An ongoing serious disagreement was uncharacteristic for us, and was, I believe, made worse by her deteriorating condition. That it took a while to cool was most unusual in our relationship. Her analogy of 6's and 9's was apt; what I saw as being protective of her she saw as interference.

Mother's mentioning my cooking was a set piece with us. She would phone, often at dinnertime, and ask what I was warming, or having sent in. I had blown my cover as a traditional housewife by disclosing that the doctor and I subsisted on take-out as well as dinners delivered by a woman who cooked.

[JULY 9, 2000]

Dear L.B.:

We are back, once more to the 6 and the 9 . . . both looking at the same numbers, but seeing them from opposite sides of the table. You are sure it's a 6 . . . I am sure it's a 9.

This is not going to break up our loving relationship which I have cherished for so many years. Nothing can change the way I feel about you. You have been a loving daughter and have proven it in so many ways. You cannot imagine the joy your relationship with the H.D. has brought to me. A real mensch. Someone to share your life . . . travel with and . . . order carry-out for . . . (I was going to say "cook for"). Ron is the answer to my prayers. I pray for his good health . . . and for yours . . . and hope you two will enjoy your golden years together.

Right now I am trying to complete a week of copy and am on deadline . . . thanks to the birthday celebrations . . . and the dozens of thank-you notes I have had to write. You and I . . . the two sad apes are going to cheer up and keep putting one foot in front of the other. There is no other way. I have gotten thru three divorces with you, and they were a piece of cake compared to this trauma . . . so onward and upward, Tochter Miner. I love you more than you will ever know.

The Senior Shirley

P.S. I appreciate your criticizing my column. Your evaluation . . . an eye from another generation is extremely appreciated. Please keep the comments coming.

───────── ⌘ ─────────

[OCTOBER 17, 2000]

L.B.:

Yes—indeed! Yesterday was my 45th Anniversary as Ann Landers. Rick Newcombe [head of her syndicate] and I had dinner together at Ambria & we pigged out on Beluga caviar—(Double helpings!)

He presented me with a sterling silver menorah!! Engraved etc. etc. Now I will put it in the closet with my brass menorah.

<u>People Mag.</u> called about the piece they are doing on you. <u>Very nice</u>.

Gotta get moving!!

L & K,
Shirley

This letter came in response to a clipping I had sent her reporting that the Menninger Clinic was moving to the Baylor College of Medicine, in Houston.

[NOVEMBER 17, 2000]

LB:

Thanks for this—I had not heard one word about it.

So much for keeping former Trustees informed.

I fear this is curtains for Menningers. The really great ones (Bill & Will) are long gone, and the sons, Walt and "Jr." (Roy?) aren't able to carry the flag.

Last I heard Roy & Bea (second wife) were starting a Menninger Institute in Los Angeles. (Lotsa luck to them.) The current generation has never heard of the Menningers, and the present batch of shrinks have shrunk . . .

This will be faxed tomorrow AM because it's 10:40 and I don't want to awaken you and the Beloved.

XXXX
Shirley Ann

─────────── ⌇✖⌇ ───────────

Mother's investment advice was in response to my having said I was contemplating getting out of the market. Her mention of State Street Bank was interesting because I had bought that stock, and a few others, because of something she'd taught me years earlier: if you know a CEO socially, think well of him, and his stock is in good shape—get some. Following this criterion, I got us both into State Street Corp. stock once I'd met Marshall Carter, their chairman . . . just as decades earlier she had met Sol Linowitz and bought Xerox.

Mention of going west to do my "gig" referred to a television show I was going to tape in Los Angeles. The old girl knew whereof she spoke. She had been doing television since 1956 when she took Ann Landers public as a contestant on the original What's My Line?

[DECEMBER 2, 2000]

Dear Lolly B:

I have done very well in the market for a long time and learned that you can never make any real money by going in and out of stocks. I pick what I perceive to be good for the long haul and stay with 'em.

The Republicans are <u>not</u> good for the market—and I wouldn't put another dime in. I'm just hanging on to what I have—<u>especially</u> Berkshire-Hathaway (Warren Buffet) and Microsoft (Bill Gates)—and of course—State Street (Thank yooooou)—

When you go west to do your gig— remember <u>BE NATURAL</u>—as if you were speaking to one person. And don't try any new make-up or hair-styles, and low-ball the jewelry. I'm sure you will do <u>very well</u>.

XXXX to the Beloved—
Shirley A.

[DECEMBER 8, 2000]

Dear LB:

I've been invited to the Whitehouse for a black tie dinner—Dec. 16—the <u>last</u> for me, I'm sure, because Bush sure as hell will not invite me, and Gore is not going to make it. Or—am I being prematurely pessimistic? RSVP—because you know everything.

XXX
Shirley Ann

I had written to Mother that a honcho at Slate *told me that "Prudie" was the only feature that brought in "Middle America."*

I figured out, after the fact, that the brevity of her faxes bespoke physical pain, which she kept from me— and almost everyone else—until it was no longer possible. Dr. Sheehan knew she was in serious difficulty a year before her multiple myeloma was confirmed. Mother kept delaying the final diagnostic tests, already knowing it was either multiple myeloma or spinal cancer. Her decision was to not treat either one. She said it was crazy, at her age, to go through chemo and radiation with no assurance of success.

Mother's inclination to hide health issues went back a long way with us. She never wanted me to worry, and I used to find out about an operation or an illness months, or even years, later. (Her traveling, or mine, often made this possible.) She felt any infirmity of hers would be very hard for me to handle. And conversely, she felt that my physical difficulties affected her—to the point where I was instructed, with each of my three pregnancies, not to have anyone call her to say I was in labor. "I only want a phone call," she said, "when there's a baby. There's no sense both of us having labor pains." It was this long-standing desire to protect me that also dictated the "schedule" for visiting her once she knew her illness was terminal. Ron and I were not allowed to roll in and out of Chicago at will. We were always invited, when she felt up to it, and never permitted to stay longer than two days. And during these visits Mother did her level best to be cheerful—or a reasonable facsimile thereof—as she tried to keep us afloat. Some people desperately wanted to say good-bye in person, but the answer was no. Mother said she simply did not have the strength, nor did she wish to deal with other people's emotions. Even with me she would plead, "No tears," only she said it in Yiddish. I asked whether she wanted to phone some friends around the country. She did not. Partly, Mother just didn't like good-byes, but her rationale likely had to do with something she told me when she knew the end was near. She said most of her life had been on a public stage; this part she wanted "just for us."

[FEBRUARY 10, 2001]

Dear L.B.:

HELL-LLL-O: "MIDDLE AMERICA" is where it's at for <u>both</u> of us—and don't forget it.

Most of the intellectuals who write to me are severely neurotic or 3/4 nuts. Give me "Middle America" any day of the week.

XXX
Shirley

April 6, 2001

Dear Margo:

I had dinner last night with Myles Sheehan. Myles recalls that he had a very sick patient and didn't know what to do with him. He was very concerned that the guy might be on his way out, so he called Dr. Weintraub at 3:00 a.m., received instructions, and then Dr. Weintraub said, "I am on my way to the hospital and should be there within a few minutes."

Myles said he then realized what a totally devoted physician Weintraub was.

Give him a hug for me and have one yourself.

Shirley Ann

———————— ⌘ ————————

Cricket, by this time a fourth-year medical student, was home in Brooklyn Heights on September 11, 2001. A doctor who lived in her building phoned to ask if she would go with her to Ground Zero. Without thinking about it, Cricket agreed. A police cruiser drove them into Manhattan, where Cricket worked for four days, mostly helping firemen rinse their eyes, and doing whatever was asked of her. Tragically, medical personnel did not have a lot to do at the site.

[SEPTEMBER 11, 2001]

CRICKET CALLED ME. SHE IS FINE . . . AND OF COURSE SHE WENT DOWN TO "HELP" AND SAID THERE WASN'T MUCH TO DO . . . THEY HAD A LOT OF PROFESSIONALS AND VOLUNTEERS. IT ALL SEEMS LIKE A BAD DREAM. TOMORROW THE PAPERS WILL BE FILLED WITH THE DETAILS . . .

I AM GOING TO BED NOW. . . . IT'S ONLY 2:15 . . . EARLY FOR ME . . . BUT I AM EXHAUSTED.

LOVE TO YOU AND DR. PUSSYCAT.

SHIRLEY ANN

[NOVEMBER 28, 2001]

I'm still far-crochen,* but tomorrow is sure to be better. <u>Love</u> the little one, who is soon to be blonde again.

xxxx to the Beloved. Dr. Myles said he's one of the "unforgettable teachers . . . so caring."

It's only 10:05 here now. I'll work till 11—then to bed with a great book by G.E.'s Jack Welch.

———————————— ⸎ ————————————

I had sent on a note from a woman friend of mine, in which she had written: "When I read your mother's column it reminds me of my mother. So much of what she says sounds just like her."

[DECEMBER 4, 2001]

Dear Lolly B.:

It's 1 AM (Chicago time) so this will be faxed by my office . . . in the morning.

I <u>love</u> it when a reader says I sound like her mother. It means I'm connecting.

—————

*"Far-crochen" means ailing; falling apart.

Love to Dr. Pussycat, too. I can't thank him enough for taking my homely kid off my hands.

xxxxxx
Shirley Ann

This note was written on her last Mother's Day, five weeks before Mother died. Ron and I had been to Chicago to see her a few days earlier. By this time we were married—though it had been extremely low-key . . . in our living room, just us and the rabbi and his wife. There was no formal announcement. I think perhaps we did this for Mother. She got such pleasure and comfort from our having made it legal, and she did, in fact, tell a few intimates that she could go peacefully, now, because she was leaving me in the care of Dr. Pussycat.

The end of this note tickled me because, sick as she was, she was still compulsive about trying to do the thoughtful thing. Or more precisely, trying to get me to do the thoughtful thing.

MAY 12, 2002

Dear Margo and Ron:

Your gorgeous double orchid plant arrived in wonderful condition, and it's one of the most elegant I've ever seen. What a beautiful way to say Happy Mother's Day.

It was a joy to see you and Ron together. Kathy Mitchell and Marcy both remarked on what a perfect fit you are. You were actually glowing like a new bride. And how smart not to have anything fancy or "social."

Phone often—which reminds me, the only glitch of the entire trip was you forgot to phone Sister Helen.

Love,
Your Mother

———————— ❧ ————————

My mother's final communication to me was written near the end of her life, but not seen by me until after she died. It was a note attached to the copy of her will she kept at home, and given to me by her accountant. Like so many of her letters to me, it was written by hand, in pencil, on yellow copy paper, with some words and lines crossed out. The scratched-out lines were from a poem called "Togetherness," which begins, "Death is nothing at all, I have only slipped away into the next room." She was apparently using that as an outline for her thoughts, because the crossed-out lines were from that poem, though not exact:

Without a trace of sorrow
Life means all that it ever meant
It is the same as it ever was
There is unbroken continuity
Why should I be out of mind because I am out of sight?
I am but waiting for you
Somewhere very near
Just around the corner

My life was full and rich. I was blessed in so many ways. I truly believe that God had his arms around me. He gave me a mission and the time and energy to fulfill that mission. I have been truly blessed.

I will live on through my daughter Margo, and through my grandchildren and their children, some not yet born. I haven't gone far away. Do not grieve for me. Be thankful for the years we had together. I lost my mother when I was 27. You had me a lot longer. We will surely meet again and enjoy eternity together.

Epilogue

My mother spent her last weeks trying to write her farewell column. It proved to be difficult for a number of reasons. The idea was tremendously sad for her; she was unsure what tack to take, and there was a little morphine added to this mix. After asking me for ideas about what should be said, she finally decided: "You do it."

Many people have asked why I did not continue as Ann Landers. Mother had in fact asked me in the 1970s—after I was established in the newspaper business—if I wanted to carry on the name when she was gone. I told her no. Advice was her big interest, not mine. She had a real sense of service. I did not. She was a high-energy workaholic personality; I was a good-time girl who never had an interest in having a big career. I also had no desire to morph into my mother. I preferred writing opinion and criticism . . . and my once-a-week "Prudie" was perfect for me. So the following message is what ran in her space—in all the papers that carried her—and it served as the very last Ann Landers column.

I write to you today in my mother's stead. She wanted to write her last column herself, but things did not work out that way. We talked about it, though, and she was quite clear about what she would have said. So I shall say it for her. She felt profoundly privileged to have been able to shed some light and offer guidance for forty-seven years . . . more than half her life. This column was her mission, her *raison d'etre,* and she worked on it, daily, almost until the end.

She believed she got as much sustenance from you, her readers, as you had gotten from her. The chance to come into your homes and into your lives meant the world to her. And she was convinced that if any one thing could serve as a solution to all manner of problems, it was kindness.

The more senior among you might remember when she announced that she and my father were parting after many years. In that shorter-than-usual column she asked her editors to leave a white space at the bottom, as a memorial to quite a good marriage that didn't make it to the finish line. I would ask her editors again, today, to leave a white space . . . this time in honor of a gutsy, old-school newspaper dame who believed there was no better job in all the world and who would, if she could have, wished you a fond and grateful farewell herself. And she wanted you to know that hers had been "a simply wonderful ride."

Margo Howard

Friends & Family

My Children:

Abra. My firstborn, whose primary occupation is that of superb wife and mother.

Adam. My middle child and only son is a filmmaker.

Cricket. Born Andrea, she has been called Cricket since she was six days old. Now she is "Dr. Cricket," a forensic pathologist.

"A.B., Mr." (Abraham Friedman). My grandfather, Mother's father, to whom she felt especially close.

Andreas, Dwayne. The chairman of Archer-Daniels-

Midland, he was a close friend and financial supporter of Hubert Humphrey, though he gave enormous amounts of money to both political parties.

Annenberg, Walter H. The publisher and philanthropist and his wife, Lenore, were social friends of Mother's.

Benton, Marjorie. Political activist and a close, loyal friend of my mother's in Chicago.

Brigham, Edna ("Blondie"). Mother's "girlfriend" of longest standing. They met in Eau Claire through Democratic politics, fought the Joe McCarthy wars together, and remained friends until the end of Mother's life.

Brodkey, Bob. Aunt Helen's second son.

Brodkey, Helen. Mother's eldest sister, who had a matriarchal role in the family; she was also called Ken and Sister Kenny.

Brodkey, Ron. My cousin, Aunt Helen's first son.

Buchwald, Anne. The late wife of Art Buchwald and one of Mother's beloved girlfriends.

Buchwald, Art. The humorist and fellow syndicated columnist, with whom Mother had been friends for many decades. He always teased her about being an object of desire for many men— himself included.

Buckley, William F. The well-known Republican

commentator, with whom Mother occasionally appeared on panels and with whom she almost always tangled.

Buffett, Warren. The business giant who, with his wife, Susie, were longtime friends of Mother's. When not committed elsewhere, Mother used to love to go to the Berkshire-Hathaway shareholder meetings in Omaha.

Carter, James E. ("Jimmy"). The Democratic politician about whom Mother was most enthusiastic in the beginning. They met when he was just gearing up to try for the presidency. Mother decided to help him but gradually became disaffected.

Cody, John, Cardinal ("Louisiana Fats"). The cardinal, who moved to Chicago from New Orleans, struck Mother as rather more secular than his position would dictate.

Coleman, John ("Red"). My first husband and the father of my three children. He was problematic for our whole family, especially when we divorced. My mother tried to "manage" him but was not successful.

Cronkite, Walter. The revered newscaster and his wife, Betsy, were wonderful friends of Mother's for many years. They were two of the chums who insisted that she spend time with them on

Martha's Vineyard the summer of her divorce from my father. The other "hosts" were the Buchwalds and Barbara Walters.

Donahue, Phil. The trailblazing television host was a friend of both Mother's and mine. He, like Oprah after him, would draft Mother to come on the show with hardly any notice if a scheduled guest was circling Chicago or not able to fly in.

Douglas, Kirk. Mother met his wife, Anne, first, and the three of them enjoyed a warm friendship for many years.

Ephron, Nora. During the years Nora and I were friendly, Mother would speak of her in letters, though I doubt they ever met.

Fanning, Larry ("Lare-Bear"). A legendary newspaper editor who guided my mother and taught her how to write for newspapers. My father and I, as well, were devoted to this man, who fit the classic mold of the hard-drinking, seen-it-all newspaperman. His name for me was "Child."

Field, Marshal IV. Mother always called him "my publisher." He inherited the *Sun-Times* and *Chicago Daily-News* from his father. *His* son, known to some as "5," was called "Marsh" by Mother.

Friedman, Abraham. See "A.B., Mr."

Friedman, Becky. A.B.'s wife, my maternal grandmother, whom Mother always referred to as "Mama."

Furth, Jules ("The Maven"). My second husband; his "mavenhood" was derived from his interest in and knowledge of hockey.

Goetz, Edie. Another of Mother's "California girlfriends," Edie Goetz was true old Hollywood royalty. The daughter of one major figure, L. B. Mayer, and the wife of another, studio head and producer Billy Goetz, Edie lived like royalty— the British kind. This was facilitated by much of her household staff having been "palace trained"—that is, in the households of Queen Elizabeth.

Grant, Cary. For whatever reason, Mother and the actor got on very well. She found him quite "normal," as well as modest and funny.

Herr, Dan. The head of the Thomas More Association in Chicago, a Catholic press. He and Mother were great buddies, and he called her "Laura" because of the movie.

Hesburgh, Theodore. The eminent activist president of Notre Dame University for twenty-five years, he was a supportive friend and adviser of my mother's for more than forty years. Because both of them were night owls, they would often speak on the phone during the midnight hours.

Hoge, Jim. Rising through the ranks of the *Sun-Times,* he was a favorite of my mother's, and her name for him was "Yalie."

Howard, Ken. My penultimate husband, of fourteen years, he was an actor perhaps best known for portraying "The White Shadow" on television. (My mother, ever sensitive to religious differences, called him "The Gorgeous Goy.")

Humphrey, Hubert. The Minnesota senator, famous for his ability to talk at length—about anything—was a friend of our family's dating from Mother's Democratic officeholder days in Wisconsin. He and his wife, Muriel, were among the *very* small group of friends to send me three consecutive wedding gifts.

Jackson, Jesse L. Both being Chicagoans, and Democrats, he and Mother had periodic contact. She thought he was a powerful speaker; she just didn't always like what he said.

Johnson, Claudia ("Lady Bird"). Mother long admired the former first lady for her dignity and her approach to public life.

Johnson, Eunice. The wife of the publisher of *Ebony* and *Jet,* she and Mother were walking buddies. Mother admired her for making a place for herself in the family publishing empire with the traveling *Ebony* fashion show.

Johnson, John H. The self-made owner-publisher of the most important black publications in this country. Mother loved the story of his mother borrowing on her furniture in order to lend him a small amount of money with which to start a magazine.

Kaye, Danny. The talented entertainer, whom Mother thought was just this side of sane.

Kennedy, John F. The man who would become president did not, at first, have Mother's support, due to her close ties to Hubert Humphrey. With time, she became his avid backer.

Kennedy, Ted. My mother felt that Kennedy—with whom she was friends for many years—was the most effective senator in Congress, a man whose public performance was more important than his private failings.

Kirby, Bill. The lawyer for John D. MacArthur and then his foundation, "Kirby," as Mother called him, was a beloved friend, legal adviser, and escort.

Kupcinet, Essee. The wife of newspaperman Irv Kupcinet, she was a figure in Chicago because of her support for theater and the arts.

Kupcinet, Irv ("Kup"). The premier gossip

columnist in Chicago for decades, he was already established at the *Sun-Times* when Mother began writing. They were friendly colleagues for nearly fifty years.

Lasker, Mary. This important philanthropist and social figure was perhaps the woman friend from whom my mother learned the most. Mother mourned the death of this close friend until she herself died.

Lerner, Max. The syndicated political columnist was my professor at Brandeis in the department of American civilization. While Mother referred to him as "a lecherous old coot," she understood my fascination with being included in some of his social outings with the intelligentsia in Cambridge.

Menninger, Roy. "Dr. Roy" was one of the founding brothers of the Menninger Clinic in Topeka, Kansas. Mother was on their board.

Merrill, John. A Harvard Medical School nephrologist, Mother met him when they flew, as guests of our government, on the same military aircraft to Vietnam. It was he who interested Mother in Harvard Medical School, on whose visiting committee she would serve for two decades.

Minow, Jo. The admired mother of the "Minow

girls": the three daughters Mother thought were the best kids in this hemisphere. (They were all "achievers," Mother would tell me, over and over.) This was a perfect setup for me to want nothing to do with them—but, in fact, they proved to be very likable!

Minow, Newton. Known to many people as John Kennedy's FCC commissioner who called television "a vast wasteland," he and his wife, Jo, were early friends of my parents in Chicago.

Mirkin, Morey. In Sioux City, where Mother grew up, Morey was such a close cousin that for a while, in high school, he lived in their house. Years later, it was he who persuaded my father to create Budget Rent-a-Car as a national car rental system.

Mitchell, Kathy. Mother's Number One Assistant, who was like a daughter to her and a sister to me. She went to work in the Ann Landers office at the age of nineteen and was fifty-three when my mother died.

Munnecke, Wilbur C. The man I chatted up on a train when I was twelve turned out to be instrumental in Mother becoming Ann Landers three years later. He was an executive at Field Enterprises, the corporate parent of the Chicago *Sun-Times.*

Percy, Charles H. Though a Republican senator from Illinois, he and Mother had a social friendship. With the "encouragement" of Mother and Marjorie Benton, he made an appointment to the federal bench that he later said had been his finest selection.

Peretz, Martin. My mentor in college and a lifelong friend. Because both were active in Democratic politics, Mother and Marty were to meet throughout the years.

Phillips, Jeanne ("Jeannie"). Popo's daughter, my cousin, two years junior to me. We essentially only knew each other when we both lived in Eau Claire, Wisconsin, for seven years when we were little girls. We've seen each other only sporadically over the years.

Phillips, Morton. Popo's husband.

Phillips, Pauline Esther ("Popo"). Mother's identical twin sister and the creator of "Dear Abby."

Pritzker, Rhoda ("Roder"). A close friend and neighbor of Mother's in Chicago, and I think her first friend when we moved there in 1954.

Rovner, Ilana. My dear chum for many years, who, when I moved away, became very close to my mother—almost as though she were a surrogate daughter.

Percy, Charles H. Though a Republican senator from Illinois, he and Mother had a social friendship. With the "encouragement" of Mother and Marjorie Benton, he made an appointment to the federal bench that he later said had been his finest selection.

Peretz, Martin. My mentor in college and a lifelong friend. Because both were active in Democratic politics, Mother and Marty were to meet throughout the years.

Phillips, Jeanne ("Jeannie"). Popo's daughter, my cousin, two years junior to me. We essentially only knew each other when we both lived in Eau Claire, Wisconsin, for seven years when we were little girls. We've seen each other only sporadically over the years.

Phillips, Morton. Popo's husband.

Phillips, Pauline Esther ("Popo"). Mother's identical twin sister and the creator of "Dear Abby."

Pritzker, Rhoda ("Roder"). A close friend and neighbor of Mother's in Chicago, and I think her first friend when we moved there in 1954.

Rovner, Ilana. My dear chum for many years, who, when I moved away, became very close to my mother—almost as though she were a surrogate daughter.

Rubin, Dorothy ("Dubby" or "Dub"). Mother's

sister, who was junior to Helen but older than Mother and Popo. She had a terrific sense of humor and was very warm.

Serling, Rod. The author famed for *The Twilight Zone* also inhabited the left-wing Democrat zone. His and Mother's friendship was forged on *Kup's Show,* when John Wayne called them both Communists!

Simon, Jennifer Jones. One of Mother's California "girlfriends," the former film star pulled out all the stops when she entertained for Mother on visits to Los Angeles.

Stevenson, Adlai. Adlai was the Illinois governor, UN ambassador, and presidential candidate. His son, also named Adlai, was state treasurer, then senator. The elder was Mother's friend; the younger was mine.

Stolar, Bob. The Washington, D.C., physician who was my mother's sounding board. It was his perseverance that convinced her to forge an identity apart from her twinship.

Sugar, Marcy. A key member of Mother's office staff, who spent nearly three decades with her.

Trezevant, Dick. First an editor, then an executive at Field Enterprises. He took over editing Mother's column when Larry Fanning moved to Alaska. My mother loved "Trezl's" sense of humor.

Walters, Barbara. Of all Mother's friends, she was perhaps the only one who pursued her profession with the same passion as did Mother.

Washington, Willie. Our first housekeeper when we moved to Chicago, who, to my mother's relief, stayed until she retired.

Weintraub, Ron (the "Heart Doc," "Dr. Pussycat," "Beloved"). My longtime beau and now husband, whom my mother loved to refer to as her son-in-law, the heart surgeon from Harvard. I, of course, liked his profession for a different reason: I got to travel with my own personal physician.

About the Author

Margo Howard grew up in Chicago and attended Brandeis University. Her newspaper career began at the *Chicago Tribune*, then the *Chicago Daily-News*. Her column of social commentary, "Margo," was syndicated throughout the country. She has written for the *New Republic, The Nation, People,* and *TV Guide*, and was a columnist for *Boston Magazine*. Currently, she writes for *Good Housekeeping* and is the Prudence behind "Dear Prudence" on Slate.com, as well as 200 newspapers, and N.P.R.

Margo Howard has three adult children and lives in Cambridge, Massachusetts, with her husband.